Give me ten seconds

JOHN SERGEANT

Give me ten seconds

MACMILLAN

First published 2001 by Macmillan
an imprint of Pan Macmillan Ltd
Pan Macmillan, 20 New Wharf Road, London N1 9RR
Basingstoke and Oxford
Associated companies throughout the world
www.panmacmillan.com

ISBN 0 333 90449 4

5 7 9 8 6

A CIP catalogue record for this book is available from
the British Library.

Typeset by SetSystems Ltd, Saffron Walden, Essex
Printed and bound in Great Britain by
Mackays of Chatham plc, Chatham, Kent

To Mary

Contents

Contents

Introduction

'GIVE ME TEN SECONDS' is a phrase I use most of my working days. As political editor of ITN one of my main tasks is to talk to the newsreader without a script, often outside Number Ten. The production assistant on the lunchtime news, the evening news, or *News at Ten* will tell me how long they have alloted me in the running order. I may have talked already to the newsreader, Sir Trevor Macdonald, or one of the others about the subject and the possible questions, but it is the production assistant who usually tells me the total time at my disposal: it may be a minute and thirty seconds, more often it is a minute and ten seconds. The PA will ask me whether I want to be given a warning that I am thirty seconds from the end, or just ten, to be delivered through my earpiece. I always say: 'Give me ten seconds.' It gives me time to sum up whatever I am saying, and it is a rigid deadline. It helps to concentrate my mind and – in theory – it stops me waffling. It has been much in my mind while writing this book, hence the title.

'I am thinking of writing a book,' I told some of my friends.

'What's it about?' they replied, and rather shamefacedly I had to admit that the subject of the book was me, or at least my professional life. I dreaded them telling me that my story was simply not interesting enough. Those doubts did not need to be encouraged. The moment the lights went out at home and I was trying to get to sleep I would think, 'What on earth have I let myself in for?' Then my thoughts would become more positive. Isn't it true that you have met all the British prime ministers for the past thirty years? As a war reporter weren't you in danger of being killed on several occasions? Did your grandmother speak to you in Russian when she was on her deathbed? And what about that famous occasion when Mrs Thatcher handbagged you on the steps of the British Embassy in Paris?

Other positive thoughts would begin to crowd in. As a child I lived in Jerusalem where my father, who had learned Arabic, was determined to be a Christian missionary just at the moment when the Jewish state of Israel was in violent birth. In the 1950s, as a vicar in Oxfordshire, he was called to Buckingham Palace to interpret in Russian for George VI. Both my parents met Nikita Khrushchev. When I was still eighteen, I went to the United States to work as an accountant in a failing construction company on the outskirts of Washington, DC. When Martin Luther King made his famous 'I have a dream' speech I was one of the few white people in the crowd.

My first job after leaving Oxford was appearing in a BBC television comedy series with Alan Bennett, which won the Comedy of the Year Award. I then worked as a reporter on the *Liverpool Daily Post & Echo*. After three years, I was taken on by the BBC and spent thirty years with them as a reporter of one kind or another. For a while I presented the *Today* programme and even for a brief period read the news on BBC2. I covered an enormous number of historic events, both at home and abroad. When that famous picture was taken in Vietnam of the girl covered in flaming napalm running naked down a road I saw the aircraft lining up for the attack. I was there when Turkish paratroopers took part in the invasion of Cyprus. I accompanied front-line Israeli forces when they took over Southern Lebanon. I reported from more than twenty-five countries before specializing as a political correspondent.

Most of my professional life has been centred on Westminster, and now I have notched up eight general elections. Towards the end of my BBC career there was also a satisfying return to my early roots in light entertainment. From the time I was first asked to appear on *Have I Got New for You* there followed a stream of opportunities to prove being serious did not preclude me from sometimes being funny as well. Finally, to my great surprise, I was taken on as political editor of ITN, who provided the news service for ITV.

The challenge, then, was to put away the doubts and the sinking feeling that I had bitten off more than I could chew, and try to write a book that might be interesting as well as amusing. I have a large number of people to thank, but will try to keep the list reasonably short. First is my wife Mary, who is the rock of my life. She knows that, however brisk the narrative, much of what is recounted was never quite as simple as it may appear. My grown-up sons, Will and Mike, now have an explanation for the dramas I tried to shield them from; and I hope that my mother, Olive Stevens, feels this book at least partly repays all the effort she invested in me. On the professional side, I would like to thank Toby Mundy, who was the first to encourage me as an author when he worked for Weidenfeld and Nicolson; my wonderfully committed editor at Macmillan, Georgina Morley, without whom this book would not have existed; and Mark Lucas, my agent, who cunningly showed me the way in the strange world of publishing. My bosses at ITN, Stewart Purvis, Richard Tait and Nigel Dacre, generously allowed me to work on the book as well as settle in as their new political editor; I am especially grateful to the ITN team at Westminster, led by Julie Hulme, who, while this book was being written, have not always benefited from my full concentration. I must also thank many people in the BBC, particularly those who come out well in the story I have to tell, and the BBC Archive at Caversham for allowing me to reproduced some of my early scripts. When I left the BBC at the beginning of 2000 I was determined not to come across as an embittered former employee, and I hope this book demonstrates that. I have much to thank them for: the BBC gave me quite a career.

1

'Here is the microphone'

'YOU'RE GOING TO BE FAMOUS.' A rival television correspondent was suddenly rather cross. 'You're going to be famous for making a bloody mistake.' It was difficult to take in what he was saying. We were caught up in a crowd of technicians and producers – some of whom gave every impression of knowing what to do, young men and women carrying clipboards with an earnest air – but, as usual when covering great events, I was not so sure. I was trying not to look bewildered. What we all required was time to reflect, not on how famous I might become but about what we should do next.

It was a cold November evening with a cloudless sky. The courtyard of the British embassy in Paris resembled a film set. The short rise of steps leading grandly to the entrance seemed to turn the courtyard into a stage and the television arc lights lit up the scene with a clinical glare. It had rained for much of the day and the gravel squelched underfoot. A large group of newspaper journalists had been placed, to their annoyance, as far as possible from the steps behind the sort of crash barriers used to control crowds at football matches. Some of the top names in British journalism knew what had happened and it was not to their liking. They had witnessed, but had not been able to take part in, a brilliant television event, which could only appear second-hand in the morning papers.

In the endless competition between print journalists and broadcasters everyone could see who had won. But not all the television correspondents who had been allowed to assemble in the middle of the courtyard, close to the bottom of the steps, considered themselves fortunate. Despite their perfect vantage point, many of them, too, were also-rans. The real drama, broadcast live to millions of homes, involved only a small number of players. And now it was over. My rival continued to shake his head with annoyance. It was all so dreadfully unfair. He had been there. He had asked Margaret Thatcher a question. I had clearly been out of my depth, made to look a complete fool; but he feared I would be judged to have scooped the story from under his nose.

I have many reasons to look back on that evening in November 1990 and bless my good fortune. It would have been exciting enough simply to hear Mrs Thatcher's reaction to the fact she had failed to win the first round in the leadership contest. But that news had been coupled with a wonderful pantomime scene, with me not knowing she was behind me and then appearing to be manhandled by members of her staff. For many people this was the moment when they realized that the Thatcher era was over. It was one of the great turning points in British politics. Two days later she resigned after eleven years as one of the most dominant prime ministers in British history.

On frequent occasions, sometimes on television, I have been asked to look again at what happened; I have even had to endure the embarrassment of seeing an actor play me in a television drama reconstructing the events of that night. It reminded me of a joke in Tom Stoppard's play *Rosencrantz and Guildenstern are Dead*. An Elizabethan playwright decides there should be a real hanging in his play, a man should actually die. But after trying it once he dropped the idea – it was not convincing enough. I felt the same about this chap dressed up as me. He wore the sort of fawn, double-breasted cavalry twill coat I wore on that occasion, but to my eyes at least, he could hardly have been less like me. He should have been strung up.

We had known for weeks that a big story was brewing. Despite all the attempts of loyal ministers to give the impression that nothing could be further from the truth, Mrs Thatcher's hold on power was finally looking shaky. She had held office with such confidence and determination that even the more cynical journalists found it difficult to imagine that she might soon be gone. If ever there was a case in modern times when we needed a child in the crowd to say that the emperor had no clothes, this was one. She seemed invulnerable. Many Tory MPs, without irony, used to refer to her as Mother, and when she was toppled they found no difficulty in speaking about regicide, as if the queen had been assassinated. Mrs Thatcher blatantly traded on the assumption that no one of sound mind would want to remove her, and, as in a Greek tragedy, that was one of the causes of her downfall. It was a fatal flaw.

A fortnight before the prime minister left for Paris, she had ordained that the result of the first round in any leadership contest would come while she was in France. This was one of the few aspects of the contest under her complete control and she made a tactical mistake. Under the Conservative Party's rules she could have delayed the vote for another two weeks, but she decided, with calculated disdain, that on that day she would be busy on the world stage, attending a conference in Paris, in effect a celebration of the end of the cold war, bringing together the Americans and the Russians with their key allies. Many of the leaders she knew well would be there including the US president George Bush, the Soviet leader, Mikhail Gorbachev, and the German chancellor, Helmut Kohl. The French president, François Mitterrand, would be the host.

At the time she made the decision on the timing of the first ballot, Mrs Thatcher still did not know if she would be challenged. Only three Tory MPs were required to trigger a contest but there were strong arguments against any of the potential challengers doing so. In private, Michael Heseltine, who did not hide his ambition to become prime minister, stuck firmly to the view that he who wields the dagger never wears the crown. It would be better if the dreadful deed were to be carried out by someone else, allowing him to emerge as the candidate to unite the party in its time of need. But Mrs Thatcher had decided that, whatever happened, it would look as though business was taking place very much as usual if she was in Paris, apparently above the fray. She had no idea that every single vote would count and that, as it turned out, with four more she could have won the first round and perhaps been able to hold on to the premiership. As her supporters bitterly reflected afterwards, if she had stayed in London she might have been able to sway those votes at the last moment.

I had followed her career closely ever since she had beaten Edward Heath in the Conservative leadership contest, which followed his defeats in the two general elections of 1974. She was irritating, bossy, single-minded, obsessive, illiberal and aloof, but I liked her. She provided more journalistic copy than any other recent prime minister, and when she came into a room it seemed as if the walls had to expand to contain her personality. Many people have had cause to criticize her for what she did during her long term in office; the cries of 'Maggie, Maggie, Maggie, out, out, out,' frequently resonated with good reason across the land, particularly at the time of the poll tax, but there were achievements, especially in economic policy, which have stood the test of time. In the narrow world of political reporting it was often amusing to cover her, even if her humour was almost always unintentional. At her best she was a towering figure and even at the end, turned on by her own cabinet, she was able to rise brilliantly to the occasion. But there was more than a little of the actress in her, if not the operatic diva, and, as she found in Paris, this did not always work to her advantage.

The previous month had seen a mounting crisis in her

leadership. She had been isolated at a European summit, at which, in what was later to be described as an ambush, the other European leaders had confronted Mrs Thatcher with their ambitious plans for a single currency. She gave her answer in an impassioned speech in the House of Commons, remembered largely for her defiant refrain of 'No, no, no.' But the Pro-Europeans in the cabinet were in a majority. The leader of the house, the former foreign secretary and chancellor, Sir Geoffrey Howe, one of the pillars of the government, dramatically resigned. His devastating attack on Mrs Thatcher in the Commons encouraged by far the most dangerous of her rivals, Michael Heseltine, to put aside his natural caution and throw down the gauntlet. She was now fighting for her political life.

The weekend before leaving for Paris I spent two days compiling Mrs Thatcher's political obituary. This was done with some regard to secrecy so we called the piece 'The Endgame', though no one in the television newsroom at White City in West London was in any doubt about what was going on. My producer was David Aaronovitch, my line manager at Westminster. He was sorely underused by the BBC but has since become well known as a columnist on the *Independent* and a supporter of New Labour. We would both have been amazed to know that the next time we worked closely together would be ten years later in a Radio 4 comedy series called *True Lies*. Then we would have to concentrate on making jokes; this time our job was to make sure they did not creep in by mistake.

As usual in my experience at the BBC, we had no discussion about what we really thought about Mrs Thatcher nor, heaven forbid, whether we voted for her. Maintaining the impartiality of the corporation had long since become second nature. After twenty years on the staff, half of that with the Political Unit, I did not need to be told that compiling the television piece which would accompany her resignation, if it happened, was not an excuse to air one's political views. It was, though, a moment for judgement and tight selection: there were more than thirty video cassettes piled up in the editing suite. Previous correspondents had tried to prepare a proper obituary for the prime minister's demise, but this was quite different. It should not be too solemn. We knew perfectly well that many of those who watched the piece would be thrilled that Mrs Thatcher had been knocked off her perch, even though others were likely to react as if it were a death in the family.

My problem was to avoid indulging in a nostalgic wallow. In many of the stories on the cassettes I appeared as a bit player, gradually ageing with time. There was my thumb on the microphone when she made her famous remarks quoting St Francis of Assisi when she first arrived in Downing Street in 1979. Wasn't that me trudging along behind her in a Moscow street in the run up to the 1987 election? And surely I was there when she was so moved at the seventy-fifth anniversary of the fateful Gallipoli landings in Turkey during the First World War? Weren't we in America, too, on more than one occasion? 'Yes, yes, I know, John. All that and much more,' David sighed, 'but not now.' The piece had to run for about eleven minutes, the longest item I had ever prepared for BBC news, and it had to be ready before I left for Paris the next day.

The real questions were whether it would run at all and whether I was right to go to France. Not everyone was sure that Paris was the place to be. One BBC correspondent admitted to me later he hugged himself in silent delight when the decision to send me was taken. With the political editor, John Cole, providing comment in London and with me, the chief political correspondent, stuck in Paris, perhaps merely holding a microphone for Mrs Thatcher, my colleague was hoping the main story of the Conservative leadership struggle would fall to him.

When I returned home in triumph the day after, for the first time in my career to be greeted with applause, I should have noticed that he was clapping with slightly less vigour than the others.

I had deliberately set off for Paris with a fairly heavy heart, as is my custom. For me it is a kind of defence mechanism. If you are certain that you are on a top story and success is assured, it frequently ends in disappointment. It is better to start with low expectations; there is far more room for surprise and excitement when they come. There were also plenty of reasons to worry. *Breakfast News* on BBC1 had a new political producer with a burning desire to put more politics on the programme. Ominously, even before Mrs Thatcher had arrived, they had been in touch about what I would be doing the next morning. What could I say? That she would be coming, and here is a picture of the British embassy where she will be staying? It took half an hour to persuade them that, keen as I wanted to appear, I could not conjure up coverage with no material. But it led to an uneasy night in the Hilton. Saying 'yes' and producing some kind of nonsense might have been more restful in the end.

There was, too, a self-inflicted problem. I had agreed that a second BBC camera crew could follow me around Paris in the hope of getting the story behind the story – as if dealing with the high politics in front of the camera would not be enough without another camera showing how I dealt with the low politics behind the scenes. But for some television producers the thirst for explanation can only be satisfied if they report on those who are reporting. They are like visitors to the model village at Beaconsfield. You look to see if the model village itself is represented in the model village. Then you look to see if this small model village contains an even smaller model village. Then you decide it is time to pack the children off home.

This could not be dealt with so easily. There would be a cameraman and a soundman, accompanied by an assistant producer, a producer and a correspondent. I agreed, through weakness I suppose. As so much of our time is spent filming other people and intruding on their lives can we really expect to avoid being put sometimes on the receiving end? The strongest argument in favour of a second camera crew was that the correspondent in this team was one of my early journalistic heroes, Julian Pettifer. He had been a dazzling television reporter in the 1960s when I had first become interested in journalism. He could always be relied upon to look handsome and self-assured, despite the chaos around him in Vietnam and other more outlandish places. We had not met before but we quickly fell into animated conversation, talking about Vietnam, where I had worked too, and the vagaries of a broadcaster's life. It poured with rain and we had to jump to avoid the puddles. Paris looked ravishing, reminding me, with a slight pang, of my brief period as *chef de bureau* in the BBC's Paris office. Then I had been obsessed by the dramatic change when the Left had taken power and François Mitterrand walked among the crowds clutching a red rose. Paris and politics can be a perfect combination, and you need not go hungry either. They even have a phrase for a good working lunch with politicians. It's called '*la politique gastronomique*'. But I never got the impression that Mrs Thatcher approved.

Unfortunately, that lunchtime we could not put the idea into practice. There had to be a piece from me in Paris on the one o'clock news, even though nothing had happened. The last part was reasonably straightforward: I would stand outside the British embassy in the rue du Faubourg St Honoré and say that later that day it would witness one of the most important moments in recent British politics. Before that, we decided that French people interviewed in the street could talk about Mrs

Thatcher and say how surprising it would be if she lost her job. In the trade this is called colour, a vital ingredient particularly if you have a dull story. One of my first news editors used to complain that the Paris correspondent was failing to get the garlic into his stories. On this occasion the garlic wasn't very pungent, but at least it was there.

At Westminster, meanwhile, the tension was rising. For most of the day Tory MPs had been traipsing along the vast Committee Corridor stretching right along the back of the Houses of Parliament facing the Thames. Nearly four hundred of them were eligible to vote, and one of the bigger committee rooms had been put aside for this purpose.

The ballot was due to close at 6 p.m. – the start of the BBC's six o'clock news. With rapid counting the result would be announced officially within the half-hour, and it had been decided to extend the programme after its normal finishing time of 6.30 to give reaction to the result, particularly, it was hoped, the response of Mrs Thatcher from Paris. In the corridor, the crush of politicians and journalists was almost unbearable. But when the result was read out discomfort was forgotten. There was an instant and knowing reaction. 'Second ballot,' was the comment, quickly and endlessly repeated among the crowd. For Mrs Thatcher's close supporters, it sounded like the tolling of a bell or, to put it more dramatically, the clap of doom. The stark figures gave the impression that the prime minister had won – Margaret Thatcher 204, Michael Heseltine 152, abstentions 16 – but the system then being used was designed to give the challenger an advantage. Knowing that toadies and careerists, of which there are many, would automatically support their leader in times of difficulty, the rules insisted that the winner should have not only an absolute majority but also a further 15 per cent of those entitled to vote. On this basis Mrs Thatcher had failed by only four votes. If just two of her supporters had not switched their vote to Mr Heseltine she could have claimed victory and would not have faced the prospect of a second ballot.

When I heard the result in Paris I was in no doubt that she was in very deep trouble. However you thought about it, this was an astonishing blow to a sitting prime minister. More than a hundred and fifty MPs had turned their backs on their leader. I thought of the recent comments of the eminent Conservative historian, Lord Blake. Considering all the historical parallels he had concluded that more than a hundred failing to vote for the prime minister would constitute a major revolt. Well, more than half that number again had marched behind her rival's banner. I cannot claim to have been certain that she would have to resign, but I did think it was likely. And this led me to make the mistake that would make me famous.

One of Mrs Thatcher's staff was an official seconded from the Foreign Office, Peter Bean. Prematurely bald and usually wearing a slightly worried expression, he played the straight man to the flamboyance and flair of her press secretary, Bernard Ingham. I tended to believe Peter a little more than I believed Bernard. This was almost certainly misguided, particularly because Peter rarely said anything to me which had not been cleared before by Bernard. But journalism often resembles a chain, and the strength of a chain is determined by its weakest link. On this occasion the weak link was Peter Bean.

Standing in the courtyard of the British embassy, the arc lights upon me, I was trying to assess what was really happening. It is laid down in the charter granting the BBC its right to exist that the staff should be impartial, and this usually means giving no hint of how a situation should be resolved. We do, though, have to try to work out what will happen. And so, fatefully, I turned to Peter Bean.

I felt sure that Mrs Thatcher would want to consider the result of the ballot and confer with her colleagues in London.

I put this thought to Peter and he concurred. He had been told she would not be coming out for half an hour, until she was ready to go to the official dinner and celebrations at the Palace of Versailles. He had not been told of any change of plan and no one who was actually involved in the discussions now taking place inside the embassy had thought to tell him what was going on. Nor, for that matter, had they bothered about me, or the thirteen million people, we later learned, who were watching that broadcast. I told the viewers, as firmly as I could, that Mrs Thatcher was not expected to come out for about half an hour.

Television correspondents are kept in touch with the news studio by devices which look like hearing aids. Through your ear you are supposed to receive vital instructions and information which can then be passed on, apparently effortlessly, to the viewers. But you are frequently given a stream of details oddly irrelevant to the task in hand. Just as you are listening intently for the first time to an interview which you will very soon be asked to comment on, an excited voice may break in and shout, 'John, you're on next.' I have often been tempted to say I can't comment because someone was shouting, 'You're on next.'

On this occasion the situation was more complicated than usual; I was working with a French cameraman. At no stage were we engaged in meaningful communication and, for once, no one was saying anything in my ear. The only voice I heard was my own saying that Mrs Thatcher wouldn't be coming out. There was an eerie silence, which seemed to go on and on, and then a photographer leapt up into the air, describing a sort of arc in front of my face. At home thirteen million people knew exactly what was happening: they were watching a pantomime. Mrs Thatcher had appeared behind me on the steps of the embassy with her two aides, Bernard Ingham and Peter Bean. They were bearing down on me at speed. The newsreader, Peter Sissons, shouted, 'John, she's behind you.' I knew nothing. I heard nothing. The magic earpiece had failed.

Turning round is always dangerous on live television if you do not know what or who is behind you. Maybe there is nothing of any interest and you would have broken a cardinal rule by looking completely lost, but something – perhaps it was that photographer and his elegant leap – prompted me to swivel. I was horrified at what I saw: the prime minister and her closest aides intent it seemed on confronting me. I desperately tried to recover my poise. 'Mrs Thatcher . . .' I spluttered, trying to make it sound like the beginning of a question, and then came a wonderful moment of pure farce.

Bernard Ingham and Peter Bean pushed me roughly aside and shouted, 'Where is the microphone?' I could not understand why they thought it mattered where the microphone was; surely if that was anyone's problem it was mine. However, the microphone they were looking for had nothing to do with me, or the BBC. It had been decided that she should give her reaction to the waiting press – all the waiting press – and not just me. A microphone had been set up on a stand in front of the print journalists, corralled at the bottom end of the courtyard. But, and this is what came to symbolize the disintegration of the Thatcher regime, the principal actors had no idea where that microphone was, or where they should go. The confusion was deliciously appropriate. They gave every impression of desperately trying to find their way out of an impossible situation. They were reluctantly forced to use the only microphone they could see, which was the small blue one in my hand. I had no intention of budging. This was a BBC exclusive. I prayed that my French cameraman was showing as wide a picture as possible so that everyone could take in the scene; and I had the distinct advantage over Mrs Thatcher and her aides, knowing that this whole event was being broadcast live. Many of the audience at home, including some of the most

senior members of the government, drew an obvious conclusion from this farce: that Mrs Thatcher appeared to have
already lost her grip on government.

The transcript of this bizarre event does not do justice to
the drama:

> *John Sergeant:* Prime Minister, Mrs Thatcher, it's here,
> this is the microphone.
> *Prime Minister:* I'm naturally very pleased that I got more
> than half the parliamentary party and disappointed that
> it's not quite enough to win on the first ballot so I
> confirm it is my intention to let my name go forward
> for the second ballot.

There have been so many comments on what was sometimes referred to as the occasion when I was 'handbagged' by
Mrs Thatcher that perhaps I should lay to rest some of the
wilder assertions. She did not herself manhandle me. She was
not reacting in a fit of rage when she saw me on television
saying she would stay inside the embassy and consult her
colleagues in London; she was not watching television. She
had decided before she left London that she would stand in
the second ballot, if she failed in the first. This plan had been
worked out with her close advisers although some of them,
including the party chairman, Kenneth Baker, had argued that
in these circumstances she should delay and consult. The scene
inside the embassy was strangely downbeat where a room had
been prepared for her to receive the news. When the result
came, her closest official adviser, Charles Powell, heard it first
and gave the others in the room the thumbs down. She did
not notice this. Then her parliamentary private secretary, Peter
Morrison, wrote down the figures. He passed them to her and
said, 'Not quite as good as we had hoped.' Mrs Thatcher is
said to have reacted coolly. She left almost immediately, and
confronted me in the courtyard.

After she and her little group had swept back up the steps I had very little time to think. It was not only the comments from my rival about how famous I might become which were distracting me; a decision had to be taken quickly about whether we should break back in to the BBC1 schedule and give people who had just switched on the chance to catch up on the news. To add to my difficulties, the television crew working with Julian Pettifer was still following me around. Every time I pushed forward to discuss what to do with producers and technicians his cameraman and soundman would push in behind me. Every time I tried to make a forceful point about what I wanted and why, a microphone would be dangled over my head.

In those days, correspondents could not broadcast easily from abroad at the same time. We were given slots and the one at 7 p.m. was allocated to *Channel Four News*. Such is the logic of television production that they decided they did not want to broadcast from Paris at the start of their programme; they wanted to begin, as usual, with their presenter Jon Snow, in London. Their correspondent in Paris, Nick Gowing, was flung into gloom, but nobly agreed that I should take the slot. There was only one major difficulty: I had not seen the pictures of my confrontation with Mrs Thatcher. So when I introduced the item live at 7 p.m. and the pictures were played in from London, I had only a rough idea of what was going to be shown. Not for the first time, those watching at home could judge the story better than I could.

For the nine o'clock news we had more material. The foreign secretary, Douglas Hurd, in a strange stiff-backed appearance in the courtyard, had declared his support for Mrs Thatcher as had the chancellor, John Major. Soon afterwards and trying not to appear too downhearted, Mr Hurd left with Mrs Thatcher for Versailles and a gruelling evening with the other leaders. Then, for the first time, I had the opportunity to see what had actually happened, when I had failed to notice Mrs Thatcher behind me. As I watched the pictures through the window of the editing van, I was so apprehensive that I closed one eye.

It looked good enough for me to try with both eyes. There was also another strange twist in my favour. The camera crew working with Julian Pettifer had decided to take what's known as a top shot of the courtyard, picturing it from a high angle from some temporary scaffolding. They did this at precisely the moment Mrs Thatcher came out. We were desperate to use those pictures, along with ours, because we now learned that the prime minister had only taken six seconds to race down the embassy steps before issuing her statement. That is not a long time to set the scene with the commentary we would need for the nine o'clock news. With that top shot and some skilful editing the scene leading up to her announcement could be artificially extended to cover eleven seconds. Now that really is the magic of television. It was because we were able to convey the whole scene in the courtyard, as well as the bruising close-up of me being pushed aside, that for many viewers it really was as if they were there.

It was all a matter of luck and that evening I was on a roll.

What made this a significant piece of television was that it appeared to tell a larger truth. Many of the elements had fallen into place by chance and could have ended up as simply misleading, but, like a political cartoon, the caricature that had been created − of a prime minister who had lost touch, with officials having lost their manners as well as their sense of direction − was devastatingly accurate. When Mrs Thatcher returned to London the next day she began to carry out the consultations she had seemed to reject. Members of the cabinet were called in and even the most loyal advised her that she could not win a second round against Michael Heseltine. The game was up. At her last cabinet meeting before resigning she said that it was a funny old world, but the biggest laugh had come two days before in Paris. It would not have amused her to know that, and I have never had the nerve to talk to her about it since. In her memoirs she simply describes how she went out of the embassy and gave her prepared statement.

Mrs Thatcher might also have been surprised when a few months later I won a British Press Guild award for the most memorable outside broadcast of 1990. We managed to beat a football programme which featured the moment when Paul Gascoigne broke down in tears after being shown a yellow card during a vital game in the World Cup in Italy. Maggie vs Gazza was not the fight she thought she was involved in.

When the work was over that evening in Paris I went with one of my producers to La Coupole, the famous brasserie on the Left Bank. I would like to say it was one of the best meals of my life, but I was too tired for that. It was, though, a moment to savour, a moment for *la politique gastronomique*. Over the years I have witnessed many important events, but the most satisfying, the funniest and certainly the most memorable event occurred during my two day trip to Paris in the late autumn of 1990. And all I really said was, 'Here is the microphone.'

2

'And who is Lenin?'

THERE IS A LONG TRADITION in my family of being present at historic events; maybe it's something in the genes. Often we have no intention of being there and it is as a result of outside forces over which we have no control. In my professional life this role has frequently been played by editors of one sort or another saying, in a fairly bossy way, 'I think we should send Sergeant.' Whatever the reason, we have found ourselves in the thick of violent and unpredictable events which have a curious way of ending up in the history books. It is certainly not a cause for complaint, indeed it is a noble family tradition, to be celebrated and if possible maintained.

From my maternal grandfather's home in Odessa on the Black Sea he could look down on the grand harbour and keep a close eye on the Russian imperial fleet. Odessa was one of the most important ports in the Russian empire, a vital stepping stone between the great wheat fields of the Ukraine and the warm waters of the Mediterranean. My grandfather, Horatio William Cook, had been named after the British hero, Horatio Nelson, and – according to the completely unreliable testimony of my grandmother – was a distant relative of the Captain Cook who discovered New Zealand. Horatio Cook had been born in Odessa and spoke fluent Russian. As well as being able to observe the imperial fleet he could also keep an eye on the family warehouse alongside the dock. His grandfather had come from Lincoln in the second half of the nineteenth century to set up business in Russia importing farm machinery from England. So pleased were the good folk of Lincoln that when Cornelius Cook returned after his first successful trip overseas the horses were unhitched from his carriage on the outskirts of town to be replaced by men who pulled the coach triumphantly into the centre of the city.

But by 1905, the easy pickings of those early years in the Russian market had given way to extreme anxiety about political unrest and fears that the Tsarist regime was being fatally undermined. The violent events of that year led almost inexorably to the communist revolution of October 1917 and one of the historic clashes took place in Odessa. The great Soviet film director, Eisenstein, turned it into a propaganda epic, *The Battleship Potemkin*, a classic of the silent screen, and my grandfather saw much of what actually happened from the family home. He was twenty-three years old.

For the second year running, the harvest across most of Russia had failed. There was widespread discontent and in many places violence. Sensing the weakness of the government, peasants organized rent strikes and began to launch full-scale attacks on big estates, seizing property and setting fire to manor houses. The army was called in to put down the peasant uprisings and morale among the troops suffered grievously. They began to refuse orders and mutinies spread. In June the unrest reached the Black Sea fleet.

On the *Potemkin*, it was a piece of rotting meat which caused the trouble. The ship's doctor declared it safe to eat but the sailors complained and the situation soon swung out of control. The sailors' spokesman was shot on the orders of the captain and a mutiny broke out. Seven officers were killed and the red flag raised. The mutineers sailed to Odessa where for two weeks striking workers had been confronting the city government. The body of the dead spokesman was placed at the foot of a set of marble steps leading from the harbour up the steep cliff to the city. All the next day vast crowds gathered to pay their respects and the tension grew. The army moved in and, in scenes brilliantly re-created by Eisenstein, carried out one of the most appalling massacres in Russian history. By dawn two thousand people had been killed and three thousand wounded. My grandfather was deeply shocked by what happened but did not draw the obvious conclusion that it was time for him to leave. Our family had strong connections in Odessa and returning to England was not a simple option.

Horatio Cook was a loyal Englishman but also deeply Russian. He went to the cathedral school in Lincoln as his father, John Horatio Cook, had before him. They were both choristers and there are those in the family who are convinced that is where the distinctive Sergeant voice comes from. My elder brother Peter and I sound very similar and so do my two sons, William and Michael. But Horatio felt Russian, too; he could pass without difficulty as a Russian and in Odessa he married the daughter of a priest, Nadezhda Rozova, known as Nadya. My mother would later boast that because of the Russian Orthodox tradition where a son would automatically follow a father into the priesthood, she could lay claim to ancestors going back a thousand years to the beginning of Christianity in Russia. It certainly sounded impressive when we heard her say this as children. My grandmother, I remember, looked just like one of those tubby Russian dolls that you open up to find another one inside. Just before she died in a nursing home near London in the 1970s she spoke to me for the last time entirely in Russian, forgetting that I did not understand.

My grandparents lived a comfortable life in Odessa, despite the increasing political tension. My mother was born in 1913, just before the start of the First World War, and was christened Olive Horatia very much as a result of my grandfather's wishes. My mother only learned many years later that she had been called Olive because my grandfather had taken a fancy to a young English woman of that name in the summer before she was born. Constancy in marriage only became a feature of the Sergeant family much later, in the present generation.

The First World War had a curiously indirect but dramatic effect on our family. None of my relatives fought in the trenches; there were no widowed ladies looking wistful on Armistice Day. But we were caught, very luckily as it turned out, by a British wartime regulation which caused my grandparents to cross Russia and avoid, by only a couple of months, the upheaval of the 1917 revolution. The regulation stated that although the first child born abroad could be British the second could not, and in the summer of 1917 my grandmother was pregnant. My mother was therefore British by birth but my future aunt Tanya had to be born in England to have British nationality. By this simple twist the family came to London, not as frightened refugees but in response to the long arm of officialdom. By the time my aunt was born the revolution had taken place and the family would never live in Russia again.

This, in turn, had a profound effect on family politics. We were not White Russians; we were not Reds. We were never part of the Russian émigré community. Just before they left for Finland and eventually the sea journey to Aberdeen my grandmother and my mother were being shown around St Petersburg. Their guide pointed out the balcony Lenin used for making speeches to vast crowds. 'And who is Lenin?' my grandmother asked. She had been surprised on the long journey overland from Odessa to find the train boarded by soldiers deserting from the Russian army. It was hot and uncomfortable. My mother, then aged three, was allowed by her parents to talk to the soldiers as a way of reducing the tension. She offered them her father's cigarettes, because, as she put it, 'He's got lots of cigarettes.' She then asked other well-off passengers for more cigarettes to give to the soldiers and they quickly acquiesced. She, a little girl, had skilfully defused a crisis and turned the desperate fugitives into her friends. As she explained when she was much older, 'No wonder the other passengers gave up their cigarettes so easily; they probably thought the deserters would kill them.'

This incident had a strong and, as it turned out, unfortunate effect on my grandfather. He concluded that my mother, whatever the difficulties in future, would be able to cope. It strengthened his determination to leave his young family in England and lead an irresponsible life of his own. What he actually did is not entirely clear although it seems that he was some kind of British agent, using his perfect Russian to move easily backwards and forwards to the Soviet Union and eastern Europe. Before long my mother, the backbone of the family, had to bring up her sister and look after her mother in Berkhamsted, near London. At one point they were so poor that they had to share the only respectable pair of shoes. It was a grim introduction to England, but it gave my mother an outlook on life from which I learnt an enormous amount. We always felt as a family that we had to be tough because life was tough.

My mother used to say, 'You never get a job you don't really want.' Then we might be told how she landed her first job as a secretary in London during the economic recession of the 1930s. She was nineteen and had sixpence to spend that day in London. The interview was in the afternoon but she left Berkhamstead at 6.30 a.m because it was much cheaper on what was called the workers' train. She spent part of the morning lingering over a cup of tea in a Lyons Corner House and then, dressed up as best she could, she went to the interview. She was hungry, and desperate for the job. 'Well, my dear,' she was asked, 'what have you been doing today in London?'

'Oh, I've been shopping,' my mother replied casually. It was the winning answer. Her employer told her later how relieved he had been with that reply. So many girls pleaded with him, they were so hard up. He wanted someone who would be easy and would not moan. Her pay was two pounds ten shillings a week. Nearly seventy years later she had no difficulty recalling the amount. From that first job she was able to move on to become secretary to Sir Bernard Pares, one of Britain's foremost Russian historians.

For some people their parents' origins may not matter very much but in my early years it was difficult for me to escape the conclusion that in many ways, as a family, we were odd and different. When I was at school there was one girl who nearly floored me with a rather improbable chat up line. She had ascertained that I was called John, my brother was Peter and my sister was called Anne. 'Do your parents,' she said, 'have very odd names?' I tried, desperately, to brush the point aside. Total strangers, I thought to myself, should not be allowed to score a goal within the first few minutes of the game.

'Well, maybe,' I spluttered defensively. My voice dropped to a whisper. 'My mother is called Olive Horatia Sergeant and my father is Ernest Noel Copland Sergeant.'

'So there,' she said, giving a very good impression of that ghastly girl in the *Just William* stories, Violet Elizabeth Bott. Secretly I was rather impressed. Girls, I decided, would have to be taken far more seriously than I had imagined. They seemed to know about families, about christenings, about names, about relationships.

★

My father was certainly not an expert in this field when he knelt down to pray one evening in the summer of 1936. He was twenty-five years old and was praying for a wife. This was not a casual moment; he took prayer seriously, as you might expect from a young curate in the Church of England. His parish was in the London suburb of Northwood. Ernest Sergeant was, though, it has to be said, a rather unusual young curate. He had two degrees from the University of Oxford and had developed a remarkable skill in foreign languages. His father had been a vicar in a parish near Liverpool and himself had been to Oxford, but Ernest had been marked out from an early age as something close to a prodigy. He attended Liverpool College and as an only child spent much of his free time poring over grammars and dictionaries. His parents were so worried about his lack of friends that they bought him a monkey as a pet. However monkeys, even more than dogs, are not only for Christmas. They are difficult to look after and they need monkey friends as well. The monkey, sadly, had to be returned to the pet shop.

At Lincoln College, Oxford my father studied theology for three years and was disappointed when the examiners awarded him only a second-class honours degree. In his spare time he had continued with his linguistic studies and decided that he would now make a serious effort to master Russian in just two years. He would rise early in the morning, work hard until lunch then take the rest of the day off. During the long vacations he spoke as much Russian as he could, spending one summer with a Russian family in Paris and another with a Russian priest in Estonia. He was awarded first-class honours with a distinction in the oral. In the long years he knew my mother she never remembers him making a mistake in Russian, although he frequently corrected her. When we were children it was their secret language; whenever they spoke it, we knew they were discussing us.

But his brilliance at languages – he would eventually master more than thirty – could not provide my father with the means to support himself, or so he supposed at the time. Instead he decided to become a clergyman in the Church of England tradition of the well-educated priest. Then as now in Britain people like him did not make a point of calling themselves intellectuals, although I find it difficult to imagine anyone more intellectual than my father. He was at this stage a believer and before he died in the 1980s he went to hospital with copies of the Bible in appropriate languages, the Old Testament in Hebrew and the New Testament in ancient Greek. 'I think I am fully covered,' he told me with a smile.

My mother believes that when he prayed for a wife my father was really hoping for someone from a difficult language group, perhaps a Basque speaker. Russian was not really exotic enough. But when you are keen for a wife you cannot be too choosy and there was the young woman he had met briefly at the School of Slavonic Studies some six months before. He had been there to talk to Sir Bernard Pares about the possibility of studying for a Ph.D. Ernest met Olive because Sir Bernard had forgotten who he was and asked them to talk to each other while he got his bearings. Ernest asked Olive, in perfect Russian, whether she spoke the language. '*Konechno*,' she replied coolly, meaning, 'Of course.' This she pronounced with a slight slur so it sounded almost like '*koneschno*', giving it, she told me, a slightly aristocratic air. To him she sounded rather too grand but it was worth a try. They met again the next day and within six weeks they were engaged.

I would like to say that this was the perfect match; with her drive and his brains, she thought, at the very least he would end up a bishop. But in 1943, after six years together, there were signs of considerable strain. Once again in the family story a world war had intervened, but it was not the direct cause of the difficulty. My father had settled down as the vicar of the small village of Twyford in Buckinghamshire, but he did try to do his bit for the war effort by helping the Foreign Office with translations of newspapers from Bulgaria and other Balkan countries. There were two children already, Peter and Anne, and my mother was keen to have a third. She would later describe this desire as her response to Adolf Hitler, although I do not think that quite does it justice. From her perspective, deep in the English countryside, Adolf Hitler and the German war machine were simply not powerful enough to prevent her doing what she was determined to do.

There was also, she insisted later, another explanation as to why she had to have a third child: the attitude of her husband. She was not very impressed by the practical help she was getting from my father. Vegetables in the country were quite hard to come by so people tended to grow their own. My mother, who became a lifelong gardener, was very cross at the haphazard way my father had planted some cabbages. 'Far too close together,' she recalled years later. 'It was the last straw. I realized that I could not count on him to help and should therefore hurry up and have another child.'

It was as a result of these diverse and unpredictable events, including two world wars and a revolution, that I was given the chance of life. On 14 April 1944 I was born in the Radcliffe Hospital in Oxford. The hand I was dealt was far from perfect but it was certainly interesting, and the fun would be seeing how many unexpected tricks I could call my own.

3

Staying together, for the sake of
the children

MY FATHER WAS PLEASED I was born in Oxford. 'I thought it would look good on your passport,' he would tell me regularly. He had a touching faith in the power of the city and its university. Indeed, when he was retired and living in Somerset and he came to count his blessings, he would usually add that his doctor had gone to Oxford. Intellectual snobbery may have something to do with it; the class war, in all its guises, was a powerful feature of English life before the Second World War, when he was growing up. Among the other gods placed in his pantheon alongside Oxford was the National Trust, which happened to own a great stretch of land leading up to a hill with a windmill near where he lived in the village of Walton. He also, for some strange reason, used to thank the Lord for the AA. Why the Automobile Association should be singled out for such an honour was never fully explained. The fact that he did not learn to drive and would have been mortified if forced to change a wheel may have been relevant. Those calm efficient AA men, with their yellow motorbikes and the deferential way they saluted all association members, could cope with such matters, and perhaps that is why they were considered by my father to be a gift from God.

The Rev. E. N. C Sergeant, as he was always formally referred to, was an impractical man and in many ways it was merely being fair to the armed forces, as well as a kindness to him, that he took no active part in the defeat of Nazi Germany. True, there was his excellence in Bulgarian, which no doubt helped to keep the Foreign Office on their toes when they came to consider the intractable problems of the Balkans. But this preoccupation, perhaps better described as an obsession, had taken its toll on my mother, who had been forced to put up with a Bulgarian lodger, in order that my father could perfect his speaking knowledge of the language. Fortunately, by the time I arrived and there were three children to look after, the Bulgarian had been transferred to the house of a friendly neighbour, with my father generously paying his rent.

My father was a romantic and he was troubled that his relatively easy wartime life might be seen as unmanly, that some might look on him as a coward. He could not easily explain to strangers that, as a clergyman, he was in a reserved occupation, exempt from military service, that he was the father of young children, and that he suffered badly from piles. These were not reasons enough in his view. When the war was over he decided, rather late in the day, that the time had come for him to brave shot and shell. He set his heart on becoming a missionary in the Middle East, and he could not be persuaded that this was a deeply irresponsible act and could place his family in considerable danger.

At their headquarters in London, the Church Missionary Society were initially not too impressed by this country parson who seemed, so much against the tide of the times, to have found a passion for travel and evangelical crusade. As hundreds of thousands of British servicemen were returning from distant parts of the globe my father was determined to set out in the opposite direction. He told the organizers of the mission to Palestine that he could learn languages, any languages. 'Arabic,' they said firmly, and off he went, no doubt with a spring in his step. For my father taking on a new language was like taking on a mistress, except that it was far easier to understand and there was never a shortage of supply.

Six months later, in January 1946, he arrived in Jerusalem, which was about to be torn apart by civil war. On the following Sunday my father preached his first sermon in Arabic. However hard he tried to convey the subtleties of Christianity in his newly acquired tongue, it was largely irrelevant to the struggle then engulfing Palestine. The British mandate was coming to an end and Jews and Arabs were fighting over the establishment of a Jewish state. Passions were running extremely high, fuelled on the Jewish side by knowledge of the atrocities of the Holocaust. The British forces were limiting Jewish immigration and trying to maintain what the Foreign Office regarded as a balanced policy towards the Arabs, greatly influenced by British interests across the whole of the Middle East.

Into this cauldron stepped my father, set on being brave and uncomplaining. There was so much in Palestine to interest him and so many people with whom he could practise his newly acquired Arabic. All his life he had studied the scriptures of the Holy Land and his experiences there would form the basis of countless future sermons. At the time there was, it has to be admitted, the problem of his family, but that would be sorted out, as so many things were, by my mother.

Olive Sergeant was a formidable young woman, who many considered headstrong, with a directness of manner which some found overpowering. Still in England she heard of the explosion at Jerusalem's King David Hotel, which left about two hundred dead or wounded, but she was not too perturbed. In her eighties she would admit that her reaction had been wrong, but simple. 'I thought it was exciting,' she said. 'I was determined to go.' My mother went to the offices of the Church Missionary Society when the Middle East manager was away on holiday. She noticed from papers on his desk that four berths were available for the outgoing journey to Palestine. When he returned he was horrified to learn that those tickets had been issued to Mrs Sergeant and her three children.

So it was that in the autumn of 1946, at the age of two, with my older brother and sister, I took up residence in the Street of the Prophets in Jerusalem. Returning there many years later with the BBC's correspondent in Israel, Alex Brodie, we could still see where the mission school had been and the high wall surrounding the property. The street had been given a Hebrew name. When I lived there I apparently referred to it as 'The Tweet of the Prophets', a touch of innocence against a background of increasing violence.

Militant Jews had decided that the only way to force the British out was to resort to terrorism. Almost every evening, during the five months we were there, we heard gunfire. Barbed wire was everywhere and we were constantly stopped by military patrols. On one occasion my mother and father were coming back from a walk when they saw a man apparently following two young air force personnel on leave. As the door of our house closed a shot rang out. One of the airmen had been killed. The British authorities decided that families and non-essential personnel should be evacuated. My father stayed but we were sent home.

My mother often regaled us with stories of our family life. Sometimes, even before an event was over, the story would begin to take shape. We suspected she sometimes decided to behave in an unusual manner simply to ensure that there would be a tale to tell. On the train from Cairo to Port Said, there was some grumbling among the passengers at the way the Sergeant children were frisking about. My mother, convinced that attack was the best form of defence, declared in a loud voice, 'There is no use in complaining, my children are perfect.' It seemed to have the desired effect. Other stories from that long journey home were endlessly recycled. I saw my first film, a Charlie Chaplin comedy, in an army hut in the Ma'adi evacuation camp near the Pyramids and was not impressed. Walking back through the sand, there were tears streaming down my face. 'Silly man, silly man,' I kept saying, and ever since have regarded Charlie Chaplin as overrated and not very funny. A more encouraging discovery was that we seemed immune to seasickness. The troopship *Circassia* pitched and yawed through the Bay of Biscay, a grand piano lost its moorings and slid dangerously about the ballroom, but the three little Sergeant children went on with their games and never missed a meal.

Our adventure in the Middle East had ended though our difficulties were by no means over. Whenever I see the film *The Railway Children* I think back to that time; our father was not in prison, but he would fail to return for another two years and when he did he seemed a stranger. My mother found a job as an assistant matron in a small private school at Swimbridge in North Devon. It was there, at Dennington House, that the Reverend Jack Russell established the breed of terriers that took his name and at the age of three I seem to have adopted some of their ways. When a much older boy attacked my brother I crawled under a table and bit him fiercely on the leg. As my mother often recalled, the eight-year-old screamed, 'That baby has bitten me.'

When my father eventually returned it was not to marital bliss. In Jerusalem he had fallen in love with an Armenian nurse. On his first night back he joined me in my bed as I slept. We were staying in a tiny flat in Kensington; my mother's bed had been deemed unsuitable and there was nowhere else. It is one of my first real memories, waking up with this strange wonderful person beside me. The father I was so pleased to see, back with us at last. Before he shaved, I remember brushing my hand across the stubble on his cheek. I knew nothing of the tension between him and my mother. They would have discussed it in Russian, and only when I was grown-up was I told about Azaduki the Armenian nurse, who followed my father to England.

With my brother and sister away at boarding school, the centre of my life in London was the Round Pond in Kensington Gardens. I went to watch the little boats being sailed there and once I fell in, to the annoyance of my aunt who was accompanying me. 'You're so wet,' she kept saying to me. 'You're so wet.'

'Don't keep looding to that,' I replied crossly. 'Don't keep looding to that.' When we arrived home, she asked my mother what I could possibly mean. 'Oh,' my mother replied casually, 'he means don't keep alluding to that.'

On another occasion my mother lost me in Kensington Gardens; she had been talking to someone and I had just vanished. With an air of increasing panic, she began to ask people if they had seen a little boy with a yellow jumper. 'No,' replied a particularly irritating woman, 'but I have just seen a dear little girl in a blue dress.'

Eventually a policeman found me. I was christened John James and my family have always called me Johnny. The policeman approached me. 'Are you,' he said, 'Johnny James?'

My mother used to enjoy recounting my reply: 'Of course.'

★

It is unlikely that I ever met Azaduki, and if I had, it would have been impossible for me to work out how she fitted into the life of my parents; they found it difficult enough themselves. My mother wrote to the authorities to obtain permission for her to stay in England, having accepted that there was little chance of her own relationship with Ernest returning to a proper footing. But the affair with Azaduki soon ran out of steam and my parents were faced with what they believed was a cruel dilemma: how could they bring up the children they adored when their marriage seemed to be over?

They reached an extraordinary agreement which would

have a profound effect on my early life. For the sake of the children, they would stay together for ten years and then would both be free to marry again. It meant that I lived in a traditional family setting with a father and a mother, a brother and a sister. We went on holidays together. We always shared meal times. Although there were times when my parents quarrelled, I had a happy childhood. We children knew nothing of this ten-year agreement and to us they seemed fond of each other. For me it was far better than if they had split up; the precious years of my childhood were protected and I could plunge into a secret, enjoyable world to which adults were only sometimes permitted.

Matters were helped by a dramatic change in our circumstances. We left London for a large eighteenth-century vicarage in one of the most beautiful villages in England. Great Tew in Oxfordshire is still largely unspoilt today, with its golden sandstone walls, thatched cottages, Norman church and a grand manor house on the hill above the village. In the 1950s, there were seldom cars on the roads, few homes had television and Oxford, just seventeen miles away, seemed a distant and exciting place. The Rev. E. N. C. Sergeant became vicar of Great Tew and my mother would play a role she surprisingly relished, that of vicar's wife.

The village was heaven for children who wanted to build igloos in the winter, to ride bikes in the summer, to chase bullocks in the field, to shoot catapults and on one glorious occasion to try to escape from home altogether. We hardly needed to read the *Just William* stories or the adventures of the Swallows and Amazons, we *were* those children, anarchic and unafraid. When it rained we read them anyway, glancing up to see the drops of water slide down the windows and wishing we could be outside and free. I had the great advantage of being the youngest. When we brought out my mother's terrible temper or my father's heavy-handed discipline, I would sometimes literally hide behind my brother Peter, who was three and a half years older, or my sister Anne, tall for her age and two years my senior.

However, I usually wanted to take bigger risks than Anne or Peter and was more upset when things went wrong. Our escape from home was a case in point. I was about six at the time and could see no reason why we should not make a break for it; we had been cooped up for long enough and could do with a great adventure. My brother and sister were not so keen. We picked up a loaf of bread and clambered over the high wall enclosing the estate belonging to the squire of Great Tew, an old Etonian called Major Eustace Robb who was very keen on the vicar's wife; they would sometimes talk for more than an hour on the telephone. When we could not think of anything better to do we climbed a tree. It had a comforting familiarity. No decision had to be made. The climb itself was reason enough. So we sat in a tree on the estate wondering what to do next as the afternoon wore on. It's not exactly clear how or why it happened but, to my horror, Peter relieved himself on the loaf of bread. It was immediately obvious that with our food supplies ruined we could not run away from home. I felt cheated as we wandered back to the vicarage and was particularly annoyed when it became apparent that our mother had not even missed us.

For a time my father was keen to see if, like him, I had a gift for languages. There was a period when he taught me himself with a timetable based on the grim little refrain, 'Latin before breakfast and French after tea.' But the attempt to turn me into a linguistic prodigy failed. The more he suggested that he would have given anything for help of this kind, the more I came to believe that parents inhabited a different world. He even tried to teach me a little Chinese. He complained that he was too old to get to grips with Mandarin but, grinning broadly and rubbing his hands, he declared that in twenty years I could easily be fluent. Members of the family had accused me of being like the emperor of China because I had come down one morning and asked in an imperious voice, 'Where is my egg?' He taught me to say '*Pu Yi chen shung*,' meaning, 'My name is Pu Yi.' Only much later did I find out that Pu Yi was the last emperor of China, who while still a child abdicated in 1912.

Each morning my father would get up and start to make us breakfast before leaving to ring a bell in church at seven o'clock. Then we would have breakfast together. We would never ask him if anyone had come to church in response to the bell because no one ever did. The real reason for the bell was to prove to the parish that he was up and working. Once the bell tolled across the village, his task was done. He imagined the locals saying to each other, 'Say what you like about the vicar, he does his bit.'

Few people went to church on Sunday except for harvest thanksgiving, when the church was full, or on important dates in the calendar such as Christmas and Easter. On one memorable Sunday when snow was on the ground only the Sergeant family were present. I thought my father would insist on going through the whole service, but he said a single prayer and we were then allowed home. We spent the rest of the day in the pale winter sun, playing with our sledge and throwing snowballs. Days like that in Great Tew now seem almost unbearably perfect; they are the strongest possible argument for not growing up.

It may seem strange, but we were not a religious family. When we were little, our parents expected us to pray before going to bed, at least when they were present, but the Rev. E. N. C. Sergeant had enough doubts about miracles and the virgin birth to be careful about taking too strong a line with us. He did stress, though, that the Church was our family business. Other children from the village were given permission to leave before the sermon began, but we were not. When there was a whist drive at the vicarage we were allowed to play cards, but we were not permitted to win. In later life I was not a church goer, sometimes frivolously suggesting that my church attendance as a child should see me through. What the experience did teach us was the importance of acting properly in public, not because it was inherently good but because it could hurt your family if you let them down.

My father did not bury himself completely in the country. On one occasion he was called upon to interpret for George VI. Russian experts in the Foreign Office had decided he was the only person in the country who could cope with the special terms used to address the senior members of the Russian Orthodox Church who were to visit the king. My father duly appeared at Buckingham Palace. After his work was over the king asked why he had learned Russian. 'I thought, sir,' my father replied, 'that it would be useful.' To my father's surprise the king laughed; like so many of his subjects the king found my father's intellectual interests impossible to understand. As an old man, my father treasured the occasion as one of his concrete achievements. 'I have,' he would say with a satisfied sigh, 'interpreted for my sovereign.'

Worldly affairs had little effect on my life in Great Tew. We did not have a television set though some of the richer farmers did. My parents believed it was better for us to talk and read. But we were allowed to watch the Boat Race in 1951 and two years later saw the coronation on television. The radio was our link to the outside world and my parents took *The Times*. There were advertisements on the front page and a few photographs on the back. These proved useful for our first school project, based on the trip Princess Elizabeth made to Kenya, which came to an abrupt end when her father died. We cut out the pictures of Winston Churchill as prime minister greeting the young queen on her return at Heathrow Airport.

The village was en fête for the coronation. I appeared in an outdoor production in the stable yard at the Big House, as the manor was called. It was vaguely royal in tone, more pantomime than play, with me unconvincingly dressed up as Old King Cole. It was quite a strain being nice to the queen, who was one of the least exciting girls in the school. My brother Peter nearly fell off some scaffolding as he tried to take a picture of me with a Box Brownie camera. Then we had to queue up in front of Major Eustace Robb and my father, to be given coronation mugs stamped with the royal crest.

It was at about this time I decided I wanted to be a comedian. Maybe this was because the world of grown-ups often seemed easier to appreciate, not as something straightforward but as comedy. The professional comedians I enjoyed most were on the radio: Tony Hancock, of course, with *Hancock's Half Hour* but all the others too, Ted Ray, Arthur Askey and Jimmy Edwards among them. I was not very discriminating. Putting on the radio, pushing matchsticks into the fretwork front as the valves heated, would always raise my expectations. When *The Goon Show* became all the rage I could not understand why everyone did not want to be a comedian. How could one cope with all those self-serving reminiscences of the Second World War without thinking of Spike Milligan shouting at the generals, 'The war is over, get to your typewriters!'? One of the highlights of my young life was going to the Radio Show at Earl's Court in London and sitting in the front row for a performance by the American comedian Jack Benny; he had such an expensive suit. But the most important thing was that he was doing his best to make me laugh. If only all grown-ups had been like that.

My parents did not have a difficult decision to make about where to send me to school; there was only one. I was very happy at Great Tew Primary School and it was hardly demanding. There were thirty children, arranged in rows of five, and each year we would move up a row. The teacher was called Mrs Bury and very good she was. Sybil Bury must have had something special; she died in April 2001 at the age of 100. She taught me from the age of five and, in large measure due to her skills, when I left I was one of the best eleven-plus candidates in the county. My father was also a teacher at a minor public school at Bloxham about ten miles away, and when I was eleven I went there as a boarder to join my brother. Because my father was on the staff the fees were limited to one hundred pounds a year. There was only one serious difficulty: the school intake was usually at the age of thirteen, so for two years I was the youngest boy in the school. Fortunately the intake was not particularly bright and when Bloxham was rated in an educational survey, it came out as the worst performing public school in the country. 'I believe,' the headmaster commented, 'in endeavour from below.' I did not like its rather rough combination of bullying and homosexuality.

In the spring of 1956, events in Russia once again touched the family. Following Stalin's death several figures were competing for the leadership of the Soviet Union. The First Secretary of the Communist Party was Nikita Khrushchev and the prime minister was Nikolai Bulganin. When they arrived in Britain for a state visit they were referred to jocularly as 'B and K', but there was nothing light-hearted about the approach of the British Secret Intelligence Service. A frogman, Commander 'Buster' Crabb, died in mysterious circumstances after being sent to examine the hulls of the warships in Portsmouth harbour which had brought the Soviet leaders to Britain. It was a tense period in the cold war. Later in the year Soviet troops would quell the uprising in Hungary, while the British government came close to disaster in the Suez crisis.

Not much of this bothered my parents as they set off from Great Tew in their tiny Morris 8 car to meet the Soviet leaders in Oxford. They had been invited to a reception because my mother worked with the mayor of Oxford, Marcus Lower, at the Workers' Educational Association. There was a noisy demonstration outside the town hall, but this did not deter my mother who greeted the first distinguished guest with a torrent of Russian. He laughed in a friendly way. It was the foreign secretary, Selwyn Lloyd, amused that my mother had no idea who he was. When Bulganin arrived, he seemed morose and only cheered up when asked by my father to autograph a copy of his collected speeches. Khrushchev was characteristically ebullient. He was asked if he was tired and, with my mother interpreting, said, 'When I worked on my back in a mine all day I thought if only I could stand up I could go on for ever. Of course I am not tired.'

My idyllic life in Great Tew came to an end in 1957. My father was caught in one of those dramatic changes which at the time are very difficult to spot. The decline in the power, prestige, and influence of the Church of England had not altered the demands which some wealthy patrons were determined to place on their vicars. It seems monstrous now that my parents should be criticized for doing work other than their parish duties but, led by a woman called Lady Hunter from Little Tew, a plot was laid against my father. Through her contacts at Bloxham she had him dismissed from the school on the grounds that he was neglecting his parish. All that early morning bell ringing had not been enough. Without his teaching salary we had insufficient funds and had to leave the village. Soon the parish was amalgamated with others and Great Tew became an unpaid post. As we noted with some satisfaction, Lady Hunter was never able to find the sort of vicar she wanted. Those days were over.

It was also the end of my parents' marriage. Their ten-year agreement was almost up. We three children moved with my mother to Oxford into the first property we had ever owned; my father went to teach at the most expensive school in

England, Millfield in Somerset. My brother and I went there as boarders for the same fees as Bloxham, just one hundred pounds a year, and Anne went to grammar school in Oxford. My father had lost his job, his marriage and his home. The effects of this major family disaster were, for me at least, surprisingly benign. At thirteen, it was the beginning of proper schooling and the foundation for much of my academic success. I would meet some extraordinary people and I would be given opportunities that money alone could not have bought.

4

Playing games with the rich

MILLFIELD SCHOOL was founded in 1935 by a Cambridge graduate and fanatical cricketer, Jack Meyer, to educate the sons of Indian princes. Based on a large house in Street in Somerset which had belonged to the Clark shoe-manufacturing family, it produced more famous sportsmen and women than any similar establishment. Meyer, known reasonably affectionately as 'Boss', had a penchant for publicity and thought my father's language skills might be put to good use. Fortunately a plan for my father to appear on the television quiz show, *Double Your Money*, did not materialize, but for nearly twenty years he taught a vast range of languages at Millfield, which also provided his two sons with an education.

Getting in was not entirely straightforward. Every applicant had to undergo an IQ test, which was meant to be a scientific way of assessing intelligence. A psychologist carried out the tests; he was overweight and had an unfortunate, rather sinister manner. One of his techniques was to ask you to button your jacket. This is apparently an infallible way of finding out whether you are left-handed. I could not resist moving the two sides of my jacket together at the same time, even though I am normally right-handed. From that point on the psychologist treated me with great suspicion. He seemed baffled when I failed to work out a simple sequence of holes he had made by cutting and folding pieces of paper. 'I thought it was more difficult than that,' I explained. 'I thought it was a trick.'

'A trick?' he growled, as if in answer to Oliver Twist's

request for more. 'First there were four holes, then there were eight holes and now there are sixteen holes. Don't you understand, it's a simple sequence?' I had suggested an odd number, seven at one stage, and had not picked up the sequence at all.

I was just thirteen years old and I knew one thing for certain: I did not like this man. 'I thought it was a trick,' I tried to look him firmly in the eye, 'like there are sometimes tricks in maths.'

'Tricks in maths?' he almost exploded. 'Oh, no, there are not. In maths something is either right or wrong.' This had suddenly become the most difficult interview in my life. I tried to explain that sometimes when you think you have learned something in maths you can make a mistake if the teacher sets you a question not quite like the one you have practised. It is a trick. He was not impressed. At the door he gave me a sticky handshake and asked me one more time, 'Are there tricks in maths?'

I tried to sound conciliatory but have never been very good at bowing to authority. Once again trying to look him firmly in the eye I could only manage to say, 'Not usually.' For whatever reason, in his formal report the psychologist concluded that though I was reasonably bright I should be taught a manual trade. My parents relayed this information to me as we travelled down to Somerset for the interview with the Millfield headmaster. They hoped it would stop me coming over as too confident and in that they succeeded. My heart sank as we moved towards the metalwork shop. 'This will particularly interest you,' Boss said to me, with heavy emphasis. I tried to look as if working on sheets of metal would be my idea of bliss.

Apart from a few feeble attempts to teach me how to construct metal set squares and files after I entered the school, I heard no more of this unusual career advice. Perhaps the notes from the psychologist left out a vital word, maybe the original conclusion was that I should *not* be taught a manual trade. But I was able to take a small revenge on my rather sinister interrogator when he produced a secret list of the IQs of every pupil in the school and a small group of us cracked his code. My IQ was recorded as AJO. From all the examples we worked out that the middle letter was the initial of the pupil's first name and the other two letters had to be decoded using a nine-letter word, which turned out to be the name of one of the school houses, Wraxleigh. 'A' as the third letter was therefore 3 and 'O' was zero. This gave me an IQ of 130, but it also gave me the advantage of knowing how bright everyone in the school was supposed to be. It also left me with a lasting suspicion of educational experts and IQ tests taken on their own without any reference to a person's character or experience. Often these tests merely demonstrate how familiar you are with tests of this sort. If you have never come across them before you are likely to do badly. The system can easily be perverted if children are trained to answer such questions, as I was with great care by Mrs Bury for my eleven-plus exam. In the Millfield example, a few pupils had been given IQs of more than 160 – the norm is meant to be 100 – and these were the little geniuses sitting quietly in maths classes, turning in perfect results in a childish hand. But none of them had particularly distinguished careers after they left school.

Jack Meyer's philosophy was simple: children of the very rich were accepted however dim and they paid full fees, while the rest of us would have to prove our usefulness to the school. The most outstanding sports players in my time, such as the athlete Mary Bignal, who won three gold medals at the Tokyo Olympics, were given full scholarships. The sons of millionaires, who were there in some strength, were usually not at all bright. At my first evening meal I was surprised to find that I was the only person on my table capable of cutting slices from a loaf of bread. But then I was sitting between a boy worth a million pounds in his own right and another worth half a million pounds more. They were amazingly rich and had been pampered at home. I had thirty shillings, or £1.50, to spend each term, and my mother was far too busy to cut slices of bread whenever we were hungry.

The problem with the sports stars, like the little geniuses, was that they could make you feel inadequate. One of my friends in class was the tennis player Mark Cox, whom I would not dare to invite for a knock up in the lunch hour. Brian Barnes the golfer was another friend who made me feel ball games were not for me. I was the vice-captain of the rugby teams for the under-15s and under-16s. The captain, a genial, guitar-playing fellow called Blacks, later turned into the celebrity disc jockey Tony Blackburn. I once even managed to win my house colours, the right to wear a special tie, because I tackled the largest boy in the school. A great roar went up from the crowd because my team won as a result. But, I may as well admit, I was trying to move away from him at the time and we collided. After the age of sixteen we were allowed to choose whether we played games. I chose golf and chess. My games report said, 'Sergeant is sometimes seen leaning on a borrowed club in the vicinity of the golf course.' But I did manage to become captain of chess.

We lived a life set apart from the normal world and I thought of Millfield as a prisoner of war camp. We had, as far as I could tell, done nothing wrong but we were prisoners, and it was difficult to escape. One consoling fact was that we were in a beautiful part of the country, the mystical area of Somerset close to Glastonbury Tor. There were, too, visitors from the outside world, who would occasionally descend literally from the skies. On one occasion a small helicopter, painted a brilliant white, landed on the sports field. I did not recognize the distinguished figure emerging with a young girl to meet the headmaster, but the better connected boys were in no doubt. The Greek shipping magnate Aristotle Onassis, who was later to marry Jackie Kennedy, had a strange proposition. He would pay almost anything for his son and daughter to come to the school, but every weekend would have to be spent in either Monte Carlo or Rome, with one or other of their separated parents. Boss decided this would be disruptive and other boarders might regard this arrangement as unfair. I did not know of their tense negotiations as I attempted to chat up Christina Onassis, then aged ten but already with dark sad eyes. Our conversation was hardly exciting, but at least I tried. This is how it went:

> *Me (pointing to the helicopter):* Would you like to have one of these?
> *Christina:* Not really.

I would like to say that seeing so much conspicuous wealth at this stage in my life was good for me, and maybe it was. I certainly realized how vast sums of money were of limited use in helping children grow up. Most of the rich pupils seemed to have difficulty making friends. They often appeared mean, so anxious were they that no one should take advantage of their wealth; and it did not help them to pass exams. I wanted my relations with them not to be clouded by money, and that usually meant without the obvious intervention of their parents or mine. The only real difficulty came at the end of each term when my mother would park her battered Ford Popular with a screech of brakes and a cloud of dust alongside sleek Jaguars and Bentleys. My mother was not in the least embarrassed by the contrast and would rush across to other parents to introduce herself. It was an approach I later admired, but at the time I wanted to curl up and die. All my attempts to relate to my fellow pupils on equal terms were shattered. There seemed to be only one solution: I decided that it was better to stay an extra night and have her pick me up the day after the end of term.

Rich parents were attracted to Millfield by Boss's un-doubted charisma. He was a charmer and a showman and he appeared genuinely excited about the possibility of dramatically extending pupils' horizons. On one occasion, he assembled all the top golfers in the school to spend the morning trying to get a hole in one. His theory was that British golfers were always too modest in their approach; they merely tried to get the ball onto the green so a hole in one was an accident. He wanted them to try for the seemingly impossible. He also made sure that the *Sunday Times* was on hand to record the event. One of his other theories was that the only way people could learn properly was if they were allowed to find their own level. This was not possible in large classes so at Millfield the average class size was about eight or ten. It made for intensive lessons but required able teachers, whose personalities became of crucial importance.

I was fortunate in being taught English by Robert Bolt, who was about to become one of the foremost playwrights in the country and later found fame as the scriptwriter of epic films, including *Lawrence of Arabia* and *Dr Zhivago*. I first came across him teaching in an army-style Nissen hut at the furthest corner of the Millfield campus. Fearfully cold in winter, with a coke stove in the middle of the hut, it was there that he drummed into me the essentials of the language. My first piece of work was a precis. I was describing how 'the war clouds of Europe were gathering' and, being thirteen at the time, thought the phrase had a certain ring about it. Not for Robert Bolt; it was a cliché and had to be struck out. When he was recovering from a stroke many years later, I wrote to commis-erate and mentioned this incident. 'Perhaps,' he replied, 'I was a little harsh.' He turned into one of my heroes because of the way he triumphed from these modest beginnings in Somerset.

During the time he taught me, he conquered the West End with a play called *Flowering Cherry*, starring Ralph Richardson and Celia Johnson. We could tell he was doing well because he turned up for class in a brand-new red estate car, which he parked alongside the hut. Then he wrote *A Man for All Seasons*, which became an Oscar-winning film with Paul Scofield, and finally took Hollywood by storm with those epic productions directed by David Lean. He was almost too successful in teaching me English. At the age of fourteen, I passed O levels in a number of subjects, including English literature and English language, and then specialized in maths and physics. As it turned out Robert Bolt was my first and last proper English teacher. I have many reasons to be grateful, not least the example he set in attempting the seemingly impossible.

Life at home in Oxford was very different from Great Tew. Instead of the large beautiful vicarage, my mother had bought a post-war semi-detached house on an estate in Wolvercote. It was considerably smaller and at the end of the day we moved in our furniture stretched forlornly down the pavement outside; there was simply not enough room for it all. The mental adjustment was even harder to make, but there were compensations including, at the end of our road, the terminus for the Number 4 bus route. It was the magic carpet to take us into Oxford. My mother was happy because there was a new man in her life, who would become the most important mentor in mine. With my brother and sister, I knew that something strange had happened to her while we waited in the Ford Popular outside Magdalen College a year earlier. As part of her work in arranging adult educational classes she had found someone to talk about Roman Britain to the aspiring intellectuals of Eynsham, a village near Oxford. We waited for what seemed like hours in the car and when she came back nothing could dent her good mood. She shone like a light bulb, and only much later did we know why. She had met the love of her life.

Courtney Edward Stevens, a fellow of Magdalen College adored by generations of students, was known formally as C. E. Stevens, but for his close friends the only question was whether he should be called Tom or Tom Brown. His brother, Sir John Stevens, who was seven years younger and became a governor of the Bank of England, had exactly the same nickname for the same reason. Both of them had arrived at Winchester College with wide collars and baggy trousers as if from Victorian times and the reaction of the other pupils was the same: 'Look, there's Tom Brown.' The elder brother, with old-fashioned reserve, had not thought fit to alert his parents to the danger and the name had stuck to them both.

At one level our Tom could be very frightening. He was formidably clever, with an extraordinary breadth of knowledge and a near photographic memory. But, it has to be said, although he would hate to admit it he was also extremely eccentric. He found it difficult to keep his shirt inside his trousers. He often spilt things because he only had sight in one eye due to an accident involving a motorbike, and he had a childlike tendency to get overexcited. But he was immensely warm and likeable with a natural gift for teaching. When we met at our home in Wolvercote, he took me to one side and asked me what I thought about the Van Allen radiation belt. It was a master stroke. Like many schoolboys at the time I was fascinated by the possibility of manned space flight, following the successful launch of the Russian satellite, the Sputnik, in 1957. But Mr Van Allen had discovered a belt of radiation circling the globe, and it was feared this could make any early attempt at manned space flight difficult, if not impossible. Unlike all the other grown-ups I came across, Tom, who was one of the country's leading experts in Roman Britain, seemed to share my concern. Scientists were soon able to discount the problem, but our conversation launched a close friendship which lasted for the rest of Tom's life. Before long he came to live with us, and became my unofficial tutor. Although I was specializing in maths and physics, increasingly I was interested in politics and modern history and Tom was my guide. Two years later he married my mother.

We spent much of our time together discussing the Second World War, and in particular the role of Adolf Hitler, or 'that man' as Tom would refer to him. Like my father, Tom had not been called up, but his work in the war had been arduous and effective. He became an expert in what was called black propaganda, otherwise known as lying. His job was to think up stories, apparently true, which would be broadcast by supposedly German radio stations in order to undermine enemy morale. In one of these, a U-boat commander advertised in a local paper for his lost binoculars. 'How casual can you get?' thundered Tom's commentary. 'When the Reich is in danger some of our commanders don't bother to look after their equipment.' The offending officer was named and was subsequently brought to trial by the German authorities. This was not exactly in the spirit of English fair play but, as Tom pointed out, it was not a time to be squeamish. His greatest coup was realizing that V for victory in Morse code could be rendered as the first bar of Beethoven's Fifth Symphony. Throughout Europe the drum beat rhythm of di, di, di, dah became a great call to arms. When Tom died in the 1970s an organ transcription of the Fifth Symphony was played at his memorial service in Magdalen College chapel, and I can almost never listen to the opening part of that symphony without tears in my eyes.

Tom spoke fluent German, but with an absurd English accent; he made no attempt to give it a guttural twang. I decided this was going to be my foreign language, having failed miserably at French. Our French teacher was a small irritating man from the Channel Islands, whom we called 'Linky' because he looked like a monkey. We liked to think he was the missing evolutionary link between monkeys and Neanderthal man, much talked about at the time. German, on the other hand, was taught by an understanding Scotsman and, I wrongly assumed, it was not a language my father knew well. Only when I was writing a thank you letter to the family in Frankfurt with whom I had spent the summer did my father lean over and calmly correct my grammar. Apart from German almost all my timetable was taken up by maths and physics, an appallingly narrow education. Each year for three years I would take A-level exams in these subjects, passing on each occasion but not with dramatically different results. But my outside activities were broadening. I became the editor of the unofficial school magazine, *Focus*, I acted in and directed plays (one was described by Robert Bolt who came back to judge the drama competition as 'communist propaganda') and I learned to fly, first gliders and then powered planes, the latter through an RAF scholarship.

It was a classic example of closing the stable door after the horse has bolted. Those in charge of the RAF were determined that Britain should never again suffer from a shortage of pilots, as we had in 1940 during the Battle of Britain. So for years after the war young men, rigorously selected after a battery of tests, were given the holiday of their lives. I received my private pilot's licence after a total of ten hours of solo flying in ageing biplanes over southern England, after recently failing my driving test. The course was at Thruxton airfield in Hampshire and there were two crashes, although no one was killed. In one of them a plane tipped over on its back during a landing. We raced across the airfield to see a terrified eighteen-year-old hanging upside down in his straps with fuel pouring over his face. Right in front of his eyes, on the instrument panel, was a cartoon of a girl taking off her bra, with the caption, 'No strap hanging here.'

It was at this point that I finally managed to get a girlfriend at school. We were both staying on beyond our eighteenth birthday to try for Oxford and the competition for the small number of girls of the same age had finally been resolved in my favour. It did wonders for my morale, but not much for my work. I had decided to try to get into Magdalen College, to do politics, philosophy and economics, but I would have to take the scholarship exam in maths and physics. One Wednesday morning, with snow on the ground, I managed to do well in a paper on applied maths. It involved working out something to do with the velocities of revolving gases in three dimensions. For the last time in my life my applied mathematical skills did the trick. I was awarded an alpha in that paper and it was enough to tip the balance.

My father too had found the love of his life. Soon after arriving at Millfield he befriended Edna Cassels, a school housemother, who organized the forty pupils at Walton House, one of the dozen or so boarding houses. She had separated from her husband and it was agreed that my father should take over his role as housemaster at Walton. In those unenlightened days no one seemed to guess that they had become lovers. My only regret is that they never married. We always got on well; she had a way with young people, particularly boys, and she loved to gossip about the school. She made no attempt to try to understand my father's academic life, but she revered his scholarship. Her natural manner was uncomplicated and fun. It was exactly the sort of relationship he craved.

My father was fond of making grand statements about life; and this was not just because he was a former parson and still gave services when members of the local clergy were ill or on holiday. He was so pleased I had got into Oxford that it seemed like the moment for some fatherly advice. 'I want you,' he said, 'to move among all classes, to be as much at ease among the rich as the poor, to be a citizen of the world.' He paused to see how much of this was striking home. I smiled, wondering whether he would accept my plan for putting all this into effect. He noticed the look of someone whose mind was made up. 'Well,' he asked finally, 'what are you going to do before you start at Oxford next autumn?'

'Well, I thought I would go to America,' I replied; and was taken aback by his sharp reply.

'But that is far too ambitious,' he said, thinking of the distance and the expense. He had not reckoned on my determination or that of my mother. Three months later, after weeks of mind-numbing tedium working as a clerk at the National Institute for Research into Nuclear Science at Culham in Berkshire, I had just enough money to pay for my ticket. My mother provided me with a vital contact in the suburbs of Washington, DC. When I left home in Oxford the family were in a fairly emotional state; they felt their young soldier was off to the wars and they might never see him again.

Tom had left early to go to work, without saying goodbye, but then walked all the way to the station to give me a gruff farewell and a book on American history. My sister, Anne, then working as a nurse in London, came to see me off on the second leg of the journey, by train to Southampton. She said goodbye and then got back on the train to give me an apple. 'You won't change, will you?' she said anxiously; only long afterwards did she tell me how much she had cried.

But as I clambered up the gangway of the great Cunard liner, the *Queen Elizabeth*, I wanted to change, to change for the better, to know more and to experience more. I was overwhelmed by excitement. I had only about forty pounds in my pocket, but I felt rich beyond belief. This was going to be my great adventure; I had finally run away from home. No one could stop me doing things now, and soon the whole of America would lie at my feet.

5

'I have a dream'

BY 1963, TRAVELLING BY ocean liner across the Atlantic was already a minority sport. Millions of people preferred to go by plane and those on board the two Cunard liners, the *Queen Elizabeth* and the *Queen Mary*, would often find themselves outnumbered by the crew. When I travelled on that marvellous ship, the *Queen Elizabeth*, in the spring of that year, there were about six hundred passengers being looked after by officers and crew totalling just over a thousand. It was, though, the cheapest way to go to America and there was a twice-weekly service. For £129 10s 0d I bought a return ticket.

As a way of crossing the Atlantic it had, for the fashionable, completely lost its glamour; they had been enticed by endless advertisements featuring air hostesses and modern planes which defied space and time. The five-day voyage from Southampton, with a brief stop at Cherbourg for passengers from France, seemed like a journey into the past.

For me, of course, it was nothing of the kind. As I walked the gently heaving decks of the half-empty liner it was hard not to be overcome by the drama of it all. Out in the vast ocean, ploughing along at about thirty knots, one of the largest passengers ships ever built appeared to be taking me from one life to another; and I assumed it would be to a better life. Childhood was fast receding in the giant ship's wake. Surely, I thought, when I reach New York, I will have to be taken for an adult?

There was a report in the ship's daily newspaper, the *Ocean*

Times, which triggered a reaction in me, perhaps giving one of the first indications of the career I might follow as an adult. The minister for war, John Profumo, had denied any knowledge of a girl called Christine Keeler. It was the beginning of the scandal which would help to sweep the Conservatives from power. I distinctly remember concluding that the minister was probably lying. Otherwise why did the *Ocean Times* think it was important enough to put on the front page? It's the sort of argument I would frequently employ years later as a political correspondent.

Heading for adulthood, though, did not mean giving up silly games. The ship was split into three distinct zones for first class, cabin class and third class. There were great differences in the ticket prices, but I felt that those of us languishing on the lower decks should not meekly accept our place. A group of young people quickly formed and found no difficulty getting into the first-class ballrooms and bars. Every time the ship's clocks reached midnight they would stop for an hour so that after five nights we would be on American time. It allowed for a magic hour when there was no time at all and this, we insisted, should not be wasted in third class. I don't think the crew really minded, but they were quick to remove from the notice boards our invitation to all passengers to go to every part of the ship 'to celebrate the captain's birthday'.

Because of our late-night behaviour we missed the dawn arrival, the Statue of Liberty, and berthing alongside the Cunard pier at 42nd Street. When we woke up I said to the young man with whom I shared a cabin, 'Well, are we going to bother to look at New York?' And we then raced up the endless stairways to the top deck. It was breathtaking. The liner had berthed in the middle of the city. The skyscrapers of Manhattan seemed close enough to touch. The sky was a sharp blue. The noise of the city welled up around us. The yellow taxicabs buzzed about. There was even a band playing 'Dixie'.

There were some brisk goodbyes and then I was on my own for the long journey south by train. In those days the guard really did ring a bell and shout out, 'Washington, Washington, it's the end of the line.' I got into a cab at Union Station and said to the driver in rather a prim voice, 'Could you take me to Two six four six South June Street?'

'What?' he replied.

'Two six four six South June Street.'

He laughed, 'Hey, I like the way you talk, keep talking.'

Eventually we understood each other when I pronounced June as if I was a barman in a Hollywood film. I was staying with a family from the deep south, who as well as being family friends were also under the mistaken impression that I would be a good influence on their teenage children.

There were times when Bob and Anne Hardy treated me with quite unexpected kindness. On one occasion Bob said to me, 'Johnny, have you got transportation problems tonight?' I was on my way to rehearse with an amateur theatre group. It was a musical and I did not have a great part; I was playing a college boy from Chicago and was having problems hitting the note, although that was not in the script. I told Bob that it was indeed going to be difficult to get from their house on the outskirts of Washington into Alexandria for the rehearsal. Without a word he handed me the keys to his E-type Jaguar. Then I had to drive it out of the garage in the basement and down a very steep drive. When I revved the big engine the house seemed to shake and manoeuvring backwards was not at all easy, but Bob made no move to interfere. This was a rite of passage. He had decided that I should be trusted, even with his beloved red sports car.

Bob's most significant act of generosity was to provide me with a job. He was soon to retire as a colonel in the American air force and with a group of friends had taken over a business making concrete blocks. Before I left Oxford, he successfully applied for me to have a visa to work as an industrial trainee, 'with the intention of returning to England shortly to set up a similar business there'. And that is how, a few weeks before my nineteenth birthday, I became the accountant for a small concrete plant on the verge of bankruptcy on Telegraph Road, Alexandria.

My first task was to produce an inventory listing all our assets and estimating their value. I was not told why, but it soon became apparent; we were applying for a big loan from the bank and this was our last chance. To help me on the first Sunday was one of Bob's business colleagues, a man wearing military fatigues and a cap with a single gold star. General Delaney had retired from the air force the day before and was one of the funniest men I have ever met. He immediately used my first name, as we sat in the yard surrounded by a disparate assortment of concrete blocks. 'Johnny,' he said, 'yesterday I was in charge of twenty thousand accountants. I was lifted out of the Pentagon by helicopter to begin my retirement. Now I am sitting in a dump with just one accountant, and that's you.'

I leaped to my feet and gave him a snappy salute. 'Yes, sir.' At this point a train roared past. Neither of us had realized that there was a railway line alongside the yard.

After the train had gone by and the noise died down, he gave me a wonderfully mournful look. 'And,' he said, glancing across at the track, 'we'll have to get that shifted.'

I was slightly surprised by the method we used to value our assets. Many of the blocks came from long-forgotten projects and were either surplus to capacity or even wrongly made. Surely they were worth nothing? But this was boom time in America and the mood was infectious. We decided that the value of the blocks was the value they had had in the original contracts, and this would take some months to sort out.

There were about thirty employees in the plant and it was

a good vantage point from which to observe some of the strangeness of US life. Being British was a great advantage and for most Americans I was a novelty. The differences between our two countries were far greater than they are today. I was thrilled to have my first hamburger, my first pizza; there were barbecues and I had to learn how to open crabs on outings to Chesapeake Bay. People were outwardly more friendly, but simply because they habitually greeted you with a cheerful 'Hi' did not mean you had broken the ice. Taking a girl on a date certainly did not imply that you were about to start an affair; it seemed hard enough to win a goodnight kiss. But conversations, with both sexes, could take a personal turn far more quickly than at home. I was waiting in a car with the large amiable black foreman, and he turned to me and said, 'You and I are not that different. If you cut me I still bleed.' It was perhaps no coincidence that throughout that hot summer of 1963 the race issue was simmering.

I earned enough money to go to New York for a few weekends, sometimes meeting up with one of my Millfield millionaires whose father was an incredibly rich South African who would take us on the town at great expense. At the 21 restaurant one evening his bored mistress would only drink champagne and eat a little mashed potatoes with caviar. It was brought in, surrounded by ice, on a vast silver salver. She picked away at it, looking cross, while the waiters circled anxiously around. I tried my best to treat all this as normal behaviour. A good deal of my time was spent worrying about the stain on my suede shoes, caused by a bowl of soup pitched over them in mid-Atlantic. I was also acutely aware that my weekly pay cheque from the concrete plant would hardly pay for the cheese and biscuits.

It's impossible to say how successful I was at convincing these very rich people I was not a complete impostor. Maybe they knew I didn't have a bean, but it would be wrong to say they did not care. Like many of the wealthy people I have met, they couldn't leave the subject alone. 'You will make a lot of money,' one overdressed, middle-aged woman declared. She tucked her arm firmly inside mine and we set off with a swagger down Fifth Avenue. 'You must meet my friend Harry Winston,' she announced when we stopped outside a small shop bearing that name. The window display was full of diamonds. I wanted to run. Mr Winston was charm itself, particularly when she insisted on repeating her claim that I would make a lot of money. My side of the conversation was limited to the assertion that I did like necklaces and yes, the ones he brought out of the safe were rather fine. He did better with another Brit at around this time. It was at Harry Winston's that Richard Burton bought an engagement ring for Elizabeth Taylor.

My friend's father had good contacts in show business as some of his money had gone into films. Our party took up a whole row in the stalls for Anthony Newley's hit musical *Stop the World, I Want to Get Off*. It made my amateur efforts in Alexandria seem very tame, but it was yet another little encouragement drawing me towards a theatrical career. On another occasion we met the producer Sam Spiegel, who had worked with my old teacher Robert Bolt, and there were often celebrities at the dinners I attended in New York. They included the singer, Alma Cogan, who had lit up dull after-noons by the radio at Great Tew with 'Love and Marriage'. I also met the actor Stanley Baker, who gave me the firmest handshake of my life.

The most embarrassing moment was when one of my friends' father's close colleagues offered me the services of a call girl. Two of them were with him at the time. The four of us were in a lift at the Sherry Netherlands Hotel. 'Which one do you want?' he demanded. 'I don't need them any more; they've been paid off till the end of the week.'

I looked at these pretty girls and I looked at this dreadful man and I just about managed to smile. 'I really couldn't decide,' I said and stumbled out of the lift as soon as I could.

Manhattan was marvellous, but I very soon found that trailing along with the super rich was not the way to live. Being alone and relatively poor felt far more comfortable.

There was one occasion in New York which would have a profound effect on my life. I went to see the British satirical revue *Beyond the Fringe*, which was playing on Broadway with the original cast. Alan Bennett, Peter Cook, Dudley Moore and Jonathan Miller were dressed in black pullovers and trousers and were wonderfully funny. Whether it was the Macmillan take-off, the wartime sketch when the time had come to make a pointless sacrifice, or Alan Bennett's sermon, it all had an aura of magic. They made it look so simple, so quick and so unlike the mood then of young America; it was also gloriously political. If anyone had told me that the next time I saw Alan Bennett he would invite me to appear with him in a television comedy series I would have been amazed.

Back at the concrete plant, things were serious. Despite all our efforts the banks had decided to call in their loans. Even the electric typewriter we had on approval was whisked away by an agent acting for the sheriff; I was trying to use it at the time. My last task was to pay off the men, using a cheque machine to print out the totals. Only later was I told that my pay cheque alone would clear the bank. Commonwealth Cast Stone, as it was called, had gone bust. But, remarkably, the mood among the managers was not downcast.

There was an extraordinary atmosphere of confidence at that time in America, and having John F. Kennedy in the White House seemed to foster that spirit. We went to a celebration of Independence Day on the Fourth of July at the Washington Monument and word spread through the crowd that the president was there. There was an air of excitement and expectation. The idea that the president himself might be walking among us gripped people's imaginations. We craned our necks, we looked this way and that, but no one could confirm the sighting. When I checked the *Washington Post* the next day I found that he had been at Camp David in Maryland, but the attitude of that crowd had been very striking. When Kennedy was assassinated four months later I thought of the way those people at the Washington Monument had responded to him, even when he was not there. For anyone with direct experience of the 'Kennedy effect' it was not difficult to understand why his death was felt so personally around the world. He was the last word in political glamour. With his young wife and children he gave the impression that his leadership could achieve everything, and perhaps a bit more. After all we know now this seems hopelessly naive, but for me it provided further encouragement towards a political career.

The demise of Commonwealth Cast Stone came fortunately late in my American trip. I had enough money to travel, and there were three months before I would have to leave for home. Through an advertisement in the *Washington Post* I came into contact with a young man from Argentina called Andres, who was of German extraction, and Anne, an English student staying at Williamsburg in Virginia. We were still living in an age of comparative innocence, so the idea of driving across America with total strangers did not seem too odd, or too dangerous. Anne was engaged to be married, much to our annoyance because she was extremely pretty, and Andres was a first-year student at Princeton University. We drove a 1957 Chevrolet station wagon, bought by Andres, all the way to San Francisco and back. Mostly we camped, often in the intense heat simply falling asleep on airbeds out in the open. Sometimes we stayed in student halls of residence, empty in the summer, and, very rarely, in cheap hotels. We bought ice in plastic bags and ate large numbers of giant watermelons at a dollar apiece. It was an epic journey – the ultimate youth experience – but it was surprisingly uneventful. Yes, we concluded, Texas was very big; the Grand Canyon was very grand; and the Mojave Desert was very hot. We even made a detour into Mexico where we were struck by the poverty; one of the couples we saw being married in a church could not afford to pay for the electricity and so the lights were switched off.

It was in the southern states that our travels took on a less carefree aspect. I was shocked at the signs of discrimination, with the toilets and drinking fountains marked separately for blacks and whites. In New Orleans Andres spoke to me in German when he realized we should not have been sitting in the back of a bus; whites usually travelled in the front. With these frequent and all too visible reminders of how difficult life was then for black people in America, we could not fail to be caught up in the drama of the civil rights movement.

In 1955 Rosa Parks, a black textile worker in Montgomery, Alabama, had refused to give up her seat in the front of a bus to a white male. She was arrested and charged with breaking a local segregation law. Martin Luther King took up her case and for the first time became involved in politics. The buses in Montgomery were boycotted by blacks for more than a year and the incident sparked off the civil rights movement. When we were in the south there was a great deal of despair among politically active blacks, but the tide was to turn that year, largely due to the non-violent protests led by King. Although he was supported by white liberals and to a certain extent by the Kennedy administration which was thankful his tactics were essentially peaceful, he was hated by a large swathe of southern opinion. That summer King spent time in jail.

When I returned to Washington, I could not easily discuss my travels through the south with the Hardys. Anne Hardy was from Little Rock, Arkansas, and Bob came from a long-established family in Mississippi. They were not impressed by liberal anguish over black rights. At one stage President Kennedy suggested that families in Washington should invite black people to their homes and Anne laughed loudly and said, 'Well, I'm going to paint my face black and present myself at the White House.' The Hardys, it has to be said, treated their own black maid with great respect, although she would travel in the back of their estate car when Anne drove her home.

Because in every other way I liked and admired them I tried to avoid the subject, but that was not always possible and it was unfortunate that one of the most extraordinary political experiences of my life could not be shared with them. I was one of the comparatively small number of whites standing in front of the Lincoln Memorial in Washington when Martin Luther King made his 'I have a dream' speech. For weeks we had been aware of the build-up to 'The March on Washington', and Anne knew that I would be going to hear the speeches. As I prepared to leave she gave me a long cool look. 'Well, Johnny,' she said, 'are you going downtown?'

'Yes, I thought I would.' I tried to sound casual. I was not going because I knew this would be a great event, but because I was deeply absorbed by political argument. I had become caught up by what I saw as a simple injustice, and I was also about to become a full-time student of politics. It would have been difficult for me to stay away.

Part of King's political approach was derived directly from the success of Ghandhi's non-violent protests against British rule in India. Later on, the drive for black rights in America took on a more militant tone, with leaders such as Malcolm X openly advocating violence, but in the early 1960s the atmosphere at civil rights rallies was often open and relaxed. White sympathizers were deliberately encouraged. I did not feel in any way threatened when I joined the throng assembling in front of the Lincoln Memorial. For me it was the American nature of the rally which seemed strange, not the fact that most of the people there were black. There was a picnic atmosphere, with children eating hot dogs and hamburgers. The parks police with wide-brimmed hats moved among the crowd apparently more concerned with tidiness than imposing the law. There were nearly two hundred and fifty thousand people, most simply keen to be there, to show solidarity.

The speeches were far too long. It was a hot day in August and the crowd on either side of the mirror-like lake stretching from the Lincoln Memorial towards Capitol Hill had no shelter from the sun except among the trees further back. Most of the speakers seemed to have little new to add; it was left to that great singer Mahalia Jackson to rouse us with 'We shall overcome'. Although we were convinced we would overcome, it still seemed a long way off. I had no idea who the last speaker would be or even whether the speech would be worth waiting for.

I have often heard recordings of the 'I have a dream' speech; I have had plenty of opportunities to read the transcript in collections of great speeches of the twentieth century; I have even, for a BBC television programme, stood where Martin Luther King stood and declaimed parts of the speech to camera. But all these are nothing compared to seeing the real thing. King was only thirty-four when he spoke in front of the Lincoln Memorial, but he was by far the most charismatic of the black leaders. Well dressed in a smart suit, he had natural confidence; and if anyone criticized him for appearing to be removed from the real struggle he could point to a string of prison convictions. Above all, he had authority and presence, vital in the family business. King once said, 'Of course I was religious. I grew up in the church. My father is a preacher, my grandfather was a preacher, my great-grandfather was a preacher, my only brother is a preacher, my daddy's brother is a preacher. So I didn't have much choice.'

On that hot day in August before the vast crowd, he used all his experience to good effect. As my father taught me, a good preacher never lets go the chance to bring together time and place. King began with a powerful line, standing in front of the statue of Abraham Lincoln whose own commitment to black rights had led to the American civil war. 'Five score years ago,' King began, 'a great American, in whose symbolic shadow we stand, signed the Emancipation Proclamation. This momentous decree came as a great beacon light of hope to millions of Negro slaves who had been seared in the flames of withering injustice. It came as a joyous daybreak to end the long night of captivity. But one hundred years later, we must face the tragic fact that the Negro is still not free.'

As a teenager barely out of school, I was taken aback. The way he emphasized the words was unusually powerful. He almost sang the speech leaving his audience in no doubt they were expected to respond. On the recordings you can't hear the way the crowd took part, but when King began to repeat the refrain, 'I have a dream,' they took it as a cue, punctuating King's speech with cries of 'Oh, yeah' and 'Amen.' He mentioned his dream of equality five times, before saying with great feeling, 'I have a dream that my four children will one day live in a nation where they will not be judged by the colour of their skin but by the content of their character. I have a dream today.'

'Oh yeah,' those round me responded. He mentioned the dream another three times. And then he took up a fresh refrain: 'So let freedom ring . . .' He began to shout out a list of places, from the hilltops of New Hampshire, to the Rockies, to Chatanooga, Tennessee. Each time he mentioned a place there would be shouts from the crowd. Those in trees on either side of the lake waved furiously. Finally and trium-phantly he ended with this: 'When we let freedom ring, when we let it ring from every village and every hamlet, from every state and every city, we will be able to speed up that day when all of God's children, black men and white men, Jews and Gentiles, Protestants and Catholics, will be able to join hands and sing in the words of the old Negro spiritual, "Free at last! Thank God Almighty, we are free at last!"'

On the printed page it may be hard to see quite why this speech made such an impact; so much was in the manner of its delivery. But those of us who were there had no doubt. I wish I had been with a companion. As it was I remember walking away, on my own, muttering to myself, 'That preacher was good, he was very good, he was very, very good.' I couldn't, of course, discuss it when I arrived back at the Hardys.

It is one of life's ironies that at the age of nineteen I should hear perhaps the best speech I would ever hear. At the time, like most teenagers, I was determined not to be bowled over, to stay cool. Adults might complain that this showed a lack of feeling, but the emotion was more complicated. The teenage fear is that you may show too much emotion and therefore lose control. I was thousands of miles away from home and could not afford to be knocked off balance. Or at least that is the way I felt.

Within days I was on my way home, back on the *Queen Elizabeth* to Southampton. I had not made my fortune in America; when I reached Oxford I had twelve shillings in my pocket. But I had enormously enjoyed those life-forming experiences. I would never be thoughtlessly anti-American and, having seen so much, I was now keen, for a time, to learn about politics and economics from books.

6

A good degree of fun

'GENTLEMEN' was the way we were officially referred to as students, however unruly our behaviour. Notices would be put up at the lodge, which is the main entrance to Magdalen College, appealing to our good sense when a dangerous clash of interests between the smooth running of the college and the natural exuberance of young people seemed likely. 'Gentlemen', one notice read, 'should refrain from letting off fireworks within the college grounds.' There were many activities, from wild parties to bringing in chunks of mud on the bottom of our shoes, which gentlemen were advised against. But there was always an element of play-acting about this. We were expected to keep regular hours and be back in college before midnight when the big doors would be closed, but round the corner there was a lamp post which could easily be climbed giving us access to the college over the wall. There were some nasty-looking spikes on the post which, on close inspection, were clearly designed to help gentlemen climb in. We were treated as if we were adults on the assumption we would often continue to behave like children. It perfectly fitted my mood.

Like many students before and since I had two objectives: a good degree and a good degree of fun. All the possibilities for seriousness and the potential for just fooling about were on display from the first week, and I divided my time between work and play. But that is putting it too severely; there was far more play than work. After three years I ended up with a second-class honours degree in politics, philosophy and economics and a part in a comedy series on television. This outcome was not obvious from the start.

My study of philosophy began with an essay entitled 'Am I awake?' which I hoped to answer with a simple 'Yes.' But that was before I became acquainted with the tortuous logic of the great French philosopher René Descartes, who in the seventeenth century decided that we existed because we thought. It sounds better in Latin: *Cogito, ergo sum.* We students liked the idea that we were learning to argue – there was certainly something in that – but often we seemed to be going round in circles. I remember spending an hour discussing intentional acts with an eminent philosopher and later head of Hertford College, Geoffrey Warnock, the husband of Baroness Warnock. He was a delightful patient man and he was trying to get me to agree that sometimes it was difficult to know whether an act is intentional if, like switching the lights off before you go to bed, it has become habitual. Geoffrey treated me with great courtesy, but the discussion made me itch for closer contact with what I couldn't help thinking of as the real world, where people switched off lights before they went to bed without worrying whether they had acted intentionally or not.

The real world occasionally broke into our economics lessons, sometimes in the form of a telegram from Number 10 Downing Street. The politics of the early 1960s was the story of how Labour managed to overturn thirteen years of Conservative rule. The Tories were not helped by the Profumo scandal, nor by the image, carefully fostered by Harold Wilson and others, that they were more at home on the grouse moor than they were running a modern government. Wilson made a lot out of the fact that there were only a very small number of professional economists. He himself had a first-class degree in politics, philosophy and economics and had been a don at

Oxford. It was no surprise that he should turn to his alma mater for help.

Among the economists regularly taking the train to Paddington was Thomas Balogh, who with his fellow Hungarian, Nicholas Kaldor, became 'the terrible twins', or 'B and K', and advised Wilson on economic policy. Tommy Balogh, as we liked to call him, also continued to teach in Balliol College. Each Wednesday before lunch we would turn up to our lecture and sometimes when the subject matter was even more complicated than usual I would drift off in the back row as the sun from the skylight picked up the dust which settled gently around us. Then suddenly the door would open and there would be a messenger with a telegram. Balogh, a small eminent figure with white hair tumbling down the back of a bald head and usually wearing a natty bow tie, would give a world-weary sigh and, not to miss the moment of drama, say 'Number Ten' with a shrug. This usually brought an indrawn breath from his audience and then he would tell the messenger, 'No reply.' If, as Henry Kissinger once said, power is the great aphrodisiac, for economics students that moment was undeniably sexy.

One of the problems Balogh tried to tackle in his lectures was what governments could do to curb inflation. Much of his time was spent ridiculing the work of the American economist and later Nobel Prize winner, Milton Friedman. Balogh would write up on a blackboard the equation which forms the basis of the quantity theory of money and suggests that if you limit the amount of money in the economy you can control inflation. It was to become the basis of the monetarist theory which sustained Margaret Thatcher in most of her eleven years in power. Balogh thought it was an absurd simplification and of no value in policy terms. 'It is the work,' he would spit out in his strong Hungarian accent, 'of the much-overrated Chicago school.'

Years later I was drawn into a conversation at his home in Chelsea with a prominent member of Mrs Thatcher's government, Sir Keith Joseph. 'What did you learn at Oxford?' Sir Keith asked, in his usual forthright manner.

'Well, Tommy Balogh taught us to laugh at monetarism.' Sir Keith was intrigued; he wanted to know how we believed inflation could be tamed. 'Well,' I said, not wishing to get involved in a detailed argument, 'we were worried about bottle-necks, shortages of supply pushing up prices.' This seemed to send Sir Keith into a reverie. He was a natural enthusiast and economics was a subject he had come to rather late in life. He had all the ardour of the convert.

'Bottlenecks,' he enthused. 'Bottlenecks.' And although I tried to change the subject and move on to talk about current politics, he wanted to worry this bone. 'Bottlenecks,' he sighed, 'yes, yes, they are important.' It was late and I eased myself towards the door. He came outside to see me to my car. The word was still running round in his head. 'Goodbye,' he said, and then couldn't resist repeating with a sense of wonder, 'Ah, yes, bottlenecks.'

What we really learned at Oxford, of course, was that economists could be wrong, advisers could be prima donnas, politicians could be fools, and it was our duty to try to reach conclusions, even if we were young and inexperienced. It was hardest to do this in our studies of politics; we knew so little about how senior ministers might behave. How could they, for instance, be more interested in the power of their particular department than the good of the country? It took experience to know that if that question was posed, they would invariably reply that more power for their department would be good for the country. The most valuable lessons Tommy Balogh taught us were to think for ourselves and not to be in awe of those in government. It very much fitted in with the spirit of the times. Politicians nowadays seem to pay little attention to what students think but in the 1960s the cult of youth was in the ascendant. What we thought then did seem to matter.

More than anything else, politicians in the United States and Britain wanted to convince the younger generation that the war in Vietnam was morally justified. With me and all of my friends, they failed. One of the senior members of the US administration, Henry Cabot Lodge, ambassador in Saigon, even came to speak to students at the Oxford Union. The speech was not particularly well received, but he then made a mistake which turned it into a disaster. He was discussing the career of the North Vietnamese military leader, General Giap, with whose name we were reasonably familiar. 'That is,' he said ponderously, 'General Giap. Let me spell that for you. G-i-a-p.' We hooted with laughter. We were not expecting a spelling lesson. The poor ambassador had made an elementary error: he had patronized his audience. When that happens, particularly to students, they can be merciless.

On another occasion the South African ambassador attempted to justify the jailing of Nelson Mandela. He was addressing the Conservative Club. A group of us had member-ship cards from all the political clubs, which enabled us to go to every meeting of interest, although I was careful not to have a card from the Communist Club because it was already a reasonable assumption that the Security Service, or MI5, was keeping a close check on student communists. Outside the meeting a large angry crowd had assembled. They broke one of the windows and shouted, 'Free Mandela!' as if this would have any effect. The situation seemed to me so absurd that I could not resist writing on a piece of paper 'Mandela freed' and pushing this out of the broken window. For a moment the shouting stopped as the message was received with some puzzlement, and then the chanting continued. It would, of course, be nearly thirty years before Nelson Mandela was freed, and those youthful voices of protest would have long since become middle-aged.

On opposing apartheid in South Africa and the American involvement in Vietnam we had no doubts. Our objections were passionate. There were some Conservatives who shared this view but generally all my friends were typically Left-wing students. Most students at the time were, although there were some traditional Conservatives who continued to make their mark. It now seems rather embarrassing to recall what a dash young Jonathan Aitken cut with his actress sister, Maria. When I saw them dressed up at the Oxford Union, Jonathan resplendent in white tie and tails, I felt they had arrived from another planet. I was certainly not so confident of my own political views to want to see them tested in a union debate. When Aitken went to prison for lying, after managing to reach John Major's cabinet, I could not help reflecting that maybe, after all, the tortoise had beaten the hare.

There was a greater gap than nowadays between the generations, and it was not only politics which set us apart. We had different clothes, the boys wore reefer jackets from Carnaby Street and the girls discovered miniskirts; there was also new music, the Beatles and the Rolling Stones. However, I must not pretend that, any more than in later life, I was the epitome of fashion. If I looked remotely trendy, it was only because almost everyone of my age was buying clothes from the same shops. Sometimes we were treated with scorn. At the wedding of a friend an unpleasant uncle said, with a sneer, 'Every intelligent person is a socialist at twenty and by forty they have thought better of it.'

I got an easy laugh by looking at him in a very pointed way and saying, 'And what were you when you were twenty?'

My closest friend at Oxford was Michael Deeny, who was also at Magdalen, studying history. We met in our first term when he came into my room to ask me to lend him ten pounds, which I was not able to do. It was a prophetic moment. In later life he was one of the Lloyd's 'names' who lost an enormous amount of money underwriting American insurance policies. He was chairman of one of the leading groups of names and brokered the deal with Lloyd's which allowed many of them to survive.

Michael was an eccentric and although he would describe me to others as the funniest man in Oxford, I had no doubt that the title should have been his. He was from Northern Ireland and had a stammer which he turned to brilliant effect, making us wait to appreciate all the more the punchline to his stories. He loved taxis and telegrams, ideally travelling by cab to reach the post office, in order to send a message. If he could not think of an appropriate recipient he would ask the taxi driver to 'J-j-just cruise around for a bit.' Hours were spent in idle conversation. We once calculated that of the world's population of several billion people there were only twenty-four we could marry. This we worked out carefully using a whole series of questionable criteria, which did not include the most important point, that even if they existed how we could find them. Oxford at this time had a dreadful preponderance of males, ten times more men than women in the student body. When we did strike lucky with a girl we shared every piece of vital information. But even though we had some successes, by the time we left every one of those twenty-four girls still lay undetected.

Oxford in the 1960s had a great reputation for student theatre; there were times when it seemed to resemble a drama school more than a university. Richard Burton was so taken by his time there that at the height of his fame as a Hollywood star he could not resist returning to the Oxford Playhouse with his wife, Elizabeth Taylor. With student actors they performed in Christopher Marlowe's *Faust*. Burton had the plum part, as the man who sold his soul to the devil. Liz appeared as his reward, Helen of Troy, whose face launched a thousand ships. She spoke not a word, but spent a few glorious minutes lifting the audience out of their seats, by walking across the stage in a cloud of smoke made by a dry-ice machine. Burton was marvellous, his rich brown voice enveloping the lines, and when he had to speak in Latin and could not remember what to say there are few actors who could do so well declaiming 'Et cetera, et cetera, et cetera.'

I would have loved to have taken part and was rather annoyed not to be in the cast, particularly because they were taken off to studios in Rome to repeat the entire performance on film. But most of my acting in Oxford was in student revues, doing comic turns in the union basement, and at parties. Our inspiration was *Beyond the Fringe*, but there was also, we hoped, a faint echo of German cabaret in the 1920s and 1930s. We longed to be sophisticated and it would be even better if, like a song by Brecht and Weill, we could also be bittersweet. I had been entranced, as a sixteen-year-old staying in Frankfurt, by a performance in a cellar under the large open spaces flattened by bombs, near the cathedral. They called it *The Worst Theatre in the World*. In one sketch, in the summer heat, a young man came on in an overcoat and shivered. 'I am cold,' he announced, in German which was simple enough for me to follow. 'Not the cold that comes from snow, but the cold that comes from . . . people.' Rather heavy perhaps, but I thought rather fun too.

The stars in revue at that time were Michael Palin, who would go on to make his name in *Monty Python*, and Robert Hewison, who would become drama critic of the *Sunday Times*. They could be extremely funny. Mike had a kind of inane cheerfulness, which audiences found instantly attractive. I remember a particularly daft sketch with him bouncing a football and musing on the usefulness of the English language.

'I like it, it's really good, you can use it anywhere.' They were endlessly silly about the class war, with officers and ordinary ranks clashing incomprehensibly in far-flung parts of the empire. It was difficult to compete and I didn't really try. I was more interested in what, very loosely, can be called satire. My chance came when Harold Wilson went to Number Ten in October 1964. With a suit, a pipe, a serious look and a Yorkshire accent, I quickly took advantage of the fact that no one else in Oxford seemed as keen as I was to make jokes at the new prime minister's expense. I finished one sketch in a cloud of tobacco smoke musing on the fact that sometimes I went on to the roof of Number Ten. 'When it rains, I get wet,' I solemnly announced, 'but in the New Britain, when it rains, we'll all get wet.' It was the sort of gritty nonsense that Wilson seemed very close to at times. When I went to see him make a speech at the Albert Hall, with Clement Attlee present in a wheelchair, I couldn't help smiling when he lyrically began to describe 'the poverty lurking behind the lace curtains of the north'.

With Michael Deeny providing much of the inspiration, my regular comedy partner was Walter Merricks, who went on to become a very solid citizen and ombudsman to the insurance industry. But at Oxford, with an upper-class drawl and an accomplished double take, he could be lugubriously funny. Sometimes we would be paid for appearing in cabaret. On one occasion, Jeffrey Archer approached me afterwards and asked me whether I would like him to be my agent. He was studying for a teacher's diploma but had already made his name by getting the Beatles and the American president, Lyndon Johnson, to help him raise a million pounds for Oxfam. I was puzzled by his suggestion. Why did I need an agent, I thought, when the most serious problem I had was whether I would do well enough in my final exams? I reminded him of the incident when he became deputy chairman of the Conservative Party.

'Yes,' he said without hesitation, 'and if you had accepted you could have made a lot of money.' It was obvious, even as students, that Jeffrey and I would take very different routes.

One of my other partners was Nigel Rees, who became well known as the chairman and originator of the BBC radio quiz show, *Quote, Unquote*. Nigel and I met at the end of our first week at Oxford when Robert Hewison suggested that we would work well together. Our humour, though, was not sufficiently similar. He once dropped me from a revue he was directing on the grounds that I was 'not whimsical enough'. He was probably right; after that I secretly tried to be more whimsical, but I could never hope to emulate his Noël Coward parody, tinkling away at the piano, with oh, such a confident air. Once, in a revue, we were invited to change parts for one performance and I sang his wonderful ode to Scunthorpe with a voice so cracked it was almost funny. I did better in a *King Lear* take-off written by Simon Brett, who later became an author of detective novels and scriptwriter of many television and radio series, including *After Henry*. This involved me leaping into the air and coming down on my stomach. Once a student audience begins to laugh they can sometimes be made to go on laughing without anything very much happening. On that occasion at the Playhouse they laughed for nearly four minutes. In the small world of Oxford theatre I had made it.

My minor fame did not impress my widowed landlady, Mrs Wright, who, in my third year, provided my lodgings off the Iffley Road, as there was no question of me living at home in Headington during the term. Mrs W, as we called her, had given her heart to her previous lodger, Michael Palin. No joke we cracked in her presence was enough to compensate her for the loss of Mike; it simply seemed to remind her of what she was missing. The year before, Mike had left to seek fame as a comic actor, but this was not really, I thought, an option for me. Acting was certainly in the blood; my father was convinced that we could only earn our living, as he put it, by standing up on our two legs and talking. But my elder brother Peter had gone to drama school and become an actor, and was finding it hard going and underpaid.

I tried to get into television, but was turned down by the BBC and by ITN. The BBC did not consider me worth interviewing and I had a disastrous encounter with Sir Geoffrey Cox, then the editor of ITN. He had fought in the war with the RAF and he appeared mainly interested in my views on the effectiveness of the bombing campaign against Germany. After I had rambled on for a few minutes he said, quite sharply, 'Well, was it effective, or not?' I rambled on for a few more minutes, but I knew that whatever the bombs had done in Germany they had certainly finished me off that day. I stood up in something of a daze, and he motioned firmly for me to leave. But the door through which I had come had vanished. There was no door. All I could see was a perfectly smooth wall of polished wood panelling. I went up to the wall and stretched out my arms, hoping by touch alone to find the way out. I have since spoken to people who knew that office in Queensway, and they cannot understand why I had any difficulty. Certainly the secretary who finally showed me out gave no impression this was a common problem. Maybe I was simply not ready for a career in television news; it did take me more than thirty years before I joined ITN, as political editor.

I had better luck with the Reuters news agency. After written tests and a series of interviews I was offered a graduate traineeship and I was convinced the way was clear for me to become a journalist. All I had to do was to finish my exams and then the final holiday would start. My last great moment of student fun would be to appear in the Oxford Revue at the Edinburgh Festival.

We had a good team: Mick Sadler, Diana Quick, Nigel Rees, Alison Skilbeck and Simon Brett. We were not very impressed by the play – put on by Oxford students – which preceded us. The cast, including Nick Elliott, later head of drama at both ITV and the BBC, frequently complained about the script, which had been written by a rather improbable character in a military greatcoat who wasn't quite sure how it should end. For most of the run it seemed a flop and then one of the London reviewers declared it was the hit of the festival and its young author never looked back. This was the world premiere of *Rosencrantz and Guildenstern are Dead*, by a young chap called Tom Stoppard.

Our revue was fairly standard fare and included sketches on the foot instead of the pound being devalued; a walking test instead of a driving test; and Simon Brett's five-minute version of *King Lear*. But Diana Quick, who was later highly successful in the television version of *Brideshead Revisited*, was clearly a real actress in the making and all the cast, except for me, seemed destined for a career in television or the theatre. Then, unknown to us, Alan Bennett arrived, and the next morning he asked to meet the entire cast in the pub next to the Masonic hall where we were staying.

Everyone ordered drinks; Alan and I had glasses of orange squash. Suddenly he turned to me and asked me whether I would be prepared to take part in a television comedy series he had written. Rehearsals would start next month. Everyone's jaw dropped and Alan looked rather embarrassed. Later I discovered that he had turned down Michael Palin because he thought he was 'too showbiz', but he had plumped for the one person in the revue who would find it most difficult to say yes.

'Would it be possible,' Alan asked, 'if I were to slip the scripts under your door this evening, perhaps you could think about it?' I explained how worried my parents would be at the thought of both their sons being actors. I did not add that my father would be displeased because he partly blamed Alan for the decline of the Church of England. The parodic sermon in *Beyond the Fringe* had gone down very badly with the Rev. E. N. C. Sergeant who had set his heart on me receiving proper training with Reuters and then travelling the world in the way he would have enjoyed as a young man. Now, he explained on the phone, it looked as if I was going to throw away my hard-won education. My mother saw it differently. 'Oh go on; you obviously want to say yes.' And when I read the scripts I knew that I could not be a Reuters trainee. There would be other times in my life when seriousness would prevail, but not this time. Those scripts were just too funny.

7

'Taking the pith out of reality'

TELEVISION COMEDY is a serious business. When I accepted
Alan Bennett's offer I had visions of the best part of student
life, the silliest part, being carried on effortlessly in the outside
world. What could be better than being paid for making people
laugh? My childhood ambition would be fulfilled; difficult
choices could be postponed; and I would have an answer for
those irritating people who kept asking me about my plans
for the future. It was therefore a considerable shock to realize
that for Alan, and our fellow toilers in the BBC joke factory,
comedy was far from being just a laugh. Pulling funny faces
and making sly asides was only possible if, in that dread phrase,
it worked, and that usually meant only on the set or in
rehearsal; a dim view was taken if the working atmosphere
became too frivolous. There was almost none of the larking
about which had made student revue so enjoyable. It's easy
now to take the side of the professionals who were running
the show but for me, aged twenty-two, the more serious the
rehearsals, the more it seemed as if the prison gates were
closing. I longed to remain an amateur, a free spirit, making
jokes to amuse myself as much as other people. Learning the
truth that show business is a business was an uphill struggle;
and we only had a six-week run.

It wasn't long before my desire for frivolity came up against
the implacable force of BBC discipline. I was blowing up a
balloon during a run-through at Television Centre, an opportunity, it seemed, for a little bit of improvisation. A worried

glance at the balloon to suggest something had gone wrong, followed by a short mime. This involved removing my finger which had been clamped over the end to prevent the balloon from being blown up and, when it was released, beaming in triumph. Not brilliant, but with the right timing potentially quite funny, or so I thought. That was not the view of the director, Sydney Lotterby, one of the most successful comedy producers of recent times, with many hits including *Porridge* and *One Foot in the Grave*. During his time with *On the Margin* I never saw him laughing at any of the lines in the show. He had been watching my antics on a bank of television screens above the control panel. My every move and the reaction of all those on the set could be closely monitored. Half a dozen cameras were involved. He stormed out of the gallery, high above where the audience would sit, and down the narrow metal staircase. I could hear from his walk how cross he was. 'Look,' he said, grabbing me by the arm. 'All our jobs depend on one man, and that's him.' He pointed to Alan Bennett who was sitting curled up in embarrassment on a studio settee. I did not think it wise to attempt a reply.

When Jonathan Miller, wearing jeans and carrying a slim volume entitled *The Renaissance in Italy*, appeared in one of the dingy rehearsal rooms we used in West London it seemed as if the mood of seriousness would prevail. It was ten years since his triumph in *Beyond the Fringe*, and he was beginning to make his name as a television director, with an interesting production of *Alice in Wonderland*, packed with established stars including Alan Bennett and Peter Cook. Jonathan could not help but look amusing with his long put-upon face, his ship's prow of a nose and his gangly legs, but he was also very much the great intellectual, full of words and rapid thought. He talked earnestly about how television would change with the advent of colour. Of his own future role, he was not so sure. He used to argue, rather unconvincingly, that the *Beyond the Fringe* four-

some had an advantage over the usual run-of-the-mill comedians in that they had a greater range: they could, for instance,
make jokes about philosophy. What is surprising is how much
Jonathan, and Alan too, felt they had to justify their position.
A large part of their potential audience still needed to be
convinced. It was difficult for many people who thought of
themselves as members of the educated classes to accept that
appearing in television comedy was not demeaning. For my
father, who never saw any of the programmes in the series,
and for others, the idea that Oxford or Cambridge graduates
should be spending their time in this way seemed odd, if not
actually perverse. It was certainly a waste of all the effort that
had been put into their education. Even my mother and
stepfather, not having a television of their own, had to make
special arrangements to see what I was up to.

Sitting on an old sofa in a former drill hall in Hammersmith
and listening to Jonathan Miller and Alan Bennett in rehearsal
it was easy to forget these difficulties, and the doubts I had
about my career were temporarily put aside. Most of their
humour was not particularly intellectual. There were silly
voices, double entendres and double takes. It was Alan's voice
which was so peculiarly riveting. When playing a vicar or a
colonel or another member of the establishment, he adopted
a tortured expression, his eyes bulged, and yet the sound he
produced was amazingly unforced. His intention was not to be
weedy or ineffectual but to be strong and daft at the same
time. It was a style completely his own.

Jonathan had been brought in partly because I had failed
in my attempts to imitate actors playing heavily significant
scenes in religious epics such as Cecil B. de Mille's *The Ten
Commandments*. It should have been quite easy for me to
grasp. There is usually a moment in these films when one
of the characters looks puzzled and says something like 'Are
you saying that a carpenter's son could be the Son of God?'

Jonathan could do this effortlessly, leaning forward as if suddenly possessed by this thought which would shake the world, and then turning dumbstruck towards the audience so that no one should miss its significance. Patiently, Alan and his producer, Patrick Garland, would play snatches from these films to try to get me into the mood, but Jonathan could do it so much better and he was persuaded to make a guest appearance as a Roman soldier.

He brought to rehearsals an undoubted aura of glamour and he was, I am pleased to report, a shameless dropper of names. He would tell me of the adulation they received in America when *Beyond the Fringe* was running on Broadway, of grand parties in Washington and how strange it was to have so many women appear to want to go to bed with him. Life as a sex symbol was not, he thought, a natural outcome of his medical studies. He had some show business stories, which touched off in me if not envy, at least a suitable level of excitement. There was the one about the film producer Sam Spiegel sitting at a table in the George V restaurant in Paris. He looks out of the window and sees an airliner silhouetted against the night sky. 'That's the Rome plane,' he announces. 'And it's late.'

Jonathan also told how a famous Hollywood actress made a comeback in a musical on Broadway. At the end of her first big number, marked by high kicks and extravagant dancing, she is disturbed by the audience reaction. Coming off stage, she asks her manager, 'Why are they hissing me?'

'They're not hissing you, darling,' the manager replies. 'They're all saying, "She's sixty-six".'

The only other well-known performer in *On the Margin* was John Fortune, later to become celebrated as one of the 'Two Johns', with John Bird, on Channel Four. He was only able to appear in one of the programmes because he was contracted to appear in another series. Years later he would still complain about how, before the contract was signed, the producer of that series had phoned him to say that Alan was not very keen to have him in his show and how the same producer had phoned Alan to say that John was not keen to be in *On the Margin*. This, apparently, is one of the reasons I was given the part. There really is no business like show business.

Most of the regular cast were almost complete unknowns. Apart from me there was one of Alan's student friends from Oxford, Roland Macleod, who was determined to leave teaching and get back to his first love, acting; two actresses, Virginia Stride and Yvonne Gilan, the second the mother of the television critic, A. A. Gill; and most surprising of all, the Lady Mayoress of Blackburn, Madge Hindle. She would become a noted character actress, with appearances in *Coronation Street* among her many other roles. She was lady mayoress because her mother was lord mayor. The local paper could not decide which was more unusual: to have one of the town's amateur actresses elevated to national television, or to have the daughter of a female mayor as lady mayoress. Alan had met Madge in amateur theatricals in Blackburn through his close Oxford friend, Russell Harty.

Madge, like Thora Hird, became the embodiment of those characters whose quirky sidelong glances at northern life would become Alan's hallmark. One of the high points in the show was Alan and Madge reading out 'In Memoriam' notices from a Lancashire evening paper. Madge remembers being told how his observational skills surfaced very early on. As a child, Alan was travelling with an aunt on a Leeds bus when she pointed out of the window. 'That,' she said with great emphasis, 'is the biggest gasometer in Europe,' she paused for effect, 'and I know the manager.' Not only did Alan see the joke, he remembered it. During *On the Margin* the most flattering moments would come when Alan took out his black notebook. It was not clear whether he was writing down what you had said or merely making a note of something he had thought of, but the impression of a writer at work could not fail to impress; and the magpie effect was not misleading. His best work usually has an element of found poetry. He suggests there is much more to everyday life than the rest of us generally see and he never seems to cheat; his scripts, as a result, always appear to ring true.

In one of my favourite sketches from the series I narrated a television profile of an archetypal northern writer, played of course by Alan. He began, 'My father was a miner; my mother is a miner.' As a writer, he has to work in Ibiza because the blue of the Mediterranean reminds him of the blue of a miner's eyes. Then we consider the three most important influences on his life, starting with Goethe, then the obscure Spanish philosopher Ortega y Gasset, and the third? 'I can't remember.' He sums up by suggesting that what he has really tried to do over all these years is 'to take the pith out of reality'. When I presented a tribute to Alan Bennett on Radio 4 more than thirty years later the producer couldn't resist ending on that comment. It came after all sorts of worthies had compared Alan with great figures from the past, including Marcel Proust and even William Shakespeare. It brought the programme neatly down to earth in a way I hoped he would appreciate.

Most of the roles I played were fairly straight: a customer in an antique shop asking Alan, as the gay proprietor, whether he had anything which was camp; a scout being taught the facts of life by his embarrassed scout master. In this sketch, Alan accidentally hit me on the nose. We were recording the programme, as usual, in front of a fairly large audience at Television Centre, and Alan dried up. There was complete silence, broken only by the drip, drip, drip of my blood on the studio floor. I leaned forward and said quietly to Alan, 'It's all right; it's all right.' But this was amplified on all the loudspeakers. We had to wait until the bleeding was stemmed,

Above, left: My mother with my grandfather in 1917, just after the family arrived in England, having escaped the Russian Revolution.

Above, right: My father as a young man.

Below, left: My mother, just after the war, when my parents were still together.

Below, right: Me, aged five.

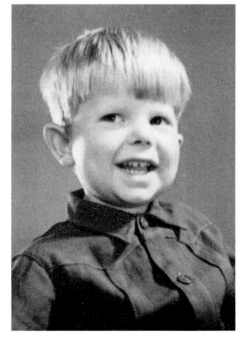

With my sister, Anne, and elder brother, Peter, safely back in Devon after our adventures in Palestine.

The Vicarage, Great Tew, the perfect childhood home.

At the Grand Canyon, aged nineteen. Pity about the hat.

With my friends Michael Deeney (on the left) and Peter Gill.
Exams over, we were able to celebrate.

Above: With Alan Bennett and Virginia Stride in a sketch from *On the Margin*.

Left: On the Margin again: Alan seems to be trying to sell me a teapot.

Right: With Mary
on our wedding day,
4 January 1969.

Below: And then there
were four. On holiday
in Devon with William
and Michael in 1976.

Left: Major Sergeant goes to war, Hué 1972.

Below: On the election trail with Edward Heath. A young and dapper Max Hastings and a rather suspicious-looking Simon Hoggart are sitting next to the Prime Minister.

With fellow BBC correspondents in Cairo for the Sadat–Begin talks, Christmas 1977. *Left to right:* Chris Drake, Bob Jobbins, Michael Elkins, Keith Graves and me.

My first party at 10 Downing Street, after Mrs Thatcher's victory in 1979. *Left to right:* me, Mary, Anne Leslie of the *Daily Mail* and her husband. Behind us is John Harrison. Later on, he and I were rivals for the post of chief political correspondent at the BBC. The powers that be could not decide which of us should appear on the television news and which on radio. In the end, in a typical BBC compromise, we did both, swapping roles every six months.

Interviewing Mrs Thatcher on the plane to Moscow in 1987.
I'm the one crouching on the floor, obscured by microphones.

With the press corps at the Sigorsk Monastery near Moscow.

then the redoubtable Sydney Lotterby set us off again, 'from the top', as we say in show business. Not for the first time I realized that a studio audience likes nothing better than to see something go wrong.

At times there were difficulties with the head of comedy, Frank Muir. For those who enjoyed him later as the amiable raconteur and star of *Call my Bluff*, it may be hard to imagine him as the BBC policeman whose job it was to keep Mr Bennett on the straight and narrow. But as I was to find out later in my career there is nothing so small that it cannot be covered by BBC policy. One particular argument was about the naming of a company which made women's corsets. For Alan the name mattered. He particularly wanted to say that the firm involved was called Kayser Bondor. It had clearly struck him as funny for most of his life. Not being allowed to say the name would wreck the joke. But Frank Muir was adamant. It was not that Alan was implying that the company did not make perfectly good corsets, it was the fact that a company name must not be mentioned on the BBC, and it was only by keeping to this rule that the corporation could defend itself against the charge that it was somehow involved in advertising. The idea that women would be so influenced by the mention of Kayser Bondor that they would rush out and buy one of their corsets seemed fairly unlikely but the head of comedy would not bend the rules, for Mr Bennett or anyone else.

Alan Bennett was determinedly non-show business. He wasn't against it; much of it he found fascinating and good fun. It was just that he did not see how he fitted in. Of the *Beyond the Fringe* foursome, his real friend was Jonathan Miller. Peter Cook and Dudley Moore had been close colleagues but also rivals. *On the Margin* was Alan's answer to their award-winning comedy series *Not Only . . . But Also*. He was deeply concerned about whether he was really funny, often pacing the streets of London for hours after a performance, filled with doubts. He was also worried about his age. Although he was only in his early thirties he felt time was against him. I remember him lying on a studio settee and saying with a deep sigh, 'Oh, I feel so old.' At that stage, ten years after graduating from university, he had still not worked out his role in life. He did not want to be just another student comic who had outstayed his welcome. Eventually he would become a play-wright and actor and win over the British public like no cultural figure since John Betjeman. But when I met him, the way forward was not at all clear. *On the Margin* won enormous acclaim; it was repeated on BBC2 and was on BBC1 within twelve months. It won the Royal Television Society award for the Best Television Comedy of the Year. But it was the only comedy series Alan ever wrote and, like me, he was in a serious quandary about what he should do next.

It was a particularly confusing time. I had started a new career as a comedy actor at the top. I was very far from making a name for myself, but some of the trappings of success had already appeared. There was one particularly disconcerting moment when a couple of young people asking for an auto-graph were sent to my dressing room. My first reaction was to decline shyly. But Sydney Lotterby would have none of that. 'It doesn't matter what you think of their request,' he announced firmly. 'If they want an autograph, give it to them.' But I was not sure if I would ever really deserve to be in such a position, and indeed whether I should even try to be. My domestic arrangements did not help to clarify the matter. I was living in a rented house in Finchley with two Oxford friends, Michael Deeny and Mark McNeil, both of whom were training to be accountants. A Hungarian memory man owned the house. He appeared on stage in Eastern Europe, showing off his skill with numbers, like the character in John Buchan's novel *The Thirty-Nine Steps*. Neither my landlord nor my friends seemed to provide obvious role models.

Michael and I shared a car, a Riley saloon built in the late forties, complete with running board and trafficators which came out, all lit up, when you needed to indicate you were about to turn. In this marvellous machine I would drive round the North Circular Road to appear in *On the Margin*. In those days you were allowed to park right in the middle of the courtyard at Television Centre, if you had successfully negotiated the commissionaires. They were all burly ex-military men who had one simple question: 'Are you an artiste?' Having swept in with a brisk affirmative, it was easy to imagine that being an artiste was exactly what one was. Only later did the nagging doubts return. Sometimes I would discuss my plight with the producer, Patrick Garland. He had been famous at Oxford for turning up to rehearsals in a silk dressing gown and behaving like Noël Coward. To me, he was, to use the old-fashioned term, incredibly smooth. Everything was possible, he would say with the sort of reassuring manner which could not fail to make me nervous. If pressed further, his voice would drop. '*Fas quo fas*,' he would intone, which he would translate as, 'Do what you are doing.' It was my first encounter with a master BBC politician. His message, delivered in such velvet tones, was really quite stark: get on with what you are being paid to do. Patrick, like so many of those associated with the show, had an immensely successful career. He directed much of Alan's best work, including his first play *Forty Years On* and *Talking Heads*. He later became director of the Chichester Festival Theatre.

My choices were limited. I could not go back to Reuters, who had offered me a job the year before, and say that I had changed my mind; I could try to make a living as an actor, though the offers were not exactly flooding in; or I could try my hand at writing a comedy series. This I did, for a time, with another Oxford friend, Baz Taylor, who went on to become a television director. But we were not successful. One of the criticisms was that we did not know enough about real life and that, of course, was true. I tried my hand in the advertising business, being auditioned for the first of a series of ads for Schweppes; William Franklyn became the cool man who didn't say Schweppes but 'Sch . . .' It was not quite clear what I would have done, but I liked the idea of going on location to Tenerife. I worked briefly in an advertising agency learning how important it was for there to be enough water in sausages, so that they would sizzle. At the BBC there was an unofficial attempt to get me reconsidered as a trainee, but when my form, which had failed to elicit an interview, was re-examined the door stayed firmly closed. I had committed the simple mistake of suggesting that I would be happy work-ing in all sorts of BBC departments. Then as now applicants have to suggest that they are keen to be one particular type of cog in the machine and not appear to be overly impressed by the machine itself. Looking back after thirty years in the BBC, it is hard to resist the conclusion that I was perfectly correct on my original form and could have been a useful member of many different departments. But that is not playing the inter-view game, which young people ignore at their peril.

Journalism seemed the answer; I had an insatiable curiosity and a yearning for adventure. But one of the problems was that I did not know any journalists. From a distance they seemed unprincipled and awful. They would stop at nothing for a story. I tried to bridge my ignorance by going to talk to Tom Stoppard. We had met briefly in Edinburgh while he was being scorned by the young cast who first put on *Rosencrantz and Guildenstern are Dead*. He had started his career on a Bristol paper, and the idea was that I would write a profile of him and submit it to the *Observer*. When he began he had had dreams of typing while the bullets flew, but he never caught a whiff of danger, indeed was never sent abroad. We met in a mansion block off Victoria Street in the centre of London, where he was living with his wife and their first child. I was somewhat flustered by the task in hand and he had to prompt me to take out a notebook. The profile was not a success. The *Observer* quite reasonably made clear that if they wanted a piece on Tom Stoppard they could commission it without my help.

Another writer and former journalist I met was Gordon M. Williams, who had been renting a cottage my mother and stepfather owned near Crediton in Devon. He had written the novel which formed the basis for *Straw Dogs*, a highly successful but very violent film directed by Sam Peckinpah. Gordon was a tough Scot, brought up in Paisley where his father was a policeman. He had worked on the *Daily Mirror* and other tabloids and was jaundiced about the whole business. 'I have had to unlearn all I learned as a journalist in order to write novels,' he would say with feeling. He was far from encouraging. Looking back on his time in Fleet Street he had come to the conclusion that the only way you could do well as a reporter on a national newspaper was if you were a permanent child. You had to be in a constant state of unnatural excitement, or at the very least give the impression you would like to be.

So at my interview for the post of trainee journalist with the *Liverpool Daily Post & Echo* I had to work hard not to give the impression that I was very apprehensive indeed. I had taken the precaution of looking up back numbers of the papers in the newspaper library at Colindale in north London and this helped me answer the obvious question: 'What do you know about our newspapers?' The proprietor, Sir Alick Jeans, an unpopular figure in the newspaper industry as I was to learn later, was ill and therefore unable to be present. It was a lucky stroke. Ian Park, his managing editor and a much more approachable man, was in the chair; he had seen me in *On the Margin* and seemed to be impressed that I was now prepared to forsake fame and fortune and settle in Liverpool as a junior trainee. He did not know that I was just desperate for the job.

The final question came at last: 'Do you think you will be able to talk to the dockers?'

'Yes,' I replied firmly, looking Mr Park in the eye. In reality I did not have a clue as to whether I would be able to talk to the tough characters in Liverpool docks. But I could hardly say 'No', and a few days later the letter of congratulations from the *Liverpool Daily Post & Echo* confirmed that he had taken me at my word.

8

Love in a cold climate

THE AMERICAN COMEDIAN W. C. Fields had a famous joke which told of the time he went to Baltimore. 'The day I went, it was closed.' Liverpool in the summer of 1967 had something of the same problem. It wasn't only the ships of the Cunard line which had deserted the city. The great Victorian port, which had for millions been the gateway to the New World, was now resting, uneasily, on its past laurels. The council was bulldozing vast sections of Liverpool to make way for the high-rise blocks which would become the infamous symbols of hopes betrayed. 'They're doing what Hitler failed to do,' was a common complaint from the older generation, as row after row of terraced streets were mangled into rubble. The proud history of Liverpool in the Blitz, the victor in the Battle of the Atlantic, was not being mocked; it was simply regarded as irrelevant. Those houses were too small and many of them had outside toilets, so the argument went, and there was a strong desire for change. But communities were lost and, to make matters worse, much of the rebuilding was long delayed. Twenty years after the war, large areas of Liverpool looked like bomb sites. Many of the old houses had gone only to be replaced by grim litter-strewn wastelands.

I arrived on the train from Bristol with an enormous blue suitcase which in a bygone age had travelled with me to boarding school. My father's partner, Edna, had driven me to the station from their home in Somerset and was surprised that I showed no signs of nervous tension. She wondered how I would fare, living on my own for the first time, in a city I did not know, doing a job I might not be suited to. 'Do you think you'll be able to manage?' she asked pensively.

'Well, if I can't, who can?' I replied with a smile. It seemed to me I had all the qualifications. I was educated, perhaps overly so, had travelled a lot and was reasonably able to cope with hardship. But when the difficulties mounted during my time at the *Liverpool Daily Post & Echo* I had reason to look back on that conversation and feel more than a little embarrassed. With hindsight it would have been more truthful to answer, 'I am sure it's going to be difficult; I'll be like a fish out of water.'

I had arranged to live in a ground-floor room in a large Victorian house on the edge of Newsham Park, not far from the Anfield football ground and a few miles from the city centre. The rent was three pounds, quite a large part of my trainee's weekly wage of fourteen pounds, which was handed to me on Friday in a brown envelope pushed through the grille of the cashier's office. Included in the rent was the heating supplied by a large gas fire, the use of a very small kitchen and, if warning had been given, a bath to be taken upstairs. The most serious problem was an overweight Dalmatian dog called Daisy, which I privately referred to as Slobberchops. She was not allowed into my room, but it was surprising how often my landlady, Mrs Arnott, had to sweep in to rescue me from her ardent attentions. Daisy was a disturbingly unattractive beast.

Mrs Arnott, a middle-aged woman with teenage daughters, found it difficult to work out what I was doing in Liverpool. Like most people in the city she took the *Liverpool Echo* and regarded it with some awe as one of the mainstays of local life. The idea that I should somehow be connected with the paper was not easy to grasp. On the first night, when I longed for her to leave me to my own thoughts, she hovered at the door, trying to seek clues as to my background. Very tentatively, she asked, 'Are your parents *also* members of the literary world?' I tried to give the impression that this was a reasonable question and hinted that the answer was yes. My real position was somewhat different. One of my first tasks on the paper was to detail the merchant navy exam results. Every name had to be properly spelled, all the postcodes had to be turned into the names of the city districts and the headline never varied: M. N. Exam Results. It was hardly the work of a member of the literary world.

The office where the reporters worked was like a school room, with a bank of telephones in wooden cubicles at one end and large windows looking out on Victoria Street at the other. For nearly a hundred years the two papers had been produced in this warren of a building, purpose built for almost round-the-clock production. Ancient Linotype machines would assemble all the separate metal pieces, forming sentences and headlines, and these would be pressed into a mould. Metal casts from the mould would be put on to the mighty printing presses, and lorries would remove the bundles of newspapers from the building. The work involved hundreds of people who all had fixed tasks. No journalist was allowed even to touch the metal type. Almost all the instructions were written out, and if we arrived, fresh-faced and hoping to change a headline, it was only, it seemed, through the goodness and generosity of the men in the print room that there was any hope this could be accomplished. The atmosphere was all too like a Victorian cotton mill, with Sir Alick Jeans brilliantly cast as the tyrannical mill owner, and the trainees unfortunately thrust into the role of the undeserving poor.

A week after I started, another trainee, Mary Smithies, arrived. She had studied classics at Cambridge, and her cousin had been a highly successful trainee on the paper some years before. She was from a village near Preston. Thin and with long dark hair, she looked in many ways as if she would be a perfect entrant. She did not, though, make a good impression on the news editor. For a start, she wore miniskirts. A great deal has been written about the wave of change during what we now call the sixties: radical politics, sexual freedom and all that. But the effect was patchy to say the least. True, the Beatles had come from Liverpool, but their influence seemed to increase the further you were from the city of their birth, and some people in Liverpool only praised them in the certain knowledge that they would not be coming back. Miniskirts, worn at work, were not a sure-fire success.

I had also misunderstood some other parts of the sixties revolution. In the canteen I made a point of not buying Mary a coffee; after all, I argued to myself, weren't men and women meant to be equal in such matters? Would I expect her to pay for my coffee? But she thought this was unfriendly and always referred to me formally, as Mr Sergeant. Asked later about this she protested that although I had only been there a week longer I gave the impression of being an established member of staff or, putting it more bluntly, a know-all. We circled each other rather warily. One Saturday afternoon she came across me at the delicatessen counter in the big Liverpool store called Coopers. 'What are you doing?' she asked.

'Buying a yoghurt and a banana,' I replied. It was only on reflection that I realized she might have meant 'What are you doing tonight?' It seemed an age later that we were talking at the back of the typing class on a Saturday morning. This time I did not need to be prompted, and that afternoon we went together with a group of trainees to a barbecue on the beach at Blundellsands. We hit it off very quickly after that slow start. Sometimes I would say, for a joke, that I married Mary because she was the only girl in Liverpool, and there was an element of truth in that: we did feel we had been marooned together on some sort of island. A woman friend later told a BBC colleague that I had married the most beautiful girl in

Lancashire and, sensing that this description was not readily believed, added, 'It was only because Mary thought he was the funniest boy in Lancashire.'

Our marriage, though, was eighteen months away and we had serious problems to overcome before that could even be contemplated. Mary faced a crisis at work. Each year Sir Alick Jeans would take on around a dozen trainees on the assumption that about half of them would not last the course. After six weeks of hard work, the blow struck and Mary was out. Mini-skirts were not mentioned, but they were certainly a factor. Far more important, it seemed, was that the small herd of trainees had to be culled. I could hardly ever think of Jeans again without a kind of shudder.

It would be nearly a year before Mary could get back on to a proper career path, by doing a postgraduate teaching course at Liverpool University. Before that we lived together in Newsham Drive. Mrs Arnott provided a sitting room upstairs, which we seldom used, and instead of just irritating me, Slobberchops frequently managed to annoy Mary as well. Against this unpromising background, we could hardly have been happier, although the effect of Mary's dismissal lingered on. I had to get used to the idea that at any point, particularly in that first year, the axe could fall on me. 'Just keep your head down,' the assistant news editor told me in what was meant to be a reassuring tone. But I was all too aware of how much I had to learn and of how the other trainees seemed to fit more easily into the matey, sporty, non-intellectual world of Liverpool journalism.

*

Journalists endlessly debate what defines a news story; in practice, it usually comes down to what you can get into the paper, or into a news programme. Young journalists, to do well as reporters, have to produce readable copy which gets published. It is, of course, far more difficult to do this when nothing much is happening, and for a junior reporter there is the added problem that they are never sent on interesting stories in the first place.

'Off you go to Sefton Park with a photographer.' The news editor, George Cregeen, rubbed his hands together as if some kind of treat was in prospect. 'We want three stories. There's no hurry. And you can take the driver.' It was rather exciting; my first job out of the office. Taking the driver was rather special, too. A handsome commanding figure with a trim moustache and well-cut suit, he sat at the desk facing the door. Most visitors assumed he was the chief reporter, and he never seemed to tire of graciously pointing out to them the small rather mousy man who held that post. The photographer said nothing when we arrived in the car at Sefton Park, and I left the two of them while I went off to search the peaceful park for something, anything, which could be described as news. There was a pond which had no fish in it. 'Why?' I demanded of the park keeper.

'Because,' he explained, 'dogs would get at the fish if there were fish in the pond.' Was that a story, or perhaps a headline? 'Dogs dish fish.' Not really. I stuck with vandalism and graffiti. The news editor was not convinced. He was a small rotund figure who bustled about, giving the impression he was about to do something important.

'This story is a bit dull.' He sighed. 'I only really wanted some captions for the pictures.' He then proceeded, with little grunts of satisfaction, to apply his skill to the pictures of flowers in Sefton Park. 'Summer is blooming,' was one of his comments; 'It's a riot of colour,' was another. Was it news? Maybe not, but it filled a large part of the *Liverpool Echo* that evening.

Sometimes, usually when no one else was about, a real story might come my way, but instead of being a vital chance to demonstrate my abilities, it all too often threw my lack of experience into vivid relief. Early one afternoon we heard that a man had been killed in one of the small engineering factories not far from the city centre. I was immediately dispatched to find out what had happened. The outside door opened out onto a large open area, which had to be crossed before reaching the main office. From the windows there the supervisors could keep an eye on what was going on within the plant. I arrived with a determined air, and placed my notebook firmly on the desk. 'Well,' I asked, 'so how did the man die?' I had a clear belief in the right of the press to information and was somewhat taken aback by the reply.

'We are not saying anything,' the manager announced. 'The whole matter will be dealt with by head office.' My disappointment, which I did nothing to hide, failed to move him. Nor did my protestations that the last edition of the *Liverpool Echo* was only minutes away. I did not know what to do. While this conversation was taking place, the door behind me opened and the chief reporter appeared. Wearing a fairly grubby mackintosh, Don McKinley projected a mood of unhurried calm.

'I suppose you're not saying anything.' He smiled sympathetically at the manager. 'I should think you'd want head office to deal with this one.' The manager nodded vigorously. 'Quite right, too,' Don continued. 'What an awful business.' He paused and looked out of the window at a pile of rubble in the centre of the plant, which I had failed to notice on the way in. 'Was that it; did the wall fall down?'

'Yes,' said the manager sadly.

'Oh dear,' said Don. 'It must have been thirty feet high?'

'No, no, twenty feet.'

'He couldn't have had a chance?'

The manager sighed. 'Not a chance.'

'Been with the firm a long time?' Don ventured.

'It was his first week in the job,' the manager sighed again.

This whole exchange lasted little more than a minute. We said our farewells and walked slowly across the plant. Immediately we were in the road outside Don made a run for a nearby telephone box; for a middle-aged man he had a surprising turn of speed. He dictated the story straight to a copy taker; at no point had he used a notebook. It made the lead in the last edition of the *Liverpool Echo*. I was beginning to realize what it was like to be a reporter.

Trainees on the *Post & Echo* were formally indentured like industrial apprentices. Once you had passed your initial training period of six months you were signed up for a total of three years and it was difficult to break that contract if you wanted to leave early. It was part of a system to discourage graduates from going straight to Fleet Street. There were only a small number of papers that took on trainees and so each had a fairly grand list of alumni. While I was on the paper, working there at the same time were Robin Oakley, later to become political editor of the BBC, Anthony Bevins, political editor of the *Independent* and later of the *Express*, and Roger Alton, who became editor of the *Observer*. The parliamentary correspondent was Frank Johnson, who had a very distinguished career including a period as editor of the *Spectator*. The trainees would usually spend their last two years working as sub-editors, not as reporters. It was regarded as a grander job and more suited to their talents. Sub-editors corrected the copy sent in by the reporters and gave it a suitable headline; they also planned how the news pages would look. I was not a very good sub-editor and in my trial weeks failed to impress. One story I puzzled over was the death of the Cuban revolutionary Che Guevara. Soldiers from the Bolivian army had killed him, and he would soon become a cult figure. I appreciated, as many young people did, that he was a charismatic leader who had fought against injustice; before long his picture would grace T-shirts across the world. But to the chief sub-editor of the *Liverpool*

Daily Post he meant very little. 'Give me an eighteen-point italic on that one,' he said, pushing the copy towards me. A snappy headline was required and I simply could not come up with anything suitable. 'Oh, give it to me,' the chief sub said crossly. He scrawled his solution on a piece of paper: 'Dissident killed.'

The decision about my future was made a short time later. I was summoned 'over the bridge', which generally signified bad news. Sir Alick Jeans had an enormous office on the other side of the building. To reach it you had to cross a bridge which spanned the road used by the lorries picking up the bundles of newspapers. I sat where Mary had sat when she had been dismissed. As Jeans had not interviewed me in the first place, I had never met him before. He was a wizened old man, whose manner and appearance seemed deliberately designed to frighten people. His defenders argued that he was simply very shy.

'Well,' he started abruptly, 'do you agree that you haven't made it as a sub?' I struggled to reply, thinking that the end was nigh. He gave me the thinnest of thin smiles. 'George Cregeen has agreed that you should be a reporter.' He raised an eyebrow. 'So you will do that.' I could not tell whether this was a statement or a question. I nodded weakly, and returned across the bridge to give my stumbling thanks to the news editor. I was delighted, in a way, not to be forced to become a sub-editor. I much preferred being a reporter and I still had visions of future adventures and even perhaps of bullets flying across my typewriter. But on that day I made a simple pledge: as soon as possible I would cease to be employed by Sir Alick Jeans.

His poor assessment of me rather cast a gloom over some aspects of my life with Mary. She was clearly 'damaged goods' in the eyes of the company, and now, it seemed, so was I. For most of our time in Liverpool we kept a low profile, not advertising our relationship to other members of the staff. When I told a columnist on the *Post* I was getting married, he was very surprised. 'Oh, Mary Smithies,' he said. 'I didn't think you knew her.'

My actor brother, Peter, put the low profile under severe strain. He arrived in Liverpool on a provincial tour of a play called *Abelard and Heloise*, prior to a West End run. It was written by Mrs Thatcher's favourite playwright, Ronald Millar, who much later provided her with the memorable riposte for those accusing her of making a U-turn in her policies: 'You turn, if you want to,' she told the Conservative Party conference. 'This lady's not for turning.' *Abelard and Heloise*, the story of a monk's illicit love affair, was notable for the first nude scene on the public stage. The fact that Diana Rigg and Keith Michell played the lovers added to the general excitement, although the naked scene took place in almost complete darkness.

Peter was the servant of Abelard's tutor, played by Timothy West. His part could not be considered long. He later described it as 'a series of thank yous and a few grunts'. But, as often happens, the smaller the part onstage, the more important it is to make an impact offstage. Peter arranged to cook for the entire cast in the basement of the Royal Court Theatre. Mary and I were invited and a great feast was prepared. Unfortunately, the cooking arrangements were far from perfect. Rows and rows of chicken pieces roasting in the oven looked marvellous, but in the hour before the matinee, the smell, which rose through the theatre, could not be contained. I had visions of the Liverpool establishment and perhaps Sir Alick Jeans himself, demanding to know how this had happened and insisting that heads should roll. Peter sprayed the auditorium with an aerosol and could not believe that a simple mistake might be taken so seriously, and in the end nobody seemed to notice. But Mary and I felt that our position in Liverpool could not be guaranteed.

As a reporter, my pay eventually rose to twenty-seven pounds a week, but money was tight and we still lived in a single room. When the Beatles album *Sgt. Pepper's Lonely Hearts Club Band* came out I was not sure whether it made sense to buy a copy but Mary was in no doubt. 'Just because we haven't got a record player,' she said, 'it doesn't mean we can't buy the record.' When reminiscing about our time in Liverpool, I would sometimes cite this remark as one of the reasons why I had to marry her. The ceremony took place on 4 January 1969 at the church in Mary's family home of Goosnargh near Preston, where for many years her parents had run the local primary school.

My troubles at the paper were still far from over. The week before our wedding I had been told I would no longer be editing the *Echo*'s diary column, called 'Over the Mersey Wall'. They had decided after a few months in the job that I had not shown sufficient interest in the silver and diamond weddings which formed its mainstay. But I did manage to improve as a general reporter. One of the regular tasks was to meet the Canadian Pacific liners when they arrived from across the Atlantic. Before the passengers left we had to provide three stories with pictures. I had learned from Don McKinley not to be pushy; the best method was to appeal to the good nature of all on board. The reporter as victim may not seem a credible role, but it used to produce dividends. It was surprising how people were prepared to help if they thought you were completely out of your depth. Quickly I would be told how the man on A deck was returning to Merseyside after fifty years away, how a woman on B deck had been a GI bride, and how a couple on C deck had become engaged on board. Back on shore, I even managed to get to grips with animal stories, appearing at the kennels when they were short of owners for strays. The technique was simple: find a dog you like and give it a name like Snap. Then run a story, with a big picture, entitled, 'Snap – the dog that is doomed to die'. The phones would not stop ringing.

As the months went by, though, I longed for something more substantial, and a year after our marriage I was thrown into a state of excitement by a BBC advertisement for national radio reporters based at Broadcasting House in London. The day before the interview our landlady took down a phone message requesting me to provide a three-minute script based on the previous day's news. Fearing that a serious piece would expose too many of my weaknesses, I wrote a humorous piece about a letter written by the headmaster of Eton to *The Times*.

On arrival at Portland Place a large commissionaire asked me gruffly, 'Have you got your script?' I was immediately shown into a windowless studio. When the interview was due to start a loudspeaker broke into life. 'Go ahead in your own time,' said an anonymous voice. I managed to read my script without a mistake. The voice did not react. 'Come up to the fifth floor,' it said.

The editor of radio news, Peter Woon, was sitting in the middle of the interview panel with his feet on the table. When it came to his turn he looked at me in a fairly unfriendly way and said, 'We weren't really meant to be listening to the content, we wanted to hear your voice; but I thought your script was suitable for a school magazine.'

I looked him coldly in the eye. 'Yes,' I said, 'it would go well in a school magazine.' And at that, to my surprise, Peter Woon took his feet off the table and began to take a serious interest. He seemed impressed when I criticized the last item on the Radio 4 programme, *The World this Weekend*. They used to have a regular slot featuring charities of different sorts. I warned of the danger of doing this too often, as it debased the currency. Not long after, the practice ceased. But I still received a formal letter of rejection from the BBC.

Mary had fixed up a job in London, teaching at Notting Hill and Ealing High School, and I was becoming increasingly worried. Then a letter arrived from the BBC saying Peter Woon would like to see me. 'What about being a producer?' he suggested.

'I don't think I would be very good at that.' I had the impression that producers had clipboards and stopwatches, and were very efficient.

'But wouldn't you like to work for the BBC in London?' Peter persisted.

'Yes, it would be a good job in a warm office, but I want to be a reporter and I think I will try the *Daily Mail*.' I had no idea that this was music to the ears of the ex-Fleet Street reporter, Peter Woon. I had said exactly what he hoped I would say. Eventually, four months after my original application, a letter from a BBC personnel officer arrived at Newsham Drive.

'Following your interview with the editor of radio news we would like to confirm that we are considering offering you a post as a radio reporter. If you accept this offer . . .' I read it a hundred times. 'If you accept this offer' presumably meant that they were making me an offer. The hesitancy was apparently caused by the need to take up my references.

When I left the BBC thirty years later I was handed a copy of the reference that Alan Bennett had written: 'He is a man of perception and intelligence, conscientious, hard-working and straightforward. He has an open and direct approach to people, together with an engaging manner, which would fit him very well for a post as News Reporter. Certainly I would far rather listen to Mr Sergeant's on the spot reports than many that are at present inflicted upon one. Last but not least, he has a good sense of humour, and I hope he gets the job.'

9

Learning to drive, the BBC way

A PLAUSIBLE MANNER, some literary skill and rat-like cunning were the qualities the journalist Nicholas Tomalin identified as the requirements for being a reporter. I copied them down in my application to the BBC. The example Tomalin gave of rat-like cunning was that he had stolen this particular phrase from another journalist, who was also trying to define the vital qualities. You should not be squeamish, he argued, about pinching other people's ideas, and it is difficult to imagine a journalist who does not do that as a matter of course. It is not simply laziness, it's a matter of practicality: you often have to work at great speed, and waiting for the perfect word, or the brilliant original thought, may not be possible. You have to deliver, and you have to do so quickly.

I was therefore expecting that very soon I would have to demonstrate these talents and was ready and eager to do so. But there was another quality required in my early days at Broadcasting House, which was completely unexpected. You had to be ready to roll up the sleeve of your shirt at a moment's notice, and be injected without protest. If you had been injected in one arm recently, the other arm could be used. Above all, you should not complain. If you had a thing about needles you should keep it to yourself. If you thought the timing of these injections was a little unfortunate, that too was better left unsaid.

As in any large organization, you were slotted into a category. I was designated a BBC reporter from my first day.

Reporters have to be ready, without warning, to be sent anywhere in the world and they have to be protected from disease. It is obviously sensible to have them injected at regular intervals, and 'keeping up to date with your jabs' is how it is described. All the vaccines – for yellow fever, typhoid, cholera and anything else they could think of – were therefore injected into my arms, as quickly as possible. This being the BBC, the man who carried out this task, the official BBC doctor, was highly intelligent and indeed could not resist showing off his all-round knowledge of all the places you might be sent to. So you were rapidly demoralized and debilitated, for no immediate benefit. Those responsible for deploying reporters would certainly not send you abroad until you were considered proficient, and that would take months. So for my first few weeks at the BBC I went around in a bit of a daze.

I discovered that the BBC was a world of its own; many senior members of the staff were convinced that anything which might carry too much of the flavour of ordinary life was better left outside the imposing entrance of Broadcasting House. It was more than forty years since the first director-general, Lord Reith, had decreed that staff who divorced could no longer be employed, and the days of announcers in dinner jackets had long since passed, but the impression was still given that you had signed up to an exclusive club and the sooner you adapted to its rules and manners the better. From now on you would not go on holiday, you would go on leave, as if you were in the armed forces and allowed a short break from your public duties. On my first day one of the senior staff smiled at me and said, 'Did you have a good leave?' He had not recognized me and thought it better to say something he assumed would be relevant. If you ever found yourself in the presence of the director-general he should be addressed as 'DG'; with all other members of the staff only first names should be used. I found it difficult not to call the editor of radio news, Peter Woon, Mr Woon, and he responded, swiftly, 'Peter, please.' In official communications, though, anyone in authority was given an acronym. Peter Woon's was Ed R.N. Sometimes these initials could be silly; the news editor of Radio Oxford had to put up with being called N.E.R.O.

An openness of manner was appreciated, but only within fairly strict limits. You were expected to respond directly if spoken to, and you had to be prepared to make suggestions about what should be done, but there were some unwritten rules which had to be obeyed, such as not making personal criticisms of your colleagues to the management. You were advised to drink beer with the editor of radio news, but that was because he liked to drink at lunchtime. Early on I was told to my surprise that I was 'not drinking enough'. Senior members of the staff did not give orders; they made suggestions. They were annoyed if you did not understand that unless there was a very strong counter-argument, their suggestions had to be carried out. 'Do you think it would be a good idea if you did x?' usually had only one meaning: 'You will do x, or there is going to be a great deal of trouble.' A general air of decorum was encouraged. It was advisable not to look as if you were in a panic, even if you were. You should move quickly if the occasion demanded, but on no account were you permitted to run in the newsroom. There was a slight relaxation allowed in the corridor outside, and it was not unknown for sub-editors to race the final few yards to the studio clutching last-minute copy for the newsreader, but any sense that events were out of control was firmly discouraged.

This did not, of course, prevent the tension rising in the period immediately before a news bulletin. One of the assistant editors in charge of the newsroom would turn bright purple in the last half hour. Everyone assumed he would die of a heart attack, but he lived on, miraculously, into old age. Another senior figure kept going on a variety of drugs, described by colleagues as uppers and downers. One day he apparently took them in the wrong order and became so cross with the assistant editor who went purple before bulletins that he threw a plastic cup full of water over him. Over the years quite a few senior journalists succumbed to drinking problems, clearly exacerbated by stress. But the BBC was determined that, on the surface, calm would reign. Our aim was an Olympian detachment – to present a sensible account of a troubled world – and that meant pretending, at least in the newsroom, that we knew what we were doing.

The BBC prided itself on the apparent looseness of its command structure. It was consciously modelled on other British institutions, particularly the army. The idea was that reporters and editors, like tank commanders, should be permitted to take decisions quickly. This was meant to encourage a certain amount of dash and style in our manoeuvres. But there was another side of the BBC which was infuriatingly bureaucratic. On any day in my thirty years with the corporation I could marvel at the freedom I was given to perform well, and be equally astonished at the way in which I was ground down by the sheer size and awkwardness of the structure.

As a reporter I was provided with a car, a brand-new Ford Escort with a two-way radio. But before I could drive it, I had to pass a BBC driving test. The one that I had passed in the conventional way, some eight years previously, was not deemed sufficient. An official from the BBC garage in south London put me through my paces. I wondered what would happen if I failed. A weekly allowance of half a crown, or twelve and a half pence, was provided to keep the car clean. This was just one of a myriad of complicated allowances covering everything from riding to work on a bike to having a meal away from a BBC canteen. It was as if nothing was normal unless it was special to the BBC. I was amused to learn that the corporation kept its own cow in Ealing, just in case a programme needed one in a hurry.

I was also given a very grand Swiss-made wristwatch, with BBC engraved on the back. It had a stopwatch facility to enable broadcasts to be timed accurately, and was said to be worth fifty pounds, some hundreds of pounds at today's prices. 'We are the only organization,' I was told with a smile, 'that makes sure that when you retire you give them a watch.' The personnel department did not think this was a laughing matter. When Frederick Forsyth, the novelist who would make his name with *The Day of the Jackal*, decided suddenly to leave the staff and support the breakaway state of Biafra in the Nigerian civil war it caused an enormous upset at Broadcasting House. There was concern that, in Africa particularly, the impartiality of our radio services might be called into question. But in one of the small offices off the bleak corridors of Broadcasting House, Freddy Forsyth's administrative officer was worried about quite a different issue. 'He must see the importance of this,' he fumed. 'We must get his watch back.'

You might think that preparations for me to begin the actual business of broadcasting would have proceeded smoothly; an organization that equipped you with almost everything from a new car to what seemed like a new personality should surely find the induction of new reporting staff a relatively simple matter. But that is to underestimate the BBC's capacity to surprise. Over the years I would come to take it for granted that a task which might seem straightforward from the outside could prove unexpectedly difficult from the inside. The problem of becoming a broadcaster at the British Broadcasting Corporation proved to be just the first of many surprises.

It was on my second day that those responsible for the news on Radio 4 decided that I was ready to meet the audience. The previous Friday I had been writing my last story for the *Liverpool*

Echo, and it was now Tuesday. I was given a large document containing an independent report detailing plans for housing, roads and transport in the south-east of England. 'Would you give us something on that for the *One O'clock News*?' I was asked. There then followed a bizarre dialogue in which I struggled to come to terms with my new career as a radio journalist.

'Would you like me to type out the script?' I ventured.

'Well, that's pretty well up to you. You can if you want.'

'Where do you want me to write it, in the reporters' room or in the newsroom, and when does it have to be ready?'

'You can write it wherever, and it should be ready for one o'clock.'

Puzzled but undaunted, I tried to get to grips with this long boring document. I knew nothing of the planning problems of the south-east of England, except there seemed to be rather a lot of them and over the years it seemed many of the grandest of the plans had not been implemented. With this gloss and with the help of my trusty BBC watch, I wrote out a script in longhand, which was meant to last for a minute. A not particularly friendly woman from the newsroom then showed me into the windowless studio and I recorded my contribution. She said nothing about the piece, which was duly broadcast. There was what I considered a fairly damning silence from the newsroom staff, but Mary, loyally listening, said how wonderful it had been to hear me and how well I was doing in my first week. In those days the news bulletins were typed out in a different part of the building and circulated to all the journalists. Most of my first broadcast was faithfully transcribed, but at the end it tailed off into a succession of dots. The terse judgement 'unintel' summed up the problem: the typist had decided that the last part of my piece was unintelligible.

It was months later, when I had improved and when even the most jaundiced member of the staff would have to concede

I could be heard and understood, that I pieced together what had happened in my first difficult days. I had suffered not only from the usual problems that any new entrant might have to cope with, but I was also getting my first experience of internal BBC politics, which can be fairly vicious.

At the time BBC news was going through one of its periodic upheavals. Looking back it seems absurd that the changes introduced by Peter Woon should have been so controversial, both inside and outside the organization. But, as a public corporation dependent on a compulsory licence fee, any major change, particularly one giving rise to accusations that standards will fall, always produces an outcry. On this occasion the change seemed particularly dramatic. The news bulletins on Radio 4, previously the Home Service, were to include pieces written and spoken by reporters and correspondents. No longer would the newsreaders, who had included such great names as John Snagge, be expected to read for ten or fifteen minutes without interruption. Correspondents – the specialists – and reporters, who covered general news, had in the past been largely confined to programmes like *Radio Newsreel*. Following the advent of Radio 4, other programmes, including *The World at One*, were created. They too had on-the-spot reports but the news itself had remained sacrosanct, and many of the newsroom staff wanted to keep it that way.

Another change was the separation of television and radio reporting. Instead of working for both, the staff would be split up into two camps. The television reporters would work at Television Centre and the radio reporters at Broadcasting House. Inevitably, the best reporters including Martin Bell, Keith Graves and Michael Sullivan went to television. Those left on radio felt aggrieved.

The advertisement for new radio reporters, which had so excited me in Liverpool, had attracted a wide field. Almost all those who were accepted, including John Simpson, already worked inside the BBC; I was the only outsider to be given a staff post. Among those who were disappointed was the woman who had shown me to the studio for my first broadcast. Many in the newsroom were still fighting a rearguard action against the changes because, apart from anything else, their own jobs would be downgraded. If reporters and correspondents told all the main stories, the journalists in the newsroom would spend most of their time writing the brief introductions read by the newsreaders. Their anger and concern were understandable, but their cause was hopeless. Before long, listeners began to appreciate the immediacy and vividness of the new 'voice pieces' and the battle against the changes was over. Nowadays no one would suggest that a newsreader completely divorced from the story was the most appropriate person to supply the colour, drama and everything else routinely provided by reporters. But for me it was an early example of the way the BBC is accused of lowering standards, or 'dumbing down' as it's now called, whenever it tries to introduce changes designed to make it more popular with audiences.

The problem caused by the split between radio and television reporting was much harder to heal. For the new boys, including John Simpson and me, it did not matter too much. We were at the start of our broadcasting careers, both in our mid-twenties, and we were ready to take our chance on the assumption that we might break into television in the end. But for the older reporters who had been consigned to radio, it was a personal blow. Television was where the glamour was; it was where you were able to make a mark and increasingly where the money was spent. Radio listeners would insist, as they still do, that the pictures are better on radio, and on complicated stories which need explaining, radio can still triumph. But by the 1970s, television had already established itself as the prime news medium for broadcasters.

The former television reporters who propped up the bar

in the BBC Club opposite Broadcasting House were nevertheless a talented humorous lot. When they were told by Peter
Woon that he had taken on 'Alan Bennett's sidekick', one of
them, Chris Underwood, said laconically, 'Why didn't you
take on Alan Bennett?' Another member of this group was
the strikingly handsome, always impeccably dressed Geoffrey
Wareham, who was told to his horror that I had 'several
degrees'. He finally cornered me, demanding to know the
truth. At that time most reporters had not been to university,
so I was reluctant to admit that I had any academic qualifications, let alone an Oxford degree. As in Liverpool, I was
endlessly lectured on the importance of experience. Some years
later the determinedly proud non-graduates would revel in the
fact that one of them would be made Washington correspondent after being asked at the interview whether he had any
A levels. 'No,' he had replied, 'but I did do mock A levels at
school.'

It was not surprising that I should form an alliance and then
a close friendship with John Simpson. He had been taken on a
few years earlier, very unusually as a news trainee, on leaving
Cambridge. He had progressed from sub-editor, to producer,
to reporter, in double-quick time. Tall and languid as he was,
I should have been frightened by his laid-back confidence, but
he was so disarmingly self-deprecating. He could also be wonderfully subversive. John tried to suggest that he had almost
none of the relevant abilities, he was not a proper reporter and
was only able to succeed because the BBC was so disorganized.
Both of us had decided not to put away childish things and
would often refer to our superiors as the grown-ups. We
delighted in jamming our feet into the lift doors so they would
be forced to open again and we would often push the enormous
iron gates on the garage with such force that the whole building
shook. Like any other tearaways, we did it because we liked to
hear the noise. In later years he became a famously brave and

distinguished correspondent and I would always fear for his safety. When he was in dangerous areas I would sit on my sofa and find myself saying to the television set, 'Just come home, John, come home.'

It was John Simpson who taught me many of the nuances of BBC life and introduced me to its strange culture of blame and advancement. He had a theory, which I was never able to disprove, that you could tell by the way members of senior management shaved whether their career was in decline. If a middle-aged man came into the office with small parts of his chin left unshaven, John would nudge me and nod vigorously. This was, he believed, a clear sign that the manager was in deep trouble. 'Haven't you noticed? Tufts, he's left tufts on his chin,' he would say, and sometimes if the man was not looking would stretch out his hand and point.

Both of us soon worked on *Newsdesk*, an evening current affairs programme presented by the brilliant and experienced Gerald Priestland, and the novelist and former ITN reporter Jacky Gillot. The programme often attracted a good deal of criticism, far more than its sister programme, *The World Tonight*. It was John Simpson who discovered how the editor dealt with this: he would always take his meal break at seven o'clock when *Newsdesk* started. If anyone complained about the programme he would immediately express his deep concern, adding quickly that unfortunately he had not heard that particular edition. He would, of course, look into the details. When I first read Michael Frayn's famous novel about journalism, *Towards the End of the Morning*, while I was still in Liverpool, I found it difficult to believe in the editor character because he was never seen in the newsroom. When I saw the editor of *Newsdesk* and *The World Tonight* head for the canteen just before seven o'clock, I was seeing what BBC editors did when their backs were against the wall, and the fact that he was competent with a razor could not dispel that view.

John and I also worked together on *Late Night Extra*, which went out between ten o'clock and midnight on Radio 2. There was a DJ, Bob Holness or David Hamilton, and the atmosphere was much more show business than the rather earnest Radio 4. It was great fun. Our task was to find, usually on the telephone, someone in the news we could interview. But the programme had other guests and this was how I first met David Frost. I knew who he was the moment he came into the studio but was reluctant to play court to the great man. Everyone else stood up to greet him and he noticed straight away that I was the only person who did not appear to be impressed. He strode across and stretched out his hand. 'Hello,' he said. 'I am David Frost.' It was a perfectly judged move. I could not help but smile and shake him by the hand. Malcolm Muggeridge's wife, Kitty, in a marvellous put-down, said of David that 'he rose without trace'. On that evening, in a studio at Broadcasting House, I learned part of the real reason why he did so well. Not only could he be charming, but he never seemed to miss an opportunity to put his charm on display.

My immediate boss was Harold Young, an old sub-editor who became news editor because he had some experience of reporting. He had never been a broadcaster but he was shrewd, and behind the rather rough exterior was a kind man. His claim to fame was that he had reported on the first thousand-bomber raid over Germany in the Second World War. The fact that he had done this merely by attending a news conference at the Air Ministry gave rise to frequent ribaldry. But Harold was useful because his experience of the BBC stretched back to those times and sometimes he was prepared to reveal his theory of how to survive. He believed that you could get away with a great deal in the BBC, but not for ever. The organization would give you the benefit of the doubt and then some more, but eventually the wheel of fortune would turn and you would be in serious trouble. He believed that two years was the danger point: if you had been involved in something you should not have been, they would find you out within two years.

Having intrigued his listeners with this preamble he would then launch into his favourite story. It concerned a couple with a bed-and-breakfast establishment near Broadcasting House. During the war they had put up members of the staff during air raids when they could not get home. It was a lucrative sideline because the BBC agreed they should be paid a retainer just in case any of the staff needed their services. 'And when,' Harold would say, with dramatic effect, 'do you think they ceased to draw that allowance?' He would hope that someone would say it was when the war ended in 1945. 'No,' Harold would shout triumphantly. 'They went on being paid until 1947.'

The BBC quickly took over much of my life. In the early morning and late at night I would scurry back and forth to our flat off Baker Street. Even on days off I was absorbed with the programmes and was sometimes called on in an emergency. From almost the very first day I was in no doubt this was the organization I wanted to work for; the only serious reservation I had was whether I was good enough, and this would be a constant source of concern. But despite these anxieties those early years at the BBC turned out to be one of the happiest periods of my life. Mary and I felt we had at last landed on our feet. She was enjoying her new teaching job and, for the first time, I began to think I might actually be a success.

10

'A bunch of ghouls'

THERE WAS A JAUNDICED old foreign news editor who used
to work at Broadcasting House who struck me, as a young
man, as the opposite of a role model. He would end his shift
in the evening after an hour in the pub, put on his brown
felt hat, and with a flourish address the small number of sub-
editors still at work in apocalyptic terms. 'All you lot,' he
would declaim, 'are waiting for something awful to happen.
You are a bunch of ghouls. The only thing you like is tragedy.'
He never waited for any reply, but with as much dignity as he
could muster would turn on his heel and walk out of the newsroom.

'Silly old twit,' was the usual response. There is nothing so
different as the world-weary journalist who has seen it all, and
the young ingénu desperate to see what the world has to offer.
Junior television reporters had to put up with a running
commentary from middle-aged cameramen, lighting men and
soundmen, who could not resist pointing out that there was
nothing new in the news business. They were always men, not
women, and had been everywhere, been involved in interviews with everyone, and were mainly interested in where
and when they would be having their dinner that evening. If
you were fortunate enough to get in front of the camera this
middle-aged gang was very intimidating. You felt young,
inexperienced and totally lacking in confidence. In my first
few years there was one great advantage in being mainly a
radio reporter: most of the time you worked alone.

Alone except for Freddy. He was the radio engineer who accompanied us on some of the more difficult assignments. His duties included driving the radio car, which was far from easy. The extra weight of equipment was enough to make the vehicle as ungainly as a tank. To begin with we used converted Land Rovers and then a specially rebuilt London taxi, which meant that another part of Freddy's duties was to tell people, in no uncertain terms, that he was not for hire. Fortunately the reporter, working in the back behind blackened windows, did not have to get involved. Who we were and what we were doing became clearer when the UHF aerial was raised, hydraulically, from the roof. About twenty feet high, it searched out a signal from the BBC transmitters located at strategic points around London.

Freddy was more than up to the job. He had already put in more than twenty years with the BBC, although he still looked a young man. Part of the ethos of the old corporation was that once you had joined you could expect to stay until you retired, and it was quite usual to move across the different departments. Freddy had started in reception at Broadcasting House at the age of fourteen, as an assistant commissionaire. He was given a smart uniform and an expensive pair of grey gloves. These came in useful every Thursday when he was sent to a shop in Oxford Street to pick up the cakes the governors were given for their tea. With his round hat, gloves, and his pile of cake boxes, the young Freddy would no doubt have melted the heart of even the sternest governor.

In his later guise as a radio engineer, Freddy was a vital anchor in the swirling waters of my new career. He was utterly reliable. It was only later, working alongside other organizations, that I came to appreciate this vital ingredient in the BBC operation. If a fellow member of the staff said they would do something, they invariably did it. If they had to be on location at five in the morning, they would be there. It was a matter of honour not to arrive late; in any case, among broadcasters, timing is often close to being an obsession. You cannot say, 'Here is the news at about six o'clock.' With my fancy BBC watch, I soon learned that seconds mattered, and if you were told your report should be a minute long, that meant sixty seconds, or sixty-five if you had the editor's permission.

Sometimes the sixty seconds seemed far too long. When a news story first breaks the details can be skimpy. Perhaps there's been an explosion and police are on the scene. Officially no one knows what has happened, and it is not in the interests of those involved to speculate. Usually the newsreader would introduce my reports with the phrase 'Here's John Sergeant' after he or she had outlined the basic facts. What I dreaded, when the information was very limited, was the alternative introduction: 'With the details, John Sergeant.' It then became blindingly obvious to the listeners that I knew none of the details. This was particularly difficult if the report was going out live from the radio car. Freddy, quite reasonably, was far more interested in whether I could be heard clearly than whether I had anything to say, and often it seemed the newsroom took the same attitude. I was filling a slot and should be grateful, at my age, to be in such a privileged position.

One of these difficult stories, the full details of which were only revealed years later, came within weeks of my joining the BBC. On 6 September 1970, Arab terrorists attempted to hijack four international airliners. Two were forced to fly to Jordan and one was taken to Cairo where it was blown up the next day. The fourth airliner was an El Al jet, which arrived at Heathrow airport after a terrorist had been killed on board by an Israeli security guard. The terrorist's female partner, Leila Khaled, was taken unhurt to Ealing police station. The radio car was soon parked outside the police station in the Uxbridge Road where it would remain for most of the next three weeks.

John Simpson and I took it in turns to try to bring the story to life when all we could see was the blank modern frontage of the police station, with some desultory comings and goings and no sign, of course, of the glamorous Arab terrorist whose fate, it was believed, could affect the future of the Middle East.

The new prime minister, Edward Heath, decided that the hijackings, by the Popular Front for the Liberation of Palestine, should not be allowed to succeed, although two of the other governments involved, those in Switzerland and West Germany, were ready to compromise. The PFLP announced that unless those governments freed six Palestinian prisoners and Britain released Leila Khaled, the two planes held in Jordan would be blown up with all their passengers on board. Not surprisingly, in the radio car outside Ealing police station we concentrated on the simple point that Leila Khaled, the ace in the pack, was firmly behind bars and would only be released on the say-so of the British prime minister. We may have been describing a rather humdrum suburban scene but the situation carried heavy implications for the world at large. If we were close to Leila Khaled, we argued to ourselves, we were close to one of the biggest news stories of our time. The fact that we had so little to say was a niggling point of detail, which we did our best to banish from our thoughts. We were very far from being world-weary reporters and wanted to prove that radio journalism could still be a force in the world.

The tension mounted. Palestinian hijackers seized a fifth plane, a British VC-10 flying from Bombay to London, which was also diverted to Dawson's Field in Jordan. The passengers, more than two hundred in all, were taken off the planes and the three aircraft were then blown up, providing graphic pictures to demonstrate that the PFLP meant business. For the next two weeks a stalemate ensued, with Leila Khaled inside Ealing police station, and the radio car, manned by reporters on shifts, mounting guard outside in the Uxbridge Road. At any moment, we believed, she might be freed and this would be the vital signal that the crisis was about to be resolved. We assumed, correctly, that if she were to leave Ealing police station the authorities would not bother to tell us until it was all over.

★

Much as I enjoyed my role as a radio reporter I was also keen to settle down domestically in London, with Mary. After living mostly in one room in Liverpool, we had gone up in the world, to a fourth-floor flat in a rather grand Victorian mansion block just off Baker Street. The previous tenants had been called Constable and, being Sergeants, we thought this highly appropriate. Our bank, a branch of Lloyds in Oxford, only reluctantly lent us the money for the carpets and curtains because they could not understand why so little of my income had passed through my account. They could not grasp why I had been paid weekly in cash as a reporter in Liverpool; I could not understand why they were being so mean, and made a special journey to Oxford to remonstrate with the manager.

But the flat was well worth the trouble. It was called 4(O) Portman Mansions; the 'O' being a letter, not a zero, designating a flat in the fourth of a series of apartment blocks which took up most of the corner between the end of Chiltern Street and the Marylebone Road. I could walk fairly easily to Broadcasting House but I was anxious to show that I needed my new car, which could be parked a short distance away in Regent's Park. We stayed there for more than three years, until soon after our first son was born, and although it was only a one-bedroom flat it was a marvellous place to live. It is still one of my favourite parts of London.

When I was ensconced in 4(O) on my day off, on a Saturday evening, it has to be said my interest in news stories, even the fate of the Middle East, was not perhaps as sharp as it should have been. To be told on the phone that I had to leave immediately and make my way to 10 Downing Street where there was a development in the Leila Khaled story did not have the instant attraction that the news desk obviously hoped to inspire. But I did my best to stifle my irritation, as I would have to, in similar circumstances, for many years to come.

It might seem fitting to report that my first visit to Number Ten filled me with awe and excitement, but it would not be true. At that stage it was not my ambition to become a political correspondent; I wanted to see more of the rough and tumble of what I still thought of as 'real reporting'. I was also rather disturbed by the insistence that even though I was not a lobby correspondent it was necessary for me to attend this particular lobby briefing because it had not been possible to get hold of the BBC's duty political correspondent.

The Westminster correspondents, often referred to as 'the lobby', held a strange position in journalistic life. They were usually treated with great respect even by their editors, often to the dismay of ordinary reporters who saw them as self-important and secretive. Much of their power came from their contact with the high and mighty at Westminster, sometimes made in the lobby itself, which is the area just outside the chamber of the House of Commons and is usually restricted to MPs, officials and the lobby journalists.

Much of the lobby's mystique has been lost in recent years, but membership is still restricted, with some news organizations only being allowed one lobby pass. But the formal lobby briefings are now held 'on the record' and a summary is published by the government on the Internet. The days when the prime minister's press secretary could never be quoted directly seem long gone.

When I settled down at the back for my first lobby briefing on that Saturday evening it was all very different. Lobby members turned to stare at me in amazement. 'Good heavens,' they seemed to be saying, 'an ordinary reporter. Who can he be?' An official from Downing Street was equally puzzled. He tapped me on the shoulder and said, 'Would you come outside, please?' In the corridor, he went on, 'We have contacted the BBC political correspondent, David Holmes, and he says he has never heard of you.'

'That's fine,' I said to his surprise. 'That's absolutely fine. I can go home.' With that I turned deliberately and began to make my way out towards the hall and the big black door. This was not quite what the official wanted: he expected some discussion at least, some argument. Reporters are meant to be voracious; they should not be put off by an initial rebuff, and they are certainly not meant to talk about going home. There was only one possible explanation: I was a proper member of the BBC staff, and it could be embarrassing if it became known that I had been ushered off the premises. So I was allowed, no, encouraged, to stay.

Soon a flustered and apologetic David Holmes arrived and I could drink in the experience without having to worry about how the briefing should be covered. It proved an alarming example of how the lobby worked. The prime minister's press secretary was Donald Maitland, the uncle of one of my Oxford friends, Ian Maitland. He spoke with exaggerated precision in an upper-class voice but, unfortunately, the story he told was a long way from being a precise account of what was happening. That would only be fully revealed many years later when Edward Heath published his autobiography in 1998.

Donald Maitland told us that the government had decided it was prepared to make a deal over Leila Khaled. They wanted this decision broadcast as soon as possible because earlier in the day our embassy in the Jordanian capital, Amman, had been threatened by a mob. This was given as the main reason for the change of heart. The only difficulty was that independent reports from Amman did not confirm the seriousness of the threat to the embassy. Not for the first time the lobby version of events did not completely square with the truth. Newspapers the next day faithfully reported the lobby version, in most cases not even trying to reconcile this account with what had actually happened in Amman.

In his book *The Course of My Life*, Sir Edward Heath admits that because of the need for secrecy it was difficult to explain the government's actions to the British public who were, he says, unused to incidents of this kind. With hindsight, it is clear that much of what we said from the radio car in the Uxbridge Road was seriously misleading. Leila Khaled, although appearing to be the ace in the pack, was in reality a busted flush. The attorney general, Peter Rawlinson, had decided that she could not be held indefinitely in police custody because she had not committed a crime under English law. The incident on the plane when she and her partner had attempted to hijack the El Al jet had taken place 'south of Clacton' and almost certainly over international waters.

On that Saturday when we were being told of the decision to make a deal, a far more interesting development had occurred than trouble with a mob in Amman. President Nasser of Egypt had responded favourably to suggestions from the prime minister that he should help in securing a deal with the Palestinians. Partly as a result of his intervention the crisis was resolved. The next week all the hostages in Jordan were freed unhurt, and the following day Leilia Khaled left Ealing police station in the back of a van, unnoticed by our team outside, and was flown in an RAF plane to Cairo. It stopped in Munich and Zurich to pick up the six other imprisoned terrorists. Edward Heath had successfully coped with his first international crisis and I had learned some of the dangers of reports introduced by the apparently innocuous phrase, 'With the details, John Sergeant.'

My caution about lobby briefings, or any occasion when

those in authority seem overly anxious to put across their views, remains to this day. One of the best definitions of news is sometimes attributed to the founder of the *Daily Mail*, Lord Northcliffe: news is something that someone, somewhere wants to suppress, all the rest is advertising. Politicians are extremely careful to avoid being caught lying, but they are often guilty of the sin of omission. Not giving reporters the relevant information is one common ploy; putting journalists off the scent by encouraging investigations into irrelevant matters is another. Governments and other interested parties often move slowly, if at all, to correct misleading impressions when they benefit from the false picture that has been created. This is where the most frequent battles take place between those in power and those whose job it is to report what is really happening. The battles are usually conducted according to a set of unwritten rules including an avoidance of the direct lie, and they are at the heart of the work I have been doing for the best part of my life.

Most of the ploys used by government in the Leila Khaled story would become familiar over the years that followed. I realized how interesting and exciting I found the struggle for information and appreciated the importance of seeing whose agenda you were following, your own or that of the government. Sometimes, much later, I would give talks and answer questions from students who suggested that working with politicians who lied must be awful. Suggesting it was a continuous battle, often in unfavourable circumstances, was one way of describing the fun of the chase. I would agree that journalists were far from perfect but sometimes, just sometimes, they were on the side of the angels. In retrospect our coverage of the Leila Khaled story was hardly impressive, but at least we had tried to find out what was going on, and I was beginning to pick up some of the tricks of the trade. The experience also countered the arguments of those like the jaundiced foreign editor who accused us of simply waiting for tragedy. My life in the BBC would be far more complicated than that.

The reaction of my friends and relatives was instructive. Mary proved to be the perfect sounding board; she listened to my broadcasts whenever possible and was always encouraging; I came to realize how important it was to know that someone on your side was listening. If she did not listen I felt, in an irrational way, that perhaps no one had heard the broadcast, that it had not gone out. Radio is such a personal medium. You could sit alone in the radio car speaking animatedly for several minutes and then afterwards, in the total silence, feel rather flat. If Mary said she had heard, and more importantly had liked, what I had said it seemed more real and more satisfying. For a broadcast journalist there is no equivalent to the book of cuttings in which a newspaper reporter can collect his best work. In all my years in the BBC there were few occasions when I could ever really look back on my efforts. It was all the more vital to enjoy the work each day.

My parents had different reactions. My mother and step-father were still living in Oxford. They secretly thought my broadcasting voice was rather monotonous, but fortunately kept this from me. To my mother the excitement of the coming years was the hope that I would be able to give her genuine political insights. All her life she had followed politics; to have her son even distantly connected with those who could affect history was heady stuff. In the Leila Khaled story she wanted to know what would happen in Jordan as a result of the terrorist action. How would King Hussein deal with the Palestinians? I did my best, in regular phone calls, to answer her questions.

Surprisingly, although he too followed political events, my father was more interested in how I was reacting intellectually to developments. He gave a great sigh of pleasure when I told him that you could stand in the middle of the newsroom, surrounded by teleprinters churning out information, and still have no idea what was going on. I was learning, he concluded, 'a greater wisdom'. For him the truth was often more interesting for being elusive and he would have been disappointed if I had suggested that understanding complicated events was anything other than difficult, if not sometimes impossible. He had a sharp nose for pretentiousness of any sort, and he wanted to make sure my arguments rang true. My closest relatives, each in their own way, kept me up to the mark.

The official BBC reaction to my first months as a reporter was rather guarded. I was called in to see Peter Woon, and to my surprise he formally handed me a letter. He deliberately ruined the effect by saying it was not as it seemed; the letter from DNCA, the director of news and current affairs, contained unqualified praise for my skills. 'Look,' Peter said. 'This is just a letter saying you are OK. Don't believe a word of it.' That was his way of keeping me up to the mark.

It would be actions, not words, which carried the greatest force, and it would be almost a year later before I knew that I had been accepted as a reporter. It was then that I set off, with barely suppressed excitement, to fly to Belfast to cover the gathering storm in Northern Ireland.

11

Bullets and bombs

IT WAS NOT the first time I had been to Northern Ireland. My Oxford friend Michael Deeny came from a Catholic family in the small town of Lurgan and, some years before, while staying with them, I had been introduced to the strange sectarian ways of the province. Michael's father was a doctor and as he drove me round Lurgan I was mystified to be told that some streets and housing estates were Catholic and some were Protestant. Even though my father had been a Church of England vicar I found it difficult to give myself a religious identity of this sort. I supposed I was a Protestant, but that had nothing to do with where I might live and how I might behave towards people from another Christian denomination, or even from another faith. It was also difficult to understand how deep the differences were when on the surface much of life in Northern Ireland was strikingly similar to life in northern England. All those Victorian terraced streets in Belfast could so easily be in Liverpool, and if you peered in through the windows those inside might well be watching exactly the same television programmes.

Travelling on the plane from London it was often possible to see, before heading out across the Irish Sea, the broad finger of the River Mersey pushed firmly against the Liverpool waterfront. I would look down to see if I could catch sight of our old home in Newsham Drive and remember happy, less earnest days. The standard joke as we were about to land at Belfast's Aldergrove Airport was that the stewardess might warn us to put our watches back three hundred years. It was hard for English reporters not to conclude that the Irish problem, and the way it was being handled, were throwbacks to the seventeenth century. Little did we realize that wars between communities, often with religious overtones, would become a familiar feature of the modern world.

My feelings on arrival were usually a mixture of apprehension and excitement, masking a sinking realization of how little I knew. When William Whitelaw became Secretary of State for Northern Ireland he gave the impression of baffled decency when confronted with the complexities of Irish history. On one occasion, when tempers were running particularly high, he stuffily declared, 'I don't think we should prejudge the past.' Like his other comments, which became known as Willie-isms, it could be considered wise or foolish, depending on your point of view. For many of those who came from the outside and were disconcerted by the strong emotions generated by this conflict, it seemed to have the makings of common sense.

On one of my first visits, Bernadette Devlin was also waiting at Gatwick for the Belfast plane and I was determined to approach her, despite her fearsome reputation as a Republican firebrand. I thought she might be able to help me make sense of the political situation. She was younger than me but had already been elected an MP, with behind-the-scenes support from the IRA; she had survived some of the most violent demonstrations yet seen in the province and had even served a short spell in prison. I could not resist trying to get to know her. It might not be easy, but what could I lose? 'Keep it brief, keep it straight,' I said to myself. 'And if it doesn't work, try again.'

The departure lounge suddenly seemed rather hot. I explained that I was a BBC reporter, new to Northern Ireland, anxious to understand, but I had one advantage which she might find useful: 'I have a hire car, waiting for me at Aldergrove.' Then, after a pause: 'If you wanted to be driven anywhere, I could drive you.'

'No,' she said, 'I live in Cookstown; it's far too far.' I smiled and noted that my offer had not been completely rejected. When we landed at Aldergrove, I tried again. 'There's a car here,' I said, 'just waiting to be used.' With a sigh she agreed, and again pointed out that it was a long drive to Cookstown. The longer the better, I thought. Unfortunately, the car rental company, not at my request, had provided an enormous brand-new car with an automatic gear change and a host of plush extras. I was anxious to convey to Bernadette that I had a keen understanding of how it must feel to be poor and oppressed; this opulent car, symbolizing all that was wrong with expense account living, would certainly not help. I apologized and muttered, 'Well, at least it'll get us there.'

We bowled along for more than an hour, deeper and deeper into the dark countryside. I had no idea where we were going, but I wished there was more street lighting or a full moon, anything to lighten the gloom. Our conversation was not of the sort to lift the spirits. Bernadette had a tough gritty voice and a relentless way of speaking, and when she referred to the Reverend Ian Paisley or other prominent Unionists it was as if a devil with horns had entered the story. Every now and then I chipped in with a question, but she understood her side of the deal was to provide an almost uninterrupted monologue, and I could hardly complain that she left so little room for optimism.

When we arrived at Cookstown, I was invited into her home for a cup of tea. 'I'll say you're a friend,' she said, 'but it might be better if you didn't say much.' Her warning was kindly meant and I took it in good part. The atmosphere in the crowded front room was tense and uncomfortable, with me trying to look relaxed eating toast and drinking tea, but believing every man who came in must be a member of the

IRA. I smiled and nodded, but said absolutely nothing, and soon, with a sense of relief, climbed into the big car and drove back to Belfast. Bernadette McAliskey, as she became, has more than her fair share of enemies. Ten years later she narrowly escaped death when she was shot seven times by a Loyalist gunman. But that evening she helped me and I was grateful.

My friends in Belfast were mostly fellow reporters from the national papers. They included Simon Winchester of the *Guardian*, who was a spectacular success, winning a major award for his work in Northern Ireland. We had met in Darlington on a newspaper course in which neither of us had distinguished ourselves. I was with the *Liverpool Echo*; he worked for the *Newcastle Journal*. We had both disliked writing fake copy for imaginary newspapers, to be judged by tutors who, we could sense, had failed in the profession; Simon would sometimes not even bother to attend classes. All those who seemed to thrive in that atmosphere sank without trace, but Belfast proved to be the real training ground for some of the best journalists of our generation. Martin Bell, ice cool and distant, was an impressive figure, often patrolling the streets alone 'to see if anything was happening'. Max Hastings adopted that air of almost reckless bravery which would become his hallmark. Robert Fisk, then of *The Times*, worried constantly about whether he was missing anything, while Simon Hoggart of the *Guardian* used to build model aircraft in his room at the Europa Hotel to ease the tension and Murray Sayle of the *Sunday Times* gave the impression that he, and only he, understood what was going on.

My first big story came during my first week in Belfast on the evening of 5 February 1971. A group of journalists were prevented from crossing the road into the Catholic Ardoyne area by a military patrol. It was soon after midnight and there had been rioting in some areas for much of the evening.

Tension had been rising for months and the soldiers, who only a few years before had been greeted in the Catholic areas as peacemakers, were now regarded as the enemy in the tough Republican districts. Searches were being carried out for weapons and the mood was ugly. As we peered into the darkness trying to work out what was happening the silence was suddenly broken. Three shots rang out, and to my amazement I could see that one of the local BBC reporters, David Capper, had recorded the sound. A young Catholic had been killed by one of those shots. The army said they had returned fire with a group of men who had been 'shooting from the shadows'. Soon afterwards, in another part of Ardoyne, a second Catholic man was shot dead by troops. Across the city there were dozens of explosions.

Some distance away in the New Lodge Road area Protestant and Catholic crowds had gathered, and soon after one o'clock burning cars were turned into a barricade. A machine gun on the Catholic side opened up on an army patrol, and all five soldiers were hit. One of them, Gunner Robert Curtis, was killed. He was the first British soldier to die on active duty in Northern Ireland for nearly fifty years.

The next morning my story led all the radio bulletins. It included the recording of the three shots and it marked a historic turning point. From then on the army's involvement in Northern Ireland was no longer seen as an attempt to keep the peace, and the conflict would take on many of the aspects of a full-blooded war. During 1971 the security forces recorded almost seven thousand violent incidents, including more than a thousand bombs. I worked as a reporter in Northern Ireland, on and off, for the next seven years, but the hardest and most dangerous time was in those first few weeks.

One evening I was going back to the Europa Hotel, which was not far from the BBC headquarters in Belfast, when I saw an army sergeant wandering, apparently aimlessly, in the road outside the hotel. 'What are you doing?' I asked him in the unembarrassed way reporters, particularly those with English accents, usually behaved towards soldiers in Northern Ireland.

'Oh, I'm looking for a bomb, sir; there's been a warning.' I briefly joined him in the search, not particularly concerned about the danger and anxious to dispel any impression that I was scared. We walked past a big red letter box and then he went on his way and I turned into the hotel. Almost immediately there was an enormous explosion. I rushed outside and saw that the sergeant, completely unhurt, had also returned to the scene. We looked at each other. The pavement, where we had been standing moments before, was covered with large pieces of cast iron, all that remained of the letter box. There is no doubt that had we delayed for even a minute we would have been caught in the blast and almost certainly killed. It was an hour or two before I fully realized how lucky I had been.

Nowadays people might say that I was 'in denial'. There was certainly an element of that when I was faced with serious danger for the first time. The instinct to argue that whatever the risk 'It can't happen to me' is strong, particularly with young reporters; there is that youthful sense of immortality which to the middle-aged seems so misplaced. An older person is more likely to believe that 'It's bound to happen to me.' I've heard Max Hastings look back ruefully on his own exploits as a reporter and take the view that you are born with a bottleful of courage and the bottle gets emptier the older you get.

I was often struck by how important it seemed not to do anything that might make you seem foolish or frightened in front of others. BBC radio reporters usually divided their spells of duty in Northern Ireland with one week in Belfast followed by a week in Londonderry, where we stayed in the City Hotel, later demolished after an explosion. One night there was a bomb alert and my room filled with acrid smoke. I followed my first instinct to get dressed and pack. I then came down the main staircase, carrying my case and ready to check out. The other guests, all in their nightclothes, clearly thought I was behaving strangely; I was certainly not being brave.

Back in London, there were times when I toyed with the idea of refusing any further assignments to Belfast, but then for no very good reason I would think about the BBC Northern Ireland Orchestra. The idea that they struggled into rehearsals in Belfast with a cello or a tuba as I was deciding that it was all too dangerous could somehow not be borne. The BBC personnel in Northern Ireland were impressive. The industrial correspondent, Eric Waugh, wrote tellingly about his fears when he was leaving the BBC headquarters in Belfast late one night and the heavy door slammed behind him. 'Then,' he admitted, 'to get to your car you have to cross the widest pavement in the world.' He worked closely with the eminent political correspondent, who insisted on being called W. D. Flackes like the old-fashioned journalist he was. *Private Eye* called him Flak Jacket, but his real name was Billy Flackes and he was much admired, not least for leaving his name in the phone book, address and all.

Many of the people in Northern Ireland – and some of their politicians – were an engaging lot with a directness and humour which lit up the darkest scene. I remember Gerry Fitt, later Lord Fitt, the MP for West Belfast, showing off the gun he had been given for his protection. As one of the leading Catholic politicians dedicated to non-violence he was in a strange position, with his home in one of the most difficult parts of the city barred and bolted against frequent attack. As Gerry waved his gun at me, explaining that he didn't know how to shoot, it was impossible to keep a straight face. We often laughed because taking everything seriously would have been far too difficult.

A master of the art of tension-relieving humour was John

Simpson, whose chosen manner was to refuse to give the impression of being under any stress. We worked together in Londonderry, which he rightly considered one of the great Georgian cities of the British Isles. A shared interest in architecture, particularly the fine doorways of Derry, was one way of passing the time; another was John's passion for first editions of Victorian novels. Once we returned to the City Hotel to find soldiers had cordoned off the whole area. An officer told us that a suspicious package had been found on top of our hired car. 'Oh, don't be silly,' said John, striding towards the car, 'that's just my parcel of books.'

The next day there was a more serious incident outside the hotel. Just as I was parking our hire car, a new Hillman Avenger, a young man wrenched open the driver's door and forced me into the middle of the car shouting something like 'Don't move or I'll blast your head off.' John, pushed against the side of the passenger seat, remained remarkably cool; I was terrified. We were being hijacked. The young man drove at breakneck speed into the Catholic Bogside, the scene of many riots, and then shouted at us to leave. John asked if we could take our tape recorders from the car boot. This we were allowed to do and then we walked disconsolately back to the hotel. We were reluctant to mention what was on our minds. Both of us started to talk at once and then immediately fell silent. Finally we had to admit the awful truth: the man had not been armed. We had lost a brand-new car simply because a man had shouted and pointed his thumb at us.

At the time of the hijacking John Simpson was the BBC's Dublin correspondent, and twice when he went on holiday in the summer, Mary and I went over to fill in and stay in his house. It was strange to be detached from the conflict and yet be meeting every day people who were watching it so closely. I tried to build up contacts with the British embassy and remember one particularly good lunch with a senior diplomat.

'Have we got any spies?' I asked, refilling his glass. 'I do hope we have.'

His voice dropped dramatically. I was hoping he would blurt out the entire operation plan of the secret services. But all he would say, talking as if his teeth were being extracted, was that they would not be James Bond types. 'We find it easier,' he said, 'to work on the idea of a common cause.' It's the old principle of finding someone who can be helped if they help you, and it's not only spies who benefit in this way. The trick for a reporter is to find out whether you can find common cause between a possible source and yourself. If it works to your mutual benefit a deal can be done.

In Dublin I was able to put this principle into effect on more than one occasion. Richard Balmforth was the correspondent for the Press Association, which supplies news to almost all the press and broadcasting organizations in the UK. Because we were the only two London correspondents in Dublin we could together control all the news from Ireland. This may sound an extravagant claim, and it would be a foolish correspondent who put it to the test, but in a small way we used the situation to our advantage. We would try not to scoop each other; if one of us heard of anything useful we would tell the other. The BBC and the Press Association would then be told at exactly the same time. There was not a great deal of news from the Irish Republic, and this arrangement, which we called News Swop International, made life a lot easier.

One of the strangest deals I have ever made also took place while I was in Dublin. A riot had started in the border town of Dundalk and the police station was under attack. I phoned from Dublin and to my surprise found myself speaking to the man in charge of the station. He was annoyed to be talking to the BBC because he was desperately keen to get in touch with his headquarters in Dublin. He told me firmly he could not help and put the phone down. Unfortunately for him it was a very old phone system and the line could not be disconnected until I too put the phone down. Both of us saw how the tables had been turned. 'Please tell me what is happening,' I said plaintively.

'And then will you put the phone down?' he growled. I agreed immediately and within minutes was broadcasting the news.

Mary was amazingly forbearing about my trips to Belfast. She was worried, of course, about the danger, but she realized how much the reporting life meant to me and knew that I had found my vocation. My parents too were supportive. It was only later that my father admitted that he would listen to the beginning of my reports to see that I was all right, but would then switch off the radio. He found the details of the Irish conflict almost too much to bear.

While writing this book, I have been reading, and in some cases listening to, a selection of my reports from Northern Ireland in the BBC archives. It has not been an easy task. My memories tend to be of companionship mixed with tension and excitement and it was in Belfast that I came of age as a reporter. But the archives tell a story of unfolding tragedy, and I must not shrink from that. Here is part of my live report for the one o'clock news the day after the explosion at McGurk's bar in Belfast on a Saturday night in December 1971. Fifteen people were killed and it was eventually found to be the work of Loyalist terrorists:

> I went to the scene a short time ago and sad groups of people are still staring at the rubble. There's nothing to show that a pub was there; it's as if a corner of the street has been ripped away. A man told me his son of fourteen was killed in the blast. The boy was upstairs and didn't stand a chance.

12

Major Sergeant goes to war

AFTER MY EXPERIENCES in Belfast, I dreamed of being a foreign correspondent, of wearing tropical suits and drinking in seedy bars, of over-tipping waiters and bringing down governments. Like a lot of journalists I had been influenced by Evelyn Waugh's account of the Abyssinian crisis of the 1930s. In *Scoop* he tells the story of the writer of a newspaper's nature notes being mistaken for a top reporter and sent, with a folding canoe and cleft sticks to carry messages, into the shambles in east Africa. It is a brilliant satire on the absurdities of reporting from far away, with little knowledge and no responsibility. Capturing at least part of that mood seemed a decent goal for any young journalist.

In the spring of 1972, flying high above the Atlantic in a chartered Britannia, I felt just like a character from one of Waugh's novels. For the past four hours the propellers had droned on, making it difficult to speak. There were only a few journalists and cameramen on board. Now we were about fifteen hundred miles out, halfway to New York, and Martin Bell had spent part of the night performing what are called pieces to camera, elegantly explaining what we were doing. I was trying to convince the crew of the plane that I should be sitting in the cockpit if I was going to have any chance of reporting for the eight o'clock morning news bulletin on Radio 4.

It had started the day before with a dramatic message from the Ministry of Defence saying they had flown out a four-man bomb-disposal team to search for explosives on board the Cunard liner *QE2*, which had left New York two days earlier. A man had phoned the company to say that bombs on board would go off unless he was given $350,000, the equivalent then of £135,000. The bomb-disposal team, later acknowledged to be members of the SAS, had parachuted into the sea near the liner. They searched the ship, but nothing had been found. Our task was simple: to find the *QE2* and make sure that the two thousand passengers and crew were safe.

It was soon after 7.30 a.m. when we swooped out of the clouds, and there before us shining in the morning light was the magnificent *QE2*, apparently unharmed. By this time I was sitting in the cockpit behind the captain and we managed to get in touch with the radio operator on board the liner. He agreed to link me up by radiotelephone to the BBC in London. There was only one snag: no one on board was prepared to make any comment about what was happening and there were only a few minutes to go before the start of the eight o'clock news. I scribbled a few words and then, shouting above the noise of the engines, delivered my verdict.

We are now circling the *QE2* and if one wasn't aware of the dramatic events of the past two days it would be easy to say: What's the fuss about? The *QE2* is steaming confidently; there's smoke from her funnel and apparently no difficulty at all on board. We're about two hundred feet above the sixty-five-thousand-ton liner. It's a clear day with good visibility. We heard about an hour ago there would be no broadcast from the liner itself, and this obviously came as a disappointment. We were hoping to talk to the captain or to some of the passengers. But at the moment we have this rather tantalizing look at the *QE2*, which leaves me to send this one message clearly back: the *QE2* is on the high seas, and is perfectly all right.

It was only when I got back to the office that I realized what an impact this had made. All night the editorial staff had worried about the cost of chartering the plane. Television news did this sort of thing, but not radio. And how could anyone be sure that I would be able to send a piece from a few hundred feet above the *QE2*? The duty editor had been applauded when he went into the morning meeting. I was treated like a returning hero. The man who tried to blackmail Cunard was eventually arrested and the events were turned into a Hollywood film. I was given the reward I really craved. It was decided that I could go to Vietnam.

For the previous few weeks I had been worrying about whether I would be chosen. A small group of reporters were taking it in turns to back up the BBC staff in that area. Since my student days I had been closely interested in events in Vietnam, and some years before had taken part in the famous demonstration against the American involvement, in Grosvenor Square in London. The war and its consequences was one of the great issues of our time and going there seemed more of a privilege than a duty. Mary inevitably saw things rather differently. For her it would mean weeks of uncertainty: not knowing when I would return, with the possibility that I might be injured or even killed. I tried to play up the excitement and play down the danger. Evelyn Waugh had not been to Vietnam – that was Graham Greene territory – but I treated both authors as useful guides. I would not be taking a folding canoe or cleft sticks, but I bought a tropical suit from a smart outfitters in Piccadilly and was determined that I would be treated, and treat myself, as a foreign correspondent. The only problem was that, like William Boot, the hero of *Scoop*, I would find the situation in the war zone itself far from easy.

The main difficulty in Vietnam was that for most of the time we were a long way from the war. The North Vietnamese, having taken heart from the partial withdrawal of the Americans, were trying to invade the South. They had tanks and a good deal of equipment, but to my surprise I learned that tanks cannot be driven for long distances; they are usually taken on tank transporters and the Communists did not have them, nor were the roads suitable. As a consequence their great offensive of 1972 was stalled in the northern province of Quang Tri, hundreds of miles from Saigon where most of the journalists were based.

Evelyn Waugh would have appreciated our position. For much of the time we had no idea what was going on; our sources were often limited to a South Vietnamese army briefing which took place each afternoon, known as the four o'clock follies. Although we knew nothing at first hand we had to decide on behalf of our news organizations whether to report the claims being made about the conduct of the war. It gave us an odd sense of power. One of those who, like me, listened to Colonel Hien of the South Vietnamese army was Jon Swain, who later became well known for his work in Cambodia after it was taken over by the Khmer Rouge. Jon was then working as a freelance for the *Daily Mail*. One Friday evening he asked me whether the BBC had captured Quang Tri, the capital of the province of the same name. There had been uncertainty all week over whether it had fallen to the Communist advance. 'No,' I said, trying to sound laconic, 'we are still fighting in the suburbs.'

The next day Jon was pleased to announce that a 'herogram' had arrived from the *Daily Mail*, a journalist's way of saying he had been congratulated. It was for a story he had sent on the fall of Quang Tri.

'How far did you go?' I asked.

'Oh, pretty far,' Jon said. 'Communist flag flying on the citadel, girls throwing flowers at the tanks, that sort of thing.' He paused. 'What about the BBC?'

'Oh,' I said, trying once again to sound laconic, 'we are

still fighting in the suburbs.' To Jon's dismay that was confirmed that afternoon by the small determined figure of
Colonel Hien. We discussed what should be done. I suggested
an unexpected counter-attack; fierce fighting in the suburbs
after the Communist flag had been wrenched off the citadel,
and the military authorities taken completely by surprise. It
was not an immediate problem for Jon, because the next day
was a Sunday; it was Monday's edition of the *Daily Mail* he
had to worry about.

On Monday afternoon Colonel Hien was still adamant:
Quang Tri remained in government hands. I gently enquired
about the *Daily Mail*'s position. Jon smiled warily. He had sent
them some sort of story, but they had not used a word of it;
they had not thought it was interesting. We went off to
celebrate with a beer. I was wearing my tropical suit, or to be
more accurate the trousers from the tropical suit; the bar was
fairly seedy, and although we had not brought down a government, we appeared to have saved a city. Or at least, that is
how we consoled ourselves, more than four hundred miles
from the actual fighting.

The BBC had a special status in Vietnam: we had far more
influence than most news organizations because as well as
broadcasting on the World Service and domestic bulletins at
home, there was also a Vietnamese language service which
operated on medium wave. It meant that my broadcasts, trans-
lated into Vietnamese, could be heard right across the country
by a large proportion of the population. The importance of this
was brought home to me on my first day when a local paper
printed a cartoon of a BBC employee with a huge dollar coin
in his mouth. The suggestion was obvious: that we were in the
pay of the Americans. On one occasion the BBC reporter I
took over from, Bob Friend, had been alarmed to be woken up
in the middle of the night by armed members of the South
Vietnamese security services. It was not immediately clear why

they were behaving in such an aggressive fashion, but the cause was eventually traced back to the work of a new translator at Bush House in London. He had made a mistake in translating the phrase 'The South Vietnamese government claim . . .' He had put this into Vietnamese as 'The South Vietnamese government boast . . .' Luckily this had been sorted out before I arrived, but it still made me ultra-cautious.

The BBC's South East Asia correspondent, Derek Wilson, a tall dapper man in his late forties, was my guardian and friend for much of the time I was in Vietnam. As we walked through the streets at night, trying not to be unnerved by the scurrying rats, he would advise me on the need to keep up standards. He, too, only wore trousers and a shirt, rather than a tropical suit, but the shirt would always be fresh on every evening. His one major problem, he confessed, was a serious dislike of helicopters; they were dangerous and should be avoided. Obstructive soldiers and policemen also annoyed him. On one occasion, approaching his favourite restaurant, he was irritated to be told that the whole area had been cordoned off. The South Vietnamese cabinet would be dining there that evening. 'I know,' a furious Derek protested, as he pushed his way through the road block. 'I have invited them to dinner.'

Saigon had seen much better days. The elegant boulevards and gracious mansions of the French colonial city had taken on a desperate air. The streets were clogged with noisy Japanese scooters, and the rickshaws had mainly been replaced by tiny Renault taxis. Beggars, many of them the Eurasian offspring of departed American soldiers, crowded round you the moment you left your hotel. I had wanted to stay in the Continental, made famous by Graham Greene, but there the rats on the terrace did not even bother to wait for nightfall. I settled in to the Caravelle, on the opposite side of the main square, which was only partially infested with cockroaches. It was a melancholy place. Telephone contact with home was very limited: Mary only managed to get through to me once, by waiting up for most of the night and booking the call well in advance.

When Derek Wilson was away I was left in sole charge of BBC operations. It was that strange period in the war known as Vietnamization. The Americans had not withdrawn, but they had no intention of sustaining any more casualties than they needed to: they had already lost 50,000 men. It was necessary to become an accredited war correspondent with the US forces, known as MACV, or Military Assistance Command Vietnam. I was rather unnerved to find that like all other correspondents I was given the honorary rank of major in the US Army, with an identity card in Vietnamese to prove it. I was not sure whether this would help if I fell into the hands of the Vietcong. Derek Wilson pointed out that the only advantage was that I could be given lifts in American helicopters.

Communications with the outside world were primitive by today's standards. I could use a teleprinter to send copy, and there was a radio circuit to London, but usually only once a week. This involved climbing up the dark staircase of a tower block and then, using bricks as stepping stones, crossing an attic flooded by rain. The radio station had taken the top floor of several blocks in order to be less vulnerable to attack. Madam Nhu, a severe tubby woman dressed in black, was in charge. She did not speak English but would wave you towards a room where a rusty microphone stood out from one of the walls. Water swirled about your feet. The voices from London were not always sympathetic. Once I was particularly interested in knowing when Derek Wilson would return. 'I don't know,' the foreign duty editor replied briskly.

'But I was told last week that you would know.' I tried not to sound too bothered.

'Well, what's a week between friends?' was the irritating response.

There were consolations. In *The Quiet American*, which is one of the best descriptions of the early part of the conflict, Graham Greene had mentioned the attractiveness of the women in Vietnam. Thomas Fowler, the seasoned correspondent at the centre of the story, says, 'Up the street came the lovely flat figures – the white silk trousers, the long tight jackets in pink and mauve patterns slit up the thigh. They are lovely, aren't they?' The street he was referring to was rue Catinat, whose name by this time had been changed to Tu Do. It was the most fashionable street in the city and ran alongside my hotel. Many of the girls there were prostitutes and the others were likely to be unfriendly, but they were a cheering sight, those beautiful tough girls. The Americans sometimes called them iron butterflies, and as they flitted about the grim streets, it was hard not to be impressed.

For a young journalist with a long interest in Vietnam, there was plenty to take in. The opera house in the middle of the main square had been rebuilt and turned into a parliament. Round the corner was the presidential palace. The Americans and their South Vietnamese allies were still trying to convince us that the real battle was between democracy and communism rather than the age-old struggle of the Vietnamese to run their own country. But it was the war itself which dominated all discussions. At night in Saigon, particularly if the cloud cover was low, the rolling thunder of the attacks in Cambodia could clearly be heard. Bombs from high-flying B-52s, based thousands of miles away on the Pacific island of Guam, would rain down on the Parrot's Beak area jutting into Vietnam.

The war would go on for another three years, but for many of the journalists the most interesting period was over. The Americans no longer believed they could win and were seeking an honourable way out. The Army of the Republic of Vietnam, known as ARVN, was doing surprisingly well, sometimes through unconventional means. One of the stories

I covered was a scheme which provided free televisions and fridges for those soldiers who agreed to stay in the front line. But there were also terrible mistakes. The worst I saw occurred on 8 June 1972 at the village of Trang Bang on Highway One. It provided one of the most notorious images of the Vietnam War.

I was with Jon Swain driving along the highway when we passed a convoy of about six hundred government troops moving towards the border with Cambodia. We drove off the road into a field and could see South Vietnamese aircraft making bombing runs down the road on the edge of a village with a small pagoda. The government forces clearly thought the area had been infiltrated by the Vietcong, but as far as we could see the countryside was peaceful. I recorded the explosions from the air attack. We were told that three South Vietnamese soldiers had been burned by napalm dropped near them by mistake. It was only when we returned to Saigon that we heard the full story. A nine-year-old girl called Kim Phuc had been caught in the exploding napalm. She ran naked down the road as the flaming chemical burned her skin. She survived and went to live in North America; but the image of a terrified and brutally wounded young girl caught up in war stirred up emotions around the world. I'd been so near but my experience that afternoon could hardly have been more distant. A famous moment, caught on camera, appeared to sum up the entire Vietnam War. Yet for us it had seemed no more than a small unpleasant incident which otherwise we would have quickly forgotten.

When Derek Wilson returned I decided that I should see as much of the country as I could. In a Boeing aircraft, so new that the cellophane wrappings were still on the seats, I flew north to the port of Da Nang. The pilot seemed as new as the plane. He missed the runway on the first approach and had to go out to sea and round again. It was quite frightening, but the passengers did not seem alarmed. Many of them were peasants and one woman was even carrying a live chicken. The unusual atmosphere was maintained at the collection of huts which formed the terminal buildings where I was grateful to see that there was a rickshaw pulled by a bicycle. Climbing in, I asked for the Grand Hotel. After twenty minutes of hard cycling I could see we had arrived at the back of the terminal buildings, having seen a good deal of the town on the way. But there was the Grand Hotel and the driver was pleased to be given an American dollar for all his hard work.

I spent a difficult night, with my ear to a transistor radio listening to the BBC World Service, trying to drown out the buzzing of mosquitoes and the crackling noise of the cockroaches. Grand it wasn't. The next morning, on the American airbase, the contrast could hardly have been starker. In air-conditioned mobile homes packed with hi-fi gear, pilots drinking Coca Cola spoke coolly about bombing raids on North Vietnam. They replied to my questions mainly in monosyllables, which does not make for good radio, but there was one moment of illumination when one of the pilots admitted to a complete lack of feeling about those on the other side who might be killed when he attacked. 'They are just targets,' he said chillingly. 'They could be trucks, they could be soldiers, but to us, we have to see them as targets.'

I left Da Nang in an American Chinook helicopter. The front doors had been removed so that on both sides heavy machine guns could be trained on the jungle as we roared up the coastline. I kept thinking of Derek Wilson's advice not to go in helicopters, but there was no other way to get to the ancient city of Hue, not far from the border with North Vietnam. I felt I had to go to the front line and had brought with me a helmet, a flak jacket, and parts of an army uniform. Major Sergeant, very temporarily attached to the US Army, was going to war.

On arrival in Hue, I spent another difficult night in a less than luxurious hotel. This time the problem was a series of explosions, which seemed all too likely to be the work of the Vietcong. I was told in the morning that it was simply some youngsters out fishing. They had been told not to, but they could not resist throwing grenades into the Perfumed River. The battered remains of the fish would then float to the surface. I put on my combat gear and decided that off to the front I would go, but first I had to visit the PTT, the post office, to find out if there were any messages. There were: Derek Wilson had to leave Saigon and I was to return there immediately. With a sigh of relief I stripped off the combat gear. A pointless sacrifice, of the sort so brilliantly outlined by Peter Cook in *Beyond the Fringe*, had been neatly avoided.

When, after six weeks, my tour of duty ended, as a treat I was allowed to fly home via Hong Kong. It was called R and R, rest and recuperation, and it felt marvellous to relax and know that I had survived. Vietnam had been an extraordinary experience and although I had not had a great deal of journalistic success I was determined this should not be the overall conclusion. If one was only allowed to be proud of doing well on stories, the list of achievements might not be a long one, but I was very proud briefly to have covered the war in Vietnam. It also had a profound effect on me, personally. The more uncertain my life, the more important it was, it seemed to me, to think about the next generation. It is not an easy matter to describe. I may have been affected by the stories I had read as a child, of how bomber pilots before their last mission were anxious to ensure the survival of their kind if not themselves. It may have been more to do with the ticking of the biological clock. After all, I was twenty-eight. But it was certainly after my time in Vietnam that Mary and I became increasingly keen to have children.

13

One last cigarette

WHEN I WAS YOUNGER there were few things that irritated me more than older people saying how life had speeded up. Deep in the English countryside they would go on about the jet plane as if they spent most of their days flying in one. They would complain about the difficulty of driving in London, where the cars whizzed about, when they seldom if ever went to London. The implication was that slower was better, while I, and it seemed every other young person stuck in the countryside, had a clear bias in the other direction. We longed for things to be done speedily and to show off the quickness of our reactions. Now, of course, I have to be careful not to catch myself saying something similar about the way that things have changed. Take a simple example: how difficult it was in the early 1970s for a woman to have a quick and reliable pregnancy test. It is so much easier and faster today.

In March 1973 Mary could wait no longer. She had to know if she was pregnant and she was not prepared to linger for a week until the GP could get back the results of a test. In the Tottenham Court Road a family planning clinic promised immediate results and she was ushered into a small room downstairs. 'Yes,' was the verdict and the staff, without hesitation, suggested she should go upstairs for a cup of tea, while they began laboriously filling in forms. 'But,' Mary said, 'I want to have this child.' There was a surprised silence.

'Oh well,' said the woman in charge. 'I suppose it's

congratulations.' It might have been a strange way of receiving life-changing information, but that did not alter its impact.

I was in Iceland covering the so-called Cod War, but when Mary got through to me in my hotel it shot straight to the top of my list of great telephone calls. The news then raced round the family, with Mary's Auntie Dorothy from Lancashire producing the most memorable response: 'It's about time, too,' she said. 'They have looked at each other for long enough.'

In the days before this momentous news broke, I had been grappling with one of the usual journalistic problems: how to follow a war on the high seas while staying in a comfortable hotel many miles away, in Reykjavik. It was, in any case, a very half-hearted war on the British side. The Icelandic government had unilaterally declared a two-hundred-mile fishing zone around its shores; in those days international waters usually started only four miles out. But times were changing not least in the North Sea where Norway and Britain would soon carve up the continental shelf in order to drill for oil. If it had not been for the understandable emotional attachment to the once mighty British fishing fleet and the compelling taste of fish and chips wrapped in newspaper the Cod War would never have started. But small countries do not like being dictated to by big countries and Iceland with its tiny population of just over 200,000 was being pushed around by Britain. Only small ships were involved and it did not develop into a shooting war, but there were close encounters in difficult conditions and tempers were rising.

Buoyed up by the news from home I asked room service for one of the local delicacies: salmon and scrambled eggs. Half an hour passed and then a waiter entered bowed under an enormous platter. For some reason, possibly a mistake in translation, he had brought no fewer than ten helpings. I was so hungry that I got through most of them – after all I was celebrating possible fatherhood – but even now, nearly thirty years later, if offered this particular dish, I tend to refuse.

Iceland, though, provided one more valuable lesson in the importance of nationalism, which cast further doubt on the argument that to be viable in the modern world, states have to be of a certain size. With a population less than a third the size of Liverpool it was amazing how well Iceland fared. You could walk down one of the main streets and be told that house was where the prime minister worked, that one the office of the foreign secretary, all on a very modest scale. The parliament, the Althing, is celebrated as one of the oldest in the world as it goes back about a thousand years. It is housed in a small building which looks like a school and had, to me at least, an unmistakable smell of Weetabix, perhaps because the windows were always closed. There are no railways and no trees, and the locals seem to drink a lot; but no one would suggest that Iceland is not a nation.

It was in partitioned countries, like Ireland and Vietnam, that I saw the most anguish; and in Cyprus, too. For most of the 1970s I was one of a disparate group of journalists who gathered in unlikely places to rekindle old friendships and rivalries. We were the international press corps, whose arrival might be greeted with relief or disdain, depending on your point of view, but without whom there could be serious events but not a big news story. Cyprus in 1974 became very big news indeed. Following a military coup by a group which favoured union with Greece, it was invaded by the Turks and has been effectively partitioned ever since. I was not fully aware of how the same reporters were following each other around the world until one night in Nicosia, crossing the Green line, as it is called, separating the Greek and Turkish sides, some shots rang out and a reporter shouted, '*Bao chi, bao chi.*' It is the Vietnamese for journalist, and was completely meaningless to those who were shooting at us, but there were enough of us there to understand and think it was funny.

Many of the older British reporters felt very much at home when we first arrived. They over-tipped the head porter at the Ledra Palace Hotel in Nicosia, and we were solemnly advised to do the same. 'He'll help you get fixed up,' we were told rather mysteriously. The old hands had memories of the Ledra Palace which went back to the terrorist campaigns against the British before Cyprus became independent in 1960. The head porter could help you get a long-distance telephone call. I duly gave him twenty pounds. But the money was completely wasted and we turned out to be the last guests he ever welcomed.

The coup, which was supported by the military junta then ruling Greece, had triggered immediate fears of a Turkish response; that was why I had been sent. Apart from the two British bases on the island, at Akrotiri and Dhekelia, there were a large number of expatriates living in Cyprus. Some of them behaved as if they were still in charge and were sometimes referred to as the Ancient Brits. Near Paphos, in the south, one of them invited a group of fellow expats to have some fun with the reporter who had arrived from the BBC. Waving his gin and tonic and sporting a large handlebar moustache this Ancient Brit roared with laughter and pointed at me. 'He seems to think there'll be war or something.' The very next morning 40,000 Turkish troops landed in the north of the island.

Back in my room at the Ledra Palace, I was woken by shouting when the invasion started. Running on to the roof we could see the sky to the north filled with parachutes and the hills above Kyrenia scorched with flames. A heavy pall of smoke lay across the horizon. Despite my efforts with the head porter it was impossible to make a phone call. It was the biggest story of my journalistic life and I could not get in touch with the office. The old hands, remarkably cool, began filling their baths with water in case supplies ran out. Greek Cypriot forces dragged heavy machine guns on to the roof and started firing into the Turkish sector. To provide cover and a certain amount of safety they decided we should be forced to stay with them. For the next thirty-six hours we were kept cooped up in the hotel, most of the time bunched together in the staircase well, protected, we hoped, from the dangers of an attack by the Turks.

It was months later that I heard how close we had come to being killed. The machine gun nest on the roof was the most effective sign of Greek Cypriot resistance, and it was decided that the Ledra Palace should be bombed from the air. I was told by Turkish Cypriot sources that their planes were already on the way when they were called back. It was argued that putting the lives of two hundred international journalists at risk would not help their cause. This did not stop Turkish forces closer to the hotel opening up with small-arms fire. The noise was deafening and, terrified, I broke my five-year ban on smoking and had one last cigarette. I have not touched one since. The BBC World Service provided the only light relief; in perfect quality we could listen to *Round the Horne*. It did not seem quite as funny as usual.

Canadian forces operating with the UN eventually freed us. Their commander, in dark olive fatigues, carried a loud-hailer and shouted into the darkness, 'Cease fire, cease fire.' The shooting continued. We managed to get out unscathed in armoured personnel carriers and were taken to the British base at Dhekelia, where we were soon queuing up to make phone calls. I was not shy to use every ounce of influence. 'Please let me jump the queue,' I said. My fellow journalists knew that if I was on the radio, everyone would know we were safe. They agreed and, as the BBC archive records, within minutes my despatch was being transmitted on the six o'clock radio news. This is what I shouted down a bad telephone line connected to Broadcasting House in London:

> The shooting began immediately after the invasion was announced at five o'clock yesterday morning. From then there was almost continuous firing. Within the first half hour a Greek machine gun post on the roof of the hotel was hit. One Greek soldier died instantly, another was carried down unconscious into the hotel lobby and died before he reached hospital. Most of the firing came from the thirty or so Greek soldiers who had taken up position in the hotel the night before the invasion. It was a strategic position because the big luxury hotel, with its swimming pool and palm trees, is right near the boundary with the Turkish sector. A massive barrage of fire was maintained by the Greeks using automatic weapons, rifles and heavy machine guns. The Turks, who knew we were there, were more restrained. But even so, the hotel was hit many times by small-arms fire. One of the other soldiers was injured and this morning three mortar bombs were lobbed in. Cement dust showered into the cellar where the women and small children were hiding. Upstairs two big glass doors were shattered. Throughout all this, a platoon of United Nations officers had tried to arrange a ceasefire. Eventually, agreement was reached and thirty-three hours after the siege began, a UN convoy came in to evacuate us. Even then, there was some firing. One of the women tourists cried with relief as she was helped into a British lorry. We were indeed lucky that none of us had been injured.

We were transferred to the other British base in the south of the island at Akrotiri. The BBC, generally, were in very poor spirits because an ITN reporter, Michael Nicholson, had pulled off a remarkable scoop. He had filmed and then interviewed Turkish paratroopers when they landed in northern Cyprus and even managed to get the film back with the help of the RAF. Impressed though I was by this feat I was in no mood to try to emulate his success. I had been badly shaken in Nicosia and had taken a conscious decision not to risk my life needlessly. This reluctance was spotted by one of my colleagues, Keith Graves, a brilliant and tough television reporter who could not resist haranguing me from the pulpit of an RAF chapel in Akrotiri. 'This man is a coward,' he shouted, having himself just returned from near Famagusta where fighting was still continuing. It would not have been so bad if there had not been a large number of fellow journalists present. Many years later, he apologized for what he called his boorish behaviour. Nonetheless, the episode reflects the enormous tension under which we were working.

There was another call to arms from Simon Dring, a television reporter who had just arrived. He announced that his task was to recover the BBC's reputation. My colleague, David Sells, was so incensed that he wrote a poem on the subject, the main character being 'Viper Dring'. Later, during a lull in the fighting, I went with Simon and a group of journalists on a visit to the north arranged by the Turkish military authorities. He gave me a lift back in his hired car and told me and the crew that we would not be going back to Nicosia; he intended to try to break through to the west and cross the front line at the village of Lapithos. 'Well, in that case,' I said firmly, 'you can drop me at the next corner – I am going with the others.' He arrived at the hotel later having been turned back by the Turkish army and prevented from getting into Lapithos. Soon after I left for home.

A week later, I was asleep in our new home in Ealing when the phone woke me. It was the BBC. One of our people in Cyprus had been killed and would I go back there straight away? We needed to send reinforcements to keep up morale. Taking a deep breath I said yes. The awful news was soon broadcast. Ted Stoddart, a soundman with a television crew, had been killed in a minefield on the front line west of Kyrenia. The reporter, Simon Dring, and the cameraman were unhurt. A BBC radio reporter with them, Christopher Morris, had been injured. I asked where they had been going and was told, 'Oh, they were on their way to Lapithos.'

That afternoon I was one of only two passengers standing on the tarmac at the military airfield at Lyneham in Wiltshire; the other was the television news editor, John Exelby. His task was to bring back Ted Stoddart's body. The VC-10 that we would travel in would return full of service families being sent home from Cyprus. The plane's captain saluted me. 'When would you like us to take off?' This was not a role I was used to. 'Straight away, fine, let's go,' I replied, and made only one special request: 'Would it be possible, in the middle of the night, to hear President Nixon's broadcast from the White House? It looks as if he will resign.' The captain readily agreed.

It was a strange scene: in a cloudless sky high above the south of France, sitting in the cockpit of an almost empty RAF VC-10 we listened to the denouement of the long-drawn-out Watergate affair. It was President Nixon's last broadcast from the White House. Leslie Stone afterwards provided the BBC comment, correctly concluding that it was the end of the Nixon presidency. I was so impressed. If only, I mused momentarily, I could become one of the BBC's political experts and give up trying to be a war correspondent; I was not sure it really suited me.

In Nicosia, the Ledra Palace had been taken over by the UN, so we checked into the Hilton, not far away. I opened the door to the room allotted to me and realized immediately that something was wrong. The previous occupant had not checked out; his clothes and equipment were lying about. I closed the door quickly and went back to reception, a wave of nausea sweeping over me. It was Ted Stoddart's room.

A ceasefire was operating while peace talks were held in Geneva. To gauge reaction on the Greek Cypriot side I decided to go to the village in the south where President Makarios had been born. My companion was a Frenchman, Michel Legrand, a photographer working for the Gamma news agency based in Paris. He offered to share the driving of my hired car and I agreed with a strict proviso. We were driving away from the front and there was no need to be reckless. If he drove in a wild fashion I would take over; I had no intention of being killed in a car accident. He immediately drove off at a crazy speed while I banged on the dashboard to get him to stop. The following year he was killed in Saigon, right at the end of the Vietnam War, when a bridge he need not have been on was blown up. He was the father of two young children. Like a number of journalists I met in Cyprus he appeared unable to resist acting dangerously in a war zone. They seemed to feel compelled to play up to events. I, on the other hand, usually attempted to stand back, trying to understand what was going on, and that could mean I was less effective. Keith Graves might have had a point – often I was also extremely scared.

In the bar on the top floor of the Hilton young Greek Cypriots used to hold forth on the iniquities of the Turks. Their blood was up and they were determined to fight. I suggested that fighting would be useless given the vastly superior Turkish forces and the determination of the British and Greeks not to intervene. Would they not do better trying to reach an agreement in Geneva? It was a classic example of how military force does not compel a change of mind; it hardens opinion. The Greek Cypriots were far less prepared to compromise than before the Turkish invasion. The talks in Geneva broke down and the Turks attacked again.

A Turkish fighter plane flew over the Hilton firing heavy-calibre rounds into the grounds, across the swimming pool and into the roof. It was all over in seconds, but the noise was terrifying and caused panic. This time I was determined that at least I would fill my bath. Once again, the phones had been cut off. I compiled a report with a Fleet Street journalist which was sent by teleprinter to all the major news organizations. He wanted to say that Nicosia had been attacked by wave after wave of bombers. I managed to persuade him that a more modest description would suffice. The Turks had decided to widen their area of occupation in the north. They took nearly 40 per cent of some of the best land in Cyprus, and the war would create such bitterness that for this generation at least it would be the end of Cyprus as a unitary state.

Eventually, I was allowed home. A Canadian Hercules aircraft lifted off from RAF Akrotiri with me as sole passenger. The vast hold was empty. I sat alone in the row of seats normally reserved for troops. It took seven hours to fly to Germany and, feeling like a less handsome version of James Bond, I changed into my best lightweight suit before landing. The big door at the back of the plane was lowered and I strolled off, looking cleaner and smarter than I had for weeks. There were no customs or passport checks. The airbase was more than a hundred miles south of Frankfurt. I drove there in a hired car and stayed in the best hotel. I have almost never felt more relieved.

Coming home there was an extra delight. William Peter Sergeant had been born the previous November. He had reddish hair and was the perfect antidote to my intense life at the BBC. In that year, 1974, I had covered a host of stories, including Sir Edward Heath's campaigns in the two general elections, of which more later. Despite all the difficulties in Vietnam, Iceland and Cyprus – and the beginnings of family life – I still hoped to become a foreign correspondent. There would be more adventures abroad before I finally settled at Westminster.

14

More foreign adventures

THE END OF the Vietnam War came as a tragic anticlimax. After traumatizing a whole generation of Vietnamese and dividing opinion in the United States like no issue since the Civil War it all came down to a few helicopters taking off from the American embassy in Saigon, young men clinging to their undercarriages, desperate to escape from the Communist advance. It was the first major war in which reporters, particularly television reporters, had a decisive effect on the outcome, and it was appropriate that those pictures underlining the American defeat should have been shown instantly around the world. Without television the American forces might have been even more ruthless and viewers would have been denied the daily diet of bad news from Vietnam which fuelled the growing peace movement.

Although I had been opposed to the war since I was a teenager it was not a moment for celebration; it was too awe-inspiring for that. After all the talk, after all the bravado and all the money, the world's greatest power had been humbled; and anyone with access to a television set could see the terrible blow to America's pride. It was the end of April 1975, and I was in Washington staying at a small hotel in Georgetown. The BBC had decided that I should fill in as a Washington correspondent for about a month and I had leapt at the chance. The main radio correspondent was a delightful, humorous, hard-working Welshman called Angus McDermid; the television correspondent fitted the same description: John Humphrys, later the famous voice of the *Today* programme.

The first call came in at about five o'clock in the morning. It was Helen Wilson, the duty producer, phoning from New York. The Americans, she told me, were leaving Vietnam. She was usually very well organized, but on this occasion she asked me what we should do. 'We should all go to our offices,' I suggested. 'Angus and I will go in here and you should go into the New York office.' I had no idea what we should do, but I knew we would have to get started; in a few hours *Today* would begin and without doubt this was one of the biggest stories we would ever cover.

It is a curious feature of reporting in Washington that the people who go to the events, the news conferences or what are called the photo opportunities, are often the more junior members of the staff. Those who do the real work stay in the office, watching it all on television. They can then react far more quickly in transmitting the news back home. It was therefore only to be expected that Angus McDermid should be left at the BBC office while I went to the White House. As I was arriving, the secretary of state, Henry Kissinger, turned up and went straight into his office. On the other side of the world, in Vietnam, the helicopters were making their final departure. The new president, Gerald Ford, who was never really to come out of the shadows left by President Nixon, would give a news conference later. There was an undeniable sense of history being made.

Angus and I dominated the *Today* programme that morning. Helen Wilson in New York recorded all the important statements from the American news networks and these we wove into the story together with separate pieces from the White House and the Washington office. When you are an inexperienced reporter, listening to the coverage of these sorts of events can be intimidating; you feel that you could not do as well in the same circumstances. But the truth is that the big stories usually write themselves; the adrenalin is flowing, and because by their nature these are events millions of people are interested in, they do not require very subtle handling. 'What's happening now?' is the best question from the programme presenters and as long as the reporters stay reasonably cool the chances are they will find the eloquence to match. If you are in the right place, even if nothing much is happening, you can always describe the calm at the centre of the storm. I think we did quite well that morning.

At his news conference Gerald Ford was anxious to appear friendly to the press. After the traumas of Watergate, only resolved after years of conflict between the president and the press, the atmosphere of reconciliation seemed rather cloying. 'I recognize the *Washington Post*,' Ford said, asking one of their senior reporters to put a question. To an outsider like me, all the drama of Vietnam and Watergate seemed to have knocked the stuffing out of both sides. In the United States they tend to take their journalists and journalism far more seriously than we do, and at their best American reporters can be very good indeed. When Gerald Ford finally had to face the electorate, having been raised from the vice-presidency after President Nixon's resignation, it was the doyenne of American television interviewers, Barbara Walters, who put him in his place. 'When I am re-elected—' he told her solemnly.

'You mean, Mr President,' she interjected, 'when you are elected.' Perhaps, after that, it was not surprising that Jimmy Carter became the next president of the United States.

John Humphrys lived with his family in the Maryland suburbs, in a vast house surrounded by a large vacant plot of land. One Sunday he invited me over for a barbecue and for the first time I appreciated how Middle America had changed since I had been there as a student. Californian wine was now marketed, as if it was cider, in jugs. John invited me to play snooker in the basement, with a jug of white wine for company. This should have set off more than one alarm bell. Drinking and playing snooker is, for me anyway, not a good idea; and why did it not occur to me that anyone who has a full-size snooker table in their basement is likely to keep on top form? What was worse, I caught him cheating. I have told this story in front of large audiences, when John Humphrys has been present, and at the reference to cheating there is usually a general intake of breath. Calm is only restored when I explain that he was cheating in my favour, altering the score on the board so that I would not seem so far behind. It was the beginning of a long friendship.

On my return to London, there was the excitement of the imminent birth of our second child. Nowadays, couples can choose whether to be told the sex of the baby, but luckily that was not an option for us. I thought a girl would be nice, because we already had a boy, and I was present at the birth in the Middlesex Hospital in central London. It was late on a Sunday night and very few staff were there. But, quickly and marvellously, Michael John Sergeant arrived, a perfect demonstration of how wrong it would be for parents to choose a baby's sex. Mike turned out to be the best possible childhood companion for Will. Our family was now complete.

Having children is as good a way as any to force you to grow up. You feel far less like playing the child when there are real children around. But that did not stop me being rather childish when, after visiting my GP, I discovered that I would need a hernia operation. It's a common complaint, a weakness in the wall of the lower abdomen which can be cut and stitched by a surgeon to stop the occasional pain and swelling. I treated the news like the clap of doom. Back from the surgery I phoned Mary at work to tell her that I would need an operation. My exact words were, 'I'm afraid it's the knife.' And with that I went smartly to bed. The phone rang in the bedroom.

The editor of radio news was convinced he was giving me good news. Guerrilla war had broken out in Rhodesia and *Today* wanted to send me there immediately. 'That should be fine,' I replied guardedly. 'Can I ring you back?' I telephoned my doctor. He was remarkably sympathetic. Yes, I could go, but on the firm understanding that I would be back within two weeks. I quickly got dressed, all symptoms forgotten as another adventure beckoned.

It was winter in London, summer in Rhodesia. In 1976 it still had the air of a British colony and we would have been very surprised to be told that in just over four years the capital, Salisbury, would be renamed Harare and the country, now Zimbabwe, would be ruled by its black majority. Off the main roads driving was dangerous because of landmines, but I was most fearful of the tough white Rhodesians, who regarded the BBC as a source of Communist propaganda. I found myself in Umtali, now known as Mutare, a small town close to the Mozambique border. Parking my hired Volkswagen outside a bar I went in for a beer. A group looking like huge rugby players followed me inside. 'The BBC is in town,' one of them spat. It was like a scene in a wild west movie. 'Oh, really,' I said. 'I wonder what they are up to.' It was not a very convincing performance, but they allowed me to edge myself gently to the door and I was soon gratefully driving off. I could not tell them what I really felt, which was that the days of white rule were coming to an end and if they listened to the BBC they would have a better understanding of why it was happening.

On the way home I stopped off in South Africa and was surprised to see along the roads newspaper billboards with bold black type carrying the stark message: 'Wilson Resigns.'

I thought Wilson must be some local politician. It was only when I reached the BBC office in Johannesburg that the mystery was solved. Harold Wilson, the Labour prime minister who went into the record books as the winner of four general elections, had suddenly, and without warning, resigned. I could not wait to get back home. I had been away for just under two weeks. My doctor's orders had been obeyed, but there was still that rendezvous with the knife which I could have done without.

The nurse who examined me was startled to find blotches on my skin. 'And what is that?' she demanded, pointing at my stomach. 'Oh, that's sunburn,' I replied. 'I have just come back from Rhodesia, where it's summer.' On a cold rainy day in the centre of London it seemed quite an exotic complaint.

People can react in a variety of ways when they find out you are a journalist. Some people immediately clam up. They are so worried about telling you something which might be published they can be discreet to the point of silliness. This nurse was one of those who react quite differently; she knew she should be more on her guard, but that made her all the keener to pass on information. It made her life just that bit more exciting.

So when I came to in the Middlesex Hospital, she was leaning over my bed. 'You'll never guess what happened,' she said. 'They lost a needle and everyone had to be injected all over again; it took ages.' Mary had been surprised to be told at one o'clock that I had still not come out of the operating theatre, even though I was the first patient of the day. She was told to ring back at three. I was still rather groggy when the nurse whispered the whole story. At the end of my operation a check was made and one of the surgeon's needles was missing. They decided to X-ray me but the radiographer was on his break and meanwhile the other patients in the queue were dangerously close to waking up. They all had to be anaesthetized again to keep them asleep.

An X-ray was taken, but nothing untoward was revealed. Finally, the staff turned to the last resort. A giant magnet was trawled across the floor of the operating theatre and the nurse told me how wonderful it was when they heard a loud 'ping'. The needle had been found.

Weeks later, when I had fully recovered, the surgeon asked me how I thought it had all gone. I conjured up an image of him on all fours, desperately searching for the needle, but I resisted the temptation to tell him how much I knew. 'What I do think,' I said, 'is how good these modern anaesthetics are; you are completely oblivious to what's going on.'

★

During my many trips abroad for the BBC it was always interesting to speculate on who had gained most from the experience: me or the BBC. If conditions were awful and especially if they were dangerous, then the BBC would draw ahead on points. But often the places and the people were of such interest, irrespective of the news story, that I would begin to believe that I was edging ahead. Every time I would try to work out in the end who had finished in front. Maybe it was the way I allocated the points, or maybe it was the way I felt about the whole enterprise, but it was uncanny how the BBC never seemed to be seriously behind. It was usually a draw.

Take one of my trips at around this time: the first occasion in my adult life that I saw the Pyramids. To be back looking at one of the great wonders of the ancient world was cause for considerable pleasure. Cairo, too, was interesting; and walking along the narrow streets playing with my new and very expensive radio. What could be more riveting than suddenly hearing one's own voice broadcasting on the medium wave relayed in Cyprus? This was clearly a trip I could enjoy, and easily win my unofficial contest with the BBC.

But, and there was always a qualification of some kind, it was not quite as simple as that. This was Christmas 1977 and I was away from my two small boys and my wife, all of whom I adored. The staff at the Cairo Hilton, who gave no impression of being Christians, had nevertheless decided to embrace the festival, no doubt encouraged by the thought of more days off. Some grim-looking turkey was warmed up for Christmas lunch and carols were piped over the music system. A rather bedraggled Father Christmas adorned a plastic tree.

To keep up my morale the news people at Broadcasting House had spoken in terms of privilege and history: 'You are,' I was told, 'privileged to be covering a story which will affect the history of the Middle East.' I could not really dispute either of those claims. This was a momentous time. Just over a month before, the Egyptian president, Anwar Sadat, had surprised the world by announcing that he would be prepared to go to the Israeli parliament, the Knesset, to make a direct appeal for peace between the two countries. After the wars of 1967 and 1973 it looked as though an extraordinary breakthrough might be possible. Sadat's visit to Jerusalem had been a great success. Now it was the turn of the hard-line Israeli prime minister, Menachem Begin, to come to Egypt. It would be the first ever visit by an Israeli prime minister.

In those days a world-class news story, and that usually meant a large degree of American interest, could attract about a thousand journalists. It was the beginning of the widespread use of satellite technology which allows television presenters to host their shows from almost anywhere. The meeting between Sadat and Begin took place by the Suez Canal at Ismailiya, a long drive across the desert from Cairo. Lines of satellite trucks were parked alongside several vast tents; and it was here that I would spend Boxing Day.

Relations between politicians and the media are often marked by frustration and in some cases downright hostility, but the truth is that wherever they are in the world, they need each other. On that tented site in the Egyptian desert this was more obvious than usual. It became apparent that the two leaders had very little to say at this stage. The importance was in the symbolism of their meeting on Egyptian soil. I was given a clear indication of this by one of the officials in Begin's office. 'What is the story?' I asked him bluntly.

'You are the story,' he replied. 'The fact that you are all here reporting their meeting: this could give momentum to the search for peace.' It was weeks later that we learned that the two leaders had met only briefly before adjourning to take a sightseeing tour of Ismailiya. At the time the impression of a much longer formal meeting was maintained. But we had not come all this way for nothing: in less than a year the Camp David accords were signed, paving the way for a peace agreement between Israel and Egypt. However, Camp David did not resolve the conflict between the Israelis and other Arab states; nor did it do much to settle the complaints of the Palestinians.

All this was brought sharply to my attention a few months after I returned to London from Cairo. A terrorist attack in Israel had convinced my news editor that there might be a military response across the border into southern Lebanon. I flew to Israel and as there were BBC reporters in Tel Aviv and Jerusalem it seemed sensible to drive to the northernmost part of the country, to the small town of Metullah. Nothing much seemed to be going on, but before leaving I went into one of the small hotels for a drink. 'So you've got here at last,' was the greeting I received. It was from John Bierman, one of the toughest and best BBC television correspondents, sitting further along the bar. 'Did you see the troops on either side of the road, coming up here?' he continued. I had not seen anything unusual, and not for the first time with John I felt inadequate. He was much more experienced, with real knowledge of warfare. 'They can't be kept in a state of readiness for much longer,' he went on. 'They'll have to strike soon or they will have to stand them down.'

Soon after midnight we saw the action. From the top of our hotel in Metullah we could see the tracer bullets lighting up the darkness inside southern Lebanon. Then the big camouflaged guns opened up from a field a short distance away. The noise was intense. Once again I was in a war zone, and as before it gave me a sinking feeling. This was the first time the Israelis had invaded Lebanon and they felt confident enough to do so because of the deal struck with President Sadat. Their aim was to drive the Palestinian forces away from the border area, which they did with their vastly superior strength. My report, complete with sound effects, appeared on the morning bulletin on Radio 4 coupled with a report from the Lebanese side by my colleague, Graham Leach.

Because I had stopped at that hotel and found John Bierman, I was one of only about ten correspondents with the advancing Israeli army; hundreds more were prevented from reaching Metullah. There is so often an irrelevant detail which sticks in your memories of these violent scenes. Mine is the fact that I was wearing a very cheap suit, which cost about twenty pounds. When we were taken in a group into the battle area I was surprised to meet an ITN reporter who looked me up and down and said, 'Like your suit.' He was dressed immaculately in combat gear. Very soon after we heard a shout that during the 1970s I learned to dread: 'Incoming, incoming.' It was a warning of shellfire from the other side. I jumped into what appeared to be a bomb shelter; there were heaps of sandbags on either side of the entrance. Cowering inside I was dismayed to read the labels on the boxes piled up inside. It was a simple and stark description: 'High explosive'. I had managed to take cover in an ammunition store.

Months later I was surprised to be told by one of the editors at Broadcasting House what a difficult night he had had when the Israelis invaded Lebanon. Correspondents were on both sides but he had been up all night wondering whether they would be able to get through. 'It had been quite a night,' he told me earnestly. I reminded him that I had been one of those correspondents. He would not be put off so easily. 'It really was a difficult night,' he went on. 'You see we really did not know what would be in the bulletin that morning.'

After the Lebanon I began to think that being a foreign correspondent might not be the answer after all. I had become used to being pushed around the world by the BBC, but if I were based abroad, my whole family would be subject to the whims of Broadcasting House. We could be told where to live and when to come home. As my sons grew older I decided this ambition would have to be abandoned. I would pursue that other interest which had been with me all my adult life: it was time to turn my passion for politics into a new stage of my career.

15

Talking to prime ministers

THE FIRST POLITICIAN I came to know just happened to be prime minister; and the only reason for our meeting was in case something strange or untoward happened to him personally. If the prime minister had been shot I would have been thrust into prominence, explaining to a large audience what had happened and, depending on the circumstances, asked to speculate why the tragedy had occurred. Not to put too fine a point on it, I was on what journalists sometimes call the Death Watch. But despite this macabre context my contact with the prime minister developed into an extremely useful and amusing introduction to politics at the highest level; and for that I must thank Sir Edward Heath.

At the beginning of 1974 there was speculation that the Conservative government, led by Mr Heath, would go for an early election. It was less than four years since they had come to office, but sharply rising oil prices combined with a bitter dispute with the miners encouraged the government to make a stand. Industry was forced to work a three-day week in order to save energy, and a junior environment minister, Patrick Jenkin, became famous for suggesting that people should brush their teeth in the dark. Mr Heath decided that the only way out of the impasse was to ask the electorate a simple question: 'Who governs Britain?' After a few weeks it was clear that the tactic had not worked. The electorate were in no mood to answer a question of that sort; they wanted to get on with the untidy business of a normal election campaign. The final result was as muddled as you might expect. Mr Heath was robbed of his majority and could only have governed with Liberal support, which was not forthcoming. The Labour leader, Harold Wilson, won the February election by default and, with a tight majority, the second general election of 1974 which followed in October.

It was not my intention to choose the losing side. In the first election I was given a choice as to which party leader I would like to follow and I thought it would be more fun to be with the person who was running the country. It would then have seemed churlish to give up my contacts with the Conservatives and switch to Labour. So in less than a year I was able to enjoy watching first a prime minister then a leader of the opposition fight for his political life. I should stress how much my role was to observe, rather than report. The BBC's political correspondents, many of whom I would get to know well in the years to come, had an extraordinary desire to stay as far away as possible from the front line of politics. They all wanted to be political commentators not reporters and tended to sit in London waiting to receive television pictures of the leader's evening speech, to which they would add what they hoped were wise words of comment. Almost all the political coverage was in the hands of the political correspondents. But the foot soldiers, of whom I was proudly in the forefront, went everywhere with the party leaders, from dawn until dusk, weekends included.

My strange role, an elaborate version of *Waiting for Godot* in which I would only come into my own if something awful happened to Ted Heath, had an extremely beneficial effect on my relations with the prime minister. Many of the political correspondents, though prepared to take part in the three-thousand-mile campaign tour, were too busy, or perhaps too partisan, to chat to Mr Heath at the end of a gruelling day. I was more than happy to do so. It was not part of my brief to become involved in acrimonious argument or to try to trick the prime minister into off-the-record remarks that could be blown up into tabloid headlines. He seemed more able to relax with me, the reporter, than with most of the political correspondents in the group.

As I was not constantly having to send copy, I was also able to be more frivolous than most of the others, ably abetted by Simon Hoggart of the *Guardian*. We spent quite a lot of the time trying to amuse each other. One of our efforts involved thinking up the most obscure slogan that could be shouted at the prime minister from the back of a crowd. The idea was to project what people might be really thinking, but it soon became an exercise in silliness. One of the big arguments at the time was about the need to control the money supply, that is the total amount of money in the economy at any one time. The only problem is that the experts could not agree on what sort of money to include and they invented more and more categories, each of which carried the name of a motorway: M1, M2 and so on. On a run-down housing estate in Cardiff Simon easily won our competition, shouting at Mr Heath, 'Redefine M3.' The prime minister was not amused.

The election campaigns of 1974, with the benefit of hindsight, seem absurdly amateurish. Even on days of major events with a key speech in the evening the prime minister would have only perhaps thirty people in the press group touring with him; and the bus to transport them was provided by Tory central office, with one of their officials acting as our guide. At the weekends, back in his constituency of Bexley and Sidcup, near London, there might be only a handful of reporters to keep Mr Heath company. Nowadays, with stations putting out twenty-four-hour television news and endless programmes requiring exclusive interviews it is easy to marshal several hundred media people during an election campaign. But in the 1970s it was possible, in the midst of a closely fought election battle, for a junior BBC reporter to get to know the prime minister.

Mr Heath's personal security was in the capable hands of Inspector Pride. Tall, with grey hair, Pride had been initially chosen because of his speed over a hundred yards in the Metropolitan Police games. He had a remarkable capacity to stand for long hours looking not at Mr Heath, but at the crowd to watch for anything suspicious. When the prime minister was alone another officer would join Inspector Pride; this was usually a large rotund figure, one of the best marksmen in the force. These two were the entire team whose job it was to protect the prime minister from attack. Unofficially, it was the group of travelling journalists who became the first line of defence. When we were around Mr Heath it would have taken a very determined terrorist to break through the ranks of Fleet Street's finest.

Even with these precautions there were strict limits on where the prime minister was allowed to go. In London, for instance, he was never able to go into a pub; the risk was thought to be too great. But outside the capital, after a speech, Mr Heath would invariably want to stop at a pub to have a Glenfiddich malt whisky. Provided that the visit was not part of the formal itinerary and the landlord had no idea he was coming, the security experts would agree. Sometimes the prime minister would have rather stilted conversations with members of the public, but often he would fall back on the travelling press for companionship.

When Mr Heath was in office he had a reputation for being wooden and without character. He was the Conservatives' answer to Labour's first grammar school leader, Harold Wilson. They were both educated by the state and both ended up with firsts from Oxford. However, Harold Wilson turned himself into a caustic wit and speechmaker, with a popular touch, whereas Mr Heath, in comparison, seemed stuffy and reserved. I can't pretend that in private all this changed. He could appear awkward and abrupt, if not sometimes downright rude. Having spoken to you at some length one day, he was quite likely to cut you dead the next. But, as became apparent to everyone at Westminster when he became the grand old man of British politics, he was also capable of being very funny; in 1974, when he was still prime minister, this came as a revelation.

I tended to ask him questions about matters which were not particularly relevant to the election campaign, often to do with Europe. I knew he would be much keener to answer these than questions on the controversy of the day. Propping up the bar of a country pub, I might ask him to discourse on subjects like why shouldn't we be allowed to protect our industries from foreign competition and if we did not, how could we be sure that the economy would grow? He would take great pains to answer, showing no impatience at having to explain the advantages of free trade and competition.

The most striking thing I learned from Mr Heath was the sheer grind of being a senior politician; how much energy was required. It seemed that one needed an obsessive interest in the myriad different issues on which the government might have to take a view. How else could one explain a prime minister at the end of a campaigning day relaxing by discussing the disadvantages of import controls? But there was another, more uncomfortable truth that I would have to come to terms with during the rest of my reporting life: much as at times I wanted to be frivolous, there was also quite a large part of *me* that found it relaxing to discuss the disadvantages of import controls at the end of a campaigning day, particularly if I could do so with someone whose views might have a dramatic effect on the way those problems were tackled. At the time I was not yet ready to give up my life as a general reporter, but it was undoubtedly during the election campaigns of 1974 that the seed of my future career was sown.

Mr Heath's relatively brief period in office would come to an end after a confusing few days following the declaration of the results, but he had agreed to give me the first interview on the evening of polling day. It was in a school hall in his Bexley constituency where the counting of votes was taking place. As the evening wore on it became clear that the Tories would not have a clear majority, and nor would Labour. Mr Heath's gamble on an early election had failed. David Dimbleby had arrived to interview the prime minister and was established at one end of the hall on what looked to me like a throne. I felt very much the poor relation, with a microphone lead trailing back to a radio link. But those late night conversations with the prime minister paid off. Mr Heath kept his word. The photographers were waved aside; the first interview would be with me. I was so excited that it took me some time to realize how little he had actually said. Then it was back to Downing Street and the beginning of a long night.

In the morning it looked no clearer. During the weekend Mr Heath held abortive talks with the Liberal leader, Jeremy Thorpe. Later Mr Thorpe would be engulfed by scandal and a notorious trial, but at that time he still looked as though he might take up the cabinet post he was offered. But the Liberals demonstrated that deep down they did not really want power; they wanted to preserve their own position. Mr Heath regarded it as the biggest political mistake of Mr Thorpe's career and it turned out to be the last time the Liberal Party, as then constituted, would have any chance of being in government. The consequences for Mr Heath were even more dramatic. The outside world knew that it was all over when his piano was unceremoniously put on to a removal van and I spent the weekend watching events from the pavement outside Number Ten.

Harold Wilson arrived in Downing Street with a muted sense of triumph. He was certainly pleased to be prime minister again, but it said a great deal that he did not want to move house. He would treat Downing Street as his office but his home remained in Lord North Street less than a mile away. When he resigned two years later to make way for Jim Callaghan it was tempting to conclude that during this final period in office he was not the man he used to be. The shine had come off Harold Wilson. Nevertheless, he had achieved a Labour victory, however narrow. In his memoirs, Mr Heath recalled his final exchange with his security officer. 'Goodbye, sir,' he said. 'Where are you going?' Mr Heath asked. The officer continued, 'Sir, you are no longer prime minister and therefore no longer entitled to special protection.' I assume he was talking to Inspector Pride.

As far as I was concerned, the second election campaign of 1974 was much less interesting than the first. As I noted in a broadcast preserved in the BBC archives, 'His (Mr Heath's) overriding theme is that there should be a government of national unity. The public, he says, are fed up to the back teeth with party bickering.' The Conservatives tried to match their style to this new policy. Mr Heath was encouraged to sit down during news conferences, and appear in question and answer sessions designed to look like television discussions. But having gone to the country on a confrontational basis earlier in the year it is not surprising that this more tolerant approach failed to convince the electorate. Harold Wilson squeaked in with an overall majority for Labour of just three seats.

After Mr Heath left office he found it easier to relax and was happy to spend time reminiscing. When Mary and I were invited to lunch at his home in Belgravia, he introduced me as 'John Sergeant, who is in charge of the BBC'. One of his stories related to a particularly difficult Commonwealth conference. At last they had agreed a final communiqué, which stressed, among other things, the evils of racial discrimination. Then the delegate from Fiji put up his hand. 'What's the matter?' Mr Heath asked crossly. 'Well,' the delegate replied, 'you don't understand; we believe in racial discrimination.'

After the election of October 1974 I went back to general reporting duties, but there were occasions when I returned to the political world. One of the stars of Harold Wilson's government was Barbara Castle; she taught me the importance of toughness in a political leader. As the minister responsible for health and social security she worked in an ugly tower block just south of the Thames. Early one evening, I arrived for an interview accompanied by a television crew. Mrs Castle greeted us briefly, holding a gin and tonic, and then swept into a lift to take us upstairs to where the interview would take place. We shot up to the seventh floor, but instead of stopping, the lift suddenly reversed and quickly descended to the basement. It did not stop there. Immediately it reached the bottom it automatically went right back up to the top of the building. It had a life of its own and the process could not be halted. We were trapped.

'If we are going to die,' Mrs Castle announced, with a confident smile, 'we may as well share the drink.' She waved the glass of gin and tonic at the small group of men with her. No one took up her offer. Her private secretary wrenched out the emergency phone and began dialling as the lift continued its crazy passage up and down the building. 'Who are you phoning?' Mrs Castle demanded.

'I'm phoning our office,' the hapless official replied.

'Well, there will be no one there,' said the secretary of state. She then devised a better plan: the next time we reached the bottom of the building we would pull the emergency stop. This was done to a collective sigh of relief and we managed to prise open the lift door.

When we staggered out into the gloomy basement one of

the television crew made immediately for the staircase. Mrs Castle would have none of that. 'Come on,' she said firmly, and strode into the adjoining lift. 'We've got to get on,' she declared, and pressed the button for the seventh floor. The interview then went ahead as planned. It was, in its own way, a remarkable demonstration of courage and leadership.

When Jim Callaghan became prime minister I was able to take a closer look at political reporting. The BBC has a system of attachments which can take you to different parts of the organization on a temporary basis. If you succeed and if a vacancy occurs you can then apply for a permanent posting. In 1977 I went to Westminster, on attachment as a political correspondent. This meant that I had the chance, for the first time, of doing some regular television reporting. It was not obvious that this would suit me, or that those at Television Centre would be particularly pleased, but, as so often happens, luck played a part. When the chief political correspondent, David Holmes, wanted to be sure that I would be acceptable he spoke to the news editor, John Exelby, unaware that he was the person who had accompanied me on that harrowing trip to Cyprus some years before; John was also a friend and neighbour in Ealing. He readily confirmed that my attachment would be accepted at Television Centre.

On the whole the attachment went well, but television news did not consider that I was a suitable person on all the stories that came up that year. One of the most extraordinary scandals of that period involved the Liberal leader, Jeremy Thorpe. He was not only accused of having a homosexual affair, but he would later be charged with conspiracy to murder his former lover. He was found not guilty, but the series of allegations and revelations destroyed his political career. At one stage, before the court case, he tried to protest his innocence at a news conference at the National Liberal Club. The BBC decided that someone should ask him if he had ever had a homosexual relationship. To my relief, it was decided that I was not up to the task. This dubious honour went to one of the hard men of television news, Keith Graves, who had so woundingly accused me of cowardice in Cyprus.

Keith was a legendary figure within the BBC. His most famous exploit followed the refusal of a BBC commissionaire to let him into a car park. His car trapped the commissionaire against a barrier and as a result his leg was broken. Accepting that this was an accident the BBC decided that Keith should be confined to the newsroom for six months, much to the annoyance of the sub-editors. Why, they demanded, should working in the newsroom be regarded as a punishment? But television news, particularly in those days, seemed to thrive on determined characters prepared to stop at nothing in their pursuit of news, and that was the role played by Keith Graves at the Jeremy Thorpe news conference.

He told the former Liberal leader, who was still an MP, 'The whole of this hinges on your private life. It is necessary to ask you if you have ever had a homosexual relationship?' The political correspondents present might have been very reluctant to ask that question, but were all agog to hear the answer. A few years before, Jeremy Thorpe had married again after his first wife had been killed in a car crash. With a handful of other journalists, I had been invited to attend a small celebration at his Westminster flat to announce his engagement. I was now about to witness Marion Thorpe leaping to her husband's defence. She pushed forward and confronted Keith Graves. 'Go on, stand up,' she shouted. 'Stand up and say that again.'

She did not know her opponent. Keith readily repeated the question. Mr Thorpe's lawyer then intervened, saying that his client could not be allowed to answer that question. Mr Thorpe remained remarkably cool, arguing that the question was not relevant to the main allegation, which was that a member of the

Liberal Party had been hired to murder someone. The whole case was extremely difficult to follow, but another journalist tried to help by suggesting that murder had been attempted because Jeremy Thorpe had had a homosexual affair with the victim. The press conference came to an unsatisfactory end. It had been arranged in order to clear the air but it only led to more confusion. Even when the case was heard in court it was impossible to get a clear picture of what had happened.

The most significant story I covered while on attachment to Westminster was the sudden death of the foreign secretary, Anthony Crosland. It was on a Saturday morning and to my surprise, as the duty correspondent, I was left to cover the story on my own, for both television and radio. The senior staff all decided that their weekends should not be interrupted, even by an event of this magnitude. I was in no mood to complain, particularly because it allowed me to spend some time with the former prime minister, Harold Wilson.

Mr Wilson had a house in the country, near Great Missenden in Buckinghamshire, and he set me a puzzle the moment I arrived. 'Don't you recognize the house? Haven't you seen it before?' I looked blank. 'Haven't you seen the film *The Dam Busters*?' Of course I had. 'This is the house that Barnes Wallis, played by Michael Redgrave, was supposed to live in.' I was intrigued to learn that it was the film home of the scientist who had invented the bouncing bombs for the famous raid on the German dams, but I also wondered how many times Mr Wilson had used this particular conversational gambit. He was obviously anxious to please as we went into his back garden to do the television interview. To my surprise he had written out what he was going to say about Anthony Crosland on some cards which he held in his hand. I thought he would ad-lib his responses, but years later I suspected this was an early sign of the loss of memory that would plague him for the rest of his life.

Suddenly a train roared past on a nearby line. 'How appropriate,' he said. 'Tony used to be transport spokesman.' He went ahead with his tribute and was his customary eloquent self; he did not seem particularly upset by the death of one of his closest colleagues. But by then Harold Wilson had probably lived the equivalent of several ordinary lives. Even in retirement he seemed an amazingly resilient figure. I just wish I could have known him in his prime. But I still counted myself extraordinarily lucky. I might not have been a full-time political correspondent yet, but I was certainly getting used to talking to prime ministers.

16

With Maggie, to Number Ten

IT IS TEMPTING to see one's life as a kind of natural progression, a march of events which on reflection can be put into some sort of order. The chanciness of everyday incidents and emotions can be deftly removed and you are left with an arrow-like certainty that what happened was logical and even inevitable. But I don't think many people who have worked at the BBC for any length of time would see it that way. It is a fascinating and wonderful organization that has produced some of the best broadcasting in the world, but it is sometimes very difficult to work out where its brain is and its behaviour towards individuals can sometimes seem arbitrary and strange.

At various times towards the end of the 1970s I was judged by senior members of the BBC management either to be the perfect person to be the main London presenter of Radio 4's *Today* programme or, alternatively, a failed political correspondent who might be able to help out on a weekly specialist TV programme on BBC2. It is only fair to stress that much of the responsibility for this switchback ride was mine; but the BBC, in its own special way, provided many of the thrills and spills.

The broadcasting business is never short of aggressive personalities: characters who have either not developed properly or flawed personalities who find it difficult to behave normally with other people. The biggest egomaniac I ever came across was the *Today* presenter Brian Redhead. He seemed at times to have enormous problems accepting that other broadcasters existed, let alone that they might be people with a legitimate but quite different approach. Whenever I met him he would immediately launch into a detailed description of the brilliance and importance of his current project. I was not expected to know anything about the subject, and if I did then Brian would pretend he had not heard what I had said and breeze on regardless, hoping that I would restrict my comments to the odd 'Ah' and 'Oh, that's good.' It was not a role to which I was well suited.

The first time I met Brian was in the Manchester studios of the BBC. I was working as a general reporter on *Today*, usually for three nights a week, beginning at nine in the evening and ending at nine the next morning. Mary had been able to go back to work part-time and I was helping to look after our two young sons, so it was not ideal when I was dispatched to Manchester for a fortnight to give the *Today* programme less of a London feel. Brian, whose home was not far away in Cheshire, presented half the programme from there and was determined not to move to London.

Whatever anyone else might think, in his view, Manchester was the centre of the world, and that is why he had to continue presenting the programme from the studio there. 'After all,' Brian went on, 'the north-west is brimming with ideas. Take Alan Bennett; isn't he brilliant?' A little warning bell went off inside me. He rattled on: 'Did you ever see that comedy series he did?' He did not pause for my reply. The warning bell rang again. Brian described one of the sketches from the programme: how Alan Bennett had dressed up as the Archbishop of Canterbury and talked to a BBC programme planner.

With an awful feeling of inevitability, I had to intervene. 'Do you know who played the part of the programme planner?' Brian shook his head. I looked him straight in the eye, preparing for the killer blow. My voice was loud and firm. 'I did.' He was so taken aback that he turned round and walked straight out of the room. He never referred to the incident, nor did he ever talk to me again about Alan Bennett or my brief career as an actor. I had shot him down in mid-flight, but it did nothing to help me in the next stage of my career.

The BBC bosses decided that if Brian Redhead would not move from Manchester there would have to be a new presenter in London, and to Brian's annoyance they came to the conclusion that I should be given that task. But I was not a great success. Sitting alone in the studio at Broadcasting House, with Brian on top form, burbling away in Manchester, it was obvious to many people that I was out of my depth. After three months I was told that my chance was over. Having been very much on the up, I was now very definitely on the way down. Nonetheless, Brian Redhead had to come to London in the end, where he was joined by John Timpson and Sue MacGregor, who together became a brilliantly successful team.

Oh well, I thought, at least I will be able to go to Westminster and become a political correspondent. Within a few months a vacancy occurred and it was only then that I realized how serious my decline had become. My main rival, David Coss, had worked with me on the *Liverpool Echo* and later became a political correspondent with the *Daily Mail* before moving into the BBC unit at Westminster which provided news for all the local radio stations. Ominously, he was invited to meet the director general, Ian Trethowan, for lunch; others were present, but I was not included. At the interview board a few days later, the political editor, David Holmes, gave the impression that he was not on my side. Needless to say, David Coss got the job.

In a smaller organization, this setback could have sounded the death knell to my career, but one of the great joys of working for the BBC is that new alliances can be formed if old ones fail. With luck and a bit of skill, you can sometimes beat the system. To succeed, though, you need patrons, and on this occasion a senior news executive, Andrew Todd, came to my aid. He believed I had been treated unfairly, and told me that my salary would be paid for a year in any part of the BBC that could be persuaded to take me on.

Partly out of devilment and partly to show my determination, the office where I chose to work produced a weekly television programme called *The Week in Westminster* for BBC2. David Holmes presented it. He found to his irritation that having rejected me one week, the next I was firmly ensconced on his pet project. This was revenge of a sort, and it was particularly sweet because there was nothing David Holmes could do. Thanks to Andrew Todd, the programme did not have to pay my salary. Having said I would 'help in any way' I ended up making short films and even did some presenting in the studio. My rehabilitation was soon under way.

There were two subjects I chose to work on which would hold me in good stead in later years: the first was the new European Monetary System, linking up currencies with an exchange rate mechanism, which was to become one of the great issues of our time. The other was a profile of the youngest member of the cabinet, the President of the Board of Trade, John Smith, who would become leader of the Labour Party. David Holmes seemed to consider these projects neither interesting nor relevant, but a very talented filmmaker, David Wickham, encouraged me. He was wonderfully ambitious in the techniques he used, often using makeshift trolleys for the camera to add movement, and rigging up elaborate lighting. It was not quite *The Ten Commandments* but we could not resist calling him Cecil B. de Wickham.

For the first time I began to see how television could be made to convey mood as well as argument. It was also fascinating to see the way politicians were prepared to jump to our tune. When David Wickham asked John Smith over and over again to come out of a lift and walk naturally down a corridor behind a trolley with a camera, the cabinet minister did what he was told. Later, we were filming at John Smith's home in Edinburgh when the messenger arrived with his government red boxes. David was not satisfied until the front of the house was bathed in light and the poor messenger was beginning to wish for an easier life. More than an hour was spent on this one scene.

It was a very good time to be working on this sort of programme, as the Labour government staggered through the season of industrial disputes which became known as the Winter of Discontent and headed towards the election of 1979. But when Jim Callaghan lost the vote of confidence and the contest began, *The Week in Westminster* was closed down for the duration of the campaign. My loyal friends in radio jumped at the chance to get me back and I was asked once again to cover the election tour of the leader of the opposition, with this time a good chance of being on the winning side. If the Conservatives succeeded, Britain would have its first woman prime minister.

I had worked with Margaret Thatcher before, when she went on a visit to Brussels as the new Tory leader in 1975. The reasoning behind my brief trip was that she might have difficulty convincing NATO bosses that a woman could be prime minister. To some of my male colleagues her grasp of military matters seemed less important than the key question, 'What is she going to do with her handbag?' It soon became apparent that Mrs Thatcher was quite capable of dealing with this and many other, more elevated problems. But she did lack confidence at the beginning, and the most striking impression was of someone who was ready to learn.

I had not covered her fight to become party leader in 1975. But at the BBC's Westminster office I heard how she grabbed the arm of the political editor, Hardiman Scott, as they crossed the road at the beginning of the leadership contest.

She squeezed his arm tightly and, dropping her voice into a conspiratorial whisper declared, 'I've got my teeth into Ted, and I am not going to let go.' She beat Edward Heath in the first round of the contest while the other strong candidate, William Whitelaw, decided not to take part, either through a failure of nerve or a misplaced sense of loyalty to Mr Heath. In the second round, when Mr Whitelaw finally entered the race, it was too late. Conservative MPs were swinging behind Mrs Thatcher and she ended up with nearly twice as many votes as Mr Whitelaw. He who had hesitated had lost.

As a veteran of both Mr Heath's election battles of five years earlier, joining Mrs Thatcher's campaign tour in 1979 made me feel like an old hand. But the differences were very marked. There would be no late-night visits to pubs, no lengthy discussions on arcane policy matters. Mrs Thatcher had none of the old-fashioned sociability which many senior Conservatives wallowed in; she was determined to sweep away conventions in order to conduct the campaign in her own style. There was no attempt to pretend she was a man in woman's clothing. If she sometimes came over as a bossy housewife, she happily accepted the comparison. Feminine virtues would be extolled and not disguised, and she made little secret of her interest in good-looking men.

As the first woman to reach the peak of British politics it was strange but some would say inevitable that she tended to treat other professional women with a certain amount of hostility. The prominent women journalists in our group, including Anne Leslie of the *Daily Mail*, were as likely to be rebuffed as welcomed. There was no question of their being treated like sisters under the skin. Mrs Thatcher seemed oblivious to the siren voices of women's liberation, and feminism as a political force seemed to pass her by. She was far and away the most successful woman in the country and she implied that if she could achieve what she had, without special help, then other women could do likewise. To Mrs Thatcher, being a woman had many obvious advantages and she was not shy to parade them in public. She was flirtatious, in a restrained way, with distinguished older men such as the political editor of *The Times*, David Wood. When a woman journalist asked her a question during a news conference, they could expect a fairly dusty response.

Mrs Thatcher was determined to come over well on television. The BBC's correspondent was Michael Cole, whose bouffant hairstyle later distinguished him when a spokesman for Mohamed Al-Fayed, the owner of Harrods. In 1979, malicious colleagues suggested that he had been chosen to follow Mrs Thatcher 'because they shared the same hair dresser'. He was in fact an extremely skilful reporter who once memorably replied to an editor asking him to cut down a piece to forty-five seconds, 'Look, I could give you the whole history of the First World War in forty-five seconds, but it might lose some of its subtlety.' The ITN correspondent was the confident Michael Brunson, who gave the impression that he had been covering political campaigns for most of his life. Mrs Thatcher referred to them as 'the two Michaels', and I was disconcerted to see how much attention she lavished on them. I am not usually the self-pitying sort, but it seemed to me that as the BBC radio correspondent I was being rather pushed to one side.

My difficulty was that more of the campaign was designed for television than in any previous election. Mr Heath had toured factories and gone on walkabouts, but it was nothing like the whirlwind whipped up by Mrs Thatcher. As she rushed round a factory, she would suddenly stop in front of some electronic device. The cameras would be summoned and she would then adopt the stance of a presenter on the BBC television programme *Tomorrow's World*. A brief lecture would follow, coupled with advice to all of us to pay attention. Then she would sweep on. There was a briskness about it all which at times seemed excessive. 'We are not,' I would complain to colleagues, 'trying to learn how to run a factory.'

On one memorable occasion we all had to wear white coats and surgical masks to tour a chocolate-making plant. Bored operatives would turn away for a moment only to find that Mrs Thatcher had taken their place and was working furiously on the production line. It was designed to show how much energy she had, and after the first week I was in no mood to disagree. She also wanted to show that she could be the boss; in a remote part of Scotland our bus got stuck in the mud and she immediately ordered us to get out and start pushing. We managed to get the bus going, in time to reach our next destination, a kipper-processing plant. Mrs Thatcher was shown how to make sure that the herrings were fresh. 'Look at their eyes, see that they are not bloodshot,' she was told. 'And then give them a good sniff; it's the only way.' It made splendid television.

There has always been a steady transfer of campaigning techniques from across the Atlantic. American experts watch UK elections, but most of the traffic comes the other way, with British politicians slowly adopting many of the habits of their American cousins. When a new method arrives, it is often poorly adapted to British conditions; and so it was with the photo opportunity. In the States this was seen as a straight-forward attempt to put the candidate against an interesting background so that photographers could get a memorable shot. In 1979 the Conservatives struggled to get to grips with the new technique.

The first British photo op took place in a field in Suffolk. About a hundred assorted media folk clambered over gates and trudged through a field before arriving at our destination. We had not been told what to expect, but there lying in the grass was a newborn calf, which Mrs Thatcher held among the racket of clicking cameras. 'It's not for me,' she told this sceptical gathering. 'It's for the photographers; they're the most important people on the campaign.' It was certainly not designed to be good radio. As we turned to make our way back to the coach the print journalists were equally disenchanted. One of them suggested we name the calf Maggie. I stayed back for a while and dearly wished I had a camera. The field was practically deserted, with the newborn calf, minutes earlier the centre of attention, now left abandoned on the grass.

The Conservatives won the election with a majority of forty-three parliamentary seats. It became obvious not long after the first results were declared that Labour would lose and Jim Callaghan would be out of office. Mrs Thatcher's first interview as prime minister was given to me at Tory central office in the early hours of the following morning. With her husband Denis and their two children Mrs Thatcher was standing on the main staircase while I was stuck at the back of a large crowd. Dignity is not an issue on such occasions. I knelt down on the floor and crawled at great speed through the legs of the assembled throng. When I surfaced near the staircase, I was relieved to see that she was still there. It was not one of the most illuminating of my interviews with Mrs Thatcher, but it captured the mood. BBC television was not able to broadcast an interview with her; amazingly, some of the technicians had decided to go home.

Later that day, I held a microphone outside Number Ten as the new prime minister intoned St Francis of Assisi's prayer calling for harmony, not division. It was the start of eleven controversial and seldom harmonious years in office. On the *PM* programme on Radio 4, the presenter, Susannah Simons, asked me a direct question: 'Will she make a good prime minister?' I quoted one of Mrs Thatcher's closest colleagues who had told me only a few days before, 'She could be a very good prime minister, but it's going to be a risk.'

One of her first official tasks was to fly to Italy to discuss European matters; it marked the beginning of her long campaign to reduce Britain's £1 billion net contribution to the EEC budget. 'Maggie's billion,' it came to be called. She announced her plans in an interview with me at the British embassy in Rome, before leaving to have talks with the Italian president. The experienced foreign secretary, Lord Carrington, gave her a guiding hand on the way to play politics in Italy. When she came out of the embassy the Italian motorcycle escort leapt on to their bikes and revved their engines. 'No, Margaret,' Lord Carrington advised. 'Not yet. We mustn't be early; we should be a little late.' The signal was given to the escort, who reluctantly dismounted. 'Oh, in that case,' the new prime minister said brightly, 'we may as well have a chat.' She leant across the roof of the embassy Rolls-Royce and talked amiably to journalists before the motorbikes were finally unleashed.

The honeymoon with the media was still in full swing when I was invited with my wife to our first party at Number Ten. All those who had taken part in her election campaign were there. Mrs Thatcher, in those early days, had a remarkable ability to listen and to answer questions from ordinary people. She did not always exhibit that skill during her period in office, but at this time she was usually refreshingly direct. I asked her how long it had taken for her to get over the excitement of winning. 'Oh, you can't stay on cloud nine for ever; you have to settle down to a routine.' Then she turned to Mary. 'Routine,' she repeated. 'Don't you agree?' Mrs Thatcher was making the startling assumption that as two simple housewives trying to go about their business, they were bound to see these matters in the same way. Mary found it amusing and possibly a little condescending. For me it was merely the beginning of a long and often difficult relationship with one of the most interesting British prime ministers ever elected.

17

Ticking a few boxes

MANAGERS IN THE BBC come in all sorts and sizes. They can be nice, nasty or just plain boring, as you find in any big organization. But observing them for thirty years as a non-manager, I found it hard, sometimes impossible, not to look down on them. They struggled to appear engaged in the real work of the BBC, which is to make programmes, but often their hearts were engaged in a quite different activity – moving up the managerial ladder. Your work might be praised on a supposedly objective basis but it was more likely to win support if, in some way, it furthered the career of a member of management.

It was not always easy to spot when you had alighted on a golden path of managerial approval. You might simply be doing what you had always done, in exactly the same way as before, but the clues would begin to multiply. If one of your bosses said, 'I thought that went well yesterday,' it could be a mistake to respond too quickly, because you needed to have an answer to the really important question: 'It went well for whom?' The manager might immediately supply the verdict: 'I've thought for some time we should be doing it that way and you proved it yesterday.'

An old journalistic adage says that your pieces are neither as good nor as bad as you think they are at the time. It is necessary to add that when you work for the BBC nothing you do of your own volition can ever attract quite the same amount of praise as something you have done which fits in with the demands of management. There is a grim little phrase that encapsulates this bureaucratic approach: 'It ticks all the boxes.' Finding out what the boxes are is an essential part of any BBC career.

One might think that reporting is more of a trade than a profession, less of an art than a task which has to be completed, usually within the constraints of a tight deadline. There are those who are better at it than others, but since everyone can see the final result, it should be fairly easy to pick out those who do it well and those who do it less well. All that is true, as far as it goes, but fashion plays a part as well, fashion in the sense of the current trend in management thinking.

Sometimes managers are gripped by the need to employ more women journalists. Sometimes the demand for more reporters from minority communities is holding sway. The search could suddenly be on for younger people, fewer graduates from Oxford and Cambridge, more reporters with regional accents. Ticking as many of these boxes as possible can shoot a candidate to the top. It can also help to decide what the management thinks at any moment about its present staff.

Fashion is important, too, in deciding the kind of stories to be covered and how this should be done. In recent years opinion research has been employed, with patchy results, to determine what people want to be informed about. Politics always comes low on the list. In the past much would depend in the BBC on the latest whims of management. One of the strongest and most persistent of these, lasting throughout my time with the corporation, was the fashion for Europe. Newsrooms might be obsessed by the Middle East and by American politics, but the constant cry from the bosses was that we must do more on Europe. There was a strong sense that following the end of the British empire, with the Commonwealth proving in no way a worthy successor, the key to Britain's future was in Europe. The difficulty was that BBC programme makers often found the subject dull and uninspiring.

For the member states of the Common Market, later the European Economic Community and finally the European Union, one of the most difficult problems was engaging the public in decisions taken at the European level. For many on the Continent this was not a serious problem. The new institutions might be costly and complicated, but they were seen as promoting peace and not conflict; and after the bloodiest century in the history of Europe, that put them almost beyond criticism. But the British approach was never so starry-eyed. Having finally joined up, the British establishment wanted to get to grips with the European institutions, and they wanted the BBC to play its part. What was later called the democratic deficit had to be filled; and Roy Jenkins and others were convinced that one way of doing this was through the European Parliament, which was directly elected, for the first time, in 1979. And this is where I came in.

A succession of senior members of BBC management had made trips to Strasbourg to sample the culinary delights of Alsace and to see how we should cover the new parliament. In London the French ambassador had been invited to expensive lunches and the hospitality had been graciously returned. But now the time for wining and dining was over and the simple question had to be answered: Who will do the work? One of the senior BBC managers, Gerard Schlesinger, not known for his gentle approach, was sent to find me in the offices of the BBC2 programme *The Week in Westminster* at Television Centre.

'We want you,' he said without preamble, 'to be responsible for covering the European Parliament.' He did not wait for my reply. 'If you don't accept, you will have to go back into the reporters' pool at Broadcasting House.'

I managed to reply, 'But I would like to accept.' He looked at me firmly and repeated the warning that there was no other place for me, except to return to being a radio reporter, a job I had left two years before. 'But,' I tried again, 'I would like to cover the European Parliament.'

If I were writing a handbook of BBC politics, one of the golden rules would be: When you have been appointed to a post the first question to ask is 'Where will I sit?' It is surprising how often this can be crucial to your success. It can also have a much wider relevance. The European Parliament almost foundered on the basis of this vital point. Their headquarters are in Luxembourg, but the monthly sessions of the parliament are in Strasbourg and committee meetings are held in Brussels. The British members have vast constituencies and they often have to run an office there and a home somewhere else. It is hardly surprising that MEPs have failed to make their mark. But with a growing sense of horror I realized that my fate was now inextricably bound up with theirs. If the new directly elected European Parliament turned out to be a dud, where would that leave the BBC's European Parliament correspondent?

With memories of delicious Alsace dinners now fading fast among BBC management there was a distinct lack of interest in where I might base myself, or indeed how I might carry out my task. They were not keen for me to be based abroad full time – that would cost too much – although I would obviously have to travel frequently to the Continent. I found myself discussing the problem in a desultory fashion with one of the managers at Broadcasting House. 'But when I am in London, couldn't I use that office?' I said, pointing out of the window and across the courtyard. He frowned and looked out across the bleak expanse. Wary of making any commitment, he said finally, 'Yes, that office does look empty.'

Eventually I was installed in Broadcasting House. I was also supplied with a car; for reasons which were never explained, that was easier than getting an office. A subscription to the French newspaper *Le Monde* was settled without difficulty, and I supplied myself with plenty of Georges Simenon's Maigret novels in the original French. It was a way of learning the language and it was sometimes comforting, when everything went wrong, to say with a suitably Gallic shrug, 'Well, what would Maigret do?'

The main difficulty was that the European Parliament only sat for one week a month. For some time I tried to put this problem out of my mind. The other weeks would have to be spent on research, I argued to myself. The key point was to make sure that those weeks in Strasbourg made an impact, and on this point my superiors were in complete agreement. It was decided that there would be a special programme on Radio 4, presented by me, on a Thursday evening, every time the parliament sat, and although that was later changed to a guaranteed part of *The World This Weekend* on Radio 4, the principle was established that the European Parliament had to be covered.

I was also given a series of producers, who accompanied me, many of them brilliant, and all good companions. Another item from any handbook of BBC politics would have to include the firm instruction: Members of staff should never travel alone. Working abroad for the BBC is difficult enough without attempting to do so on your own. One of my producers later became the BBC's legal affairs correspondent, Joshua Rozenberg. He was not particularly happy at this time, fearing that his career had been shunted into a siding, but we became firm friends; and for me this period was one of the best times in the BBC.

In covering the European Parliament in Strasbourg our first hurdle was to work out a way to make the contributions in ten languages work in radio terms. Translators were on hand, but the standard was variable and they could sound very monotonous. We needed to make sure that at all times we had a recording of the speaker and of the simultaneous translation. Joshua was despatched to the electronic shops in Tottenham Court Road in London and returned triumphant with a desktop stereo cassette recorder. On one track we would record the speaker, and on the other the translation. We would be able to fade from one to the other, or at least that was the theory.

We were slightly apprehensive when we prepared to plug in for the first time in our small office, which overlooked the hemicycle, as it was called, the floor of the European Parliament. The eighty-one British members were split between the European parties, with Labour, and their leader Barbara Castle, sitting on the left, with the socialists, and the Tories, led by Sir James Scott Hopkins, on the centre right. There was a good turnout and, unusually for the European Parliament, the debate was fairly lively. That was until Joshua plugged in our equipment.

For a few minutes we had no idea what had gone wrong. The debate seemed to have stalled. MEPs were taking off their headphones and shaking their heads. Some of them started to complain to the parliament's president, who presides over sessions like the speaker in the House of Commons. It was apparent that the parliament would have to be suspended. Then came the awful realization that our equipment, bought with such pride in Tottenham Court Road, had torpedoed the workings of the European Community. There wasn't even time to ask, 'What would Maigret do?' Quickly and rather shamefacedly we pulled out the plugs, and order was instantly restored. Instead of hearing simultaneous translations in all ten languages MEPs could once again follow what was being said.

If only their deliberations had lived up to the importance they attached to them. Although we managed to solve the technical problem of how to record what they were saying, we never conquered the far more serious difficulty of their lack of political clout. One of the founding fathers of the European institutions, Jean Monnet, said that a parliament without power becomes an academy and that is largely what happened to the Strasbourg assembly. Its debates became academic, because what the MEPs said did not matter. It was given a little more to do in later years, but it has yet to fulfil its promise of bringing Europe closer to the people.

I came to the conclusion that in politics, as in architecture, the Renaissance idea of man as the measure of all things holds sway. The European Parliament is too far removed from the experience of ordinary people, and even those of us who travelled there each month for two years found it a confusing and unsatisfying experience. I was the first and as it turned out the last full-time BBC correspondent attached to the European Parliament, and despite my best efforts the post could only be sustained by taking on work in other areas.

Tony de Lotbinière came to my rescue. Despite his name he was a former Guards officer and British to the core. His claim to fame in the BBC was that he had persuaded Kenneth Clark to make his famous TV series *Civilisation* which, apart from anything else, taught me the Renaissance idea of man being the measure of all things. Tony was a committed European; he had a house in Italy and, having fought in the war, was determined to do everything he could to bring Europe together. As a highly experienced documentary producer he had been commissioned, as I had in my small way, to put Europe on the BBC map. It was inevitable that we should meet.

As a young man my father used to go to Bertorelli's restaurant in Charlotte Street in London. Today it is a rather upmarket establishment, but for most of the twentieth century it was a family-run business, serving unpretentious Italian food.

I thought the association with my father might give me some confidence. It was typical of Tony that he made me choose not only the restaurant where we would have lunch, but also the wine. A bottle of Soave was produced, and he was happy to go along with that. He gave the impression that he knew little of Italy or indeed Europe, and explained that he was hoping to make two television programmes based on the accession of Greece to the European Community, which would happen the next year, in 1981. The programmes, each fifty minutes in length, would take the slot on BBC1 over Christmas and the New Year normally occupied by *Panorama*. He would need an expert on Europe to make this come about.

I could hardly believe what was happening. Was I really being asked to write and present a major documentary on Europe? I tried to conceal my feelings. 'If there is anything I can do to help, I would be very happy to do so,' I said cautiously. Tony admitted later that the lunch had been a test of whether we could get on. He had carefully noted all my choices and all my comments. He was pleased I had not rushed to accept.

'I thought it was a good sign,' he confided, when we started to travel together, 'that you could keep control of your emotions.' It did not occur to him that it was my natural pessimism which had been on display; I could not quickly come to terms with the fact that most of my immediate career problems had been dramatically solved.

Then, of course, I had to become an expert on Europe. Journalism is a strange business. If I had been a true European specialist I would not have been a great deal of use to Tony de Lotbinière and would almost inevitably have been swamped with too much detail. But I had to know enough to make the project work, to write the script, and to help choose the locations. It was one of the most demanding and enjoyable assignments of my career.

For nine months we criss-crossed the Continent and even went to America to look at the way the European Community was affecting opinion at the United Nations and in Washington. The most bizarre moment came in Greece when our government helper was furious that we insisted on filming donkeys; he wanted Greece to be portrayed as vibrant and modern. At one stage we had to give him the slip by driving quickly up a narrow track in our van, as he roared past in his little Volkswagen. He was also obsessed by Greece's newly found skill in growing kiwi fruit, an obsession we did not share.

Tony's most recent film had been about Covent Garden and he passed on to me his enthusiasm for opera. Whenever possible during filming we would go to the opera in the evening. In Brussels we saw *The Barber of Seville* and in New York we went to a production of *The Tales of Hoffman*. It's tough making documentaries.

The programmes, called *The Europe We Joined*, were received fairly well. The *Daily Telegraph* seemed to think that I must be an expert because I had chosen such delightful spots in Greece in which to film. Despite the good reviews, I felt rather flat when the programmes went out. When you have contributed to a news bulletin the satisfaction is immediate, but after nine months of work on these programmes, watching them at home with Mary didn't give me much of a thrill. I knew the material too well. The fun in these long documentaries is while they are being made, not on transmission. But it *was* enormous fun.

Some of the gaps during the weeks in which I continued to cover the European Parliament were filled working for BBC2's *Newsnight* programme, then edited by the brilliant George Carey. It was all part of the slow process of learning how television works. I was briefly a newsreader on the programme, delivering news summaries from a separate studio on my own. Appearing on television can be extremely nerve-racking, and the tension is often far greater if you do not have people working with you in the studio.

I was then given another lucky break, which fulfilled a long-held ambition. There was a gap in the arrangements for the Paris office. The outgoing correspondent, Stephen Jessel, was leaving to go on holiday, while the incoming correspondent, Philip Short, had not yet finished his tour of duty in China. I was delighted to be asked to be the acting Paris correspondent in the meantime. Stephen thought this would not be a problem because the incumbent president, Valéry Giscard d'Estaing, would win the presidential election, thus allowing Stephen to go on holiday with a clear conscience. That is how I came to cover the first two months in office of President François Mitterrand, who surprised many people by winning the presidential election of 1981.

I arrived in Paris on Mitterrand's first day in office, and was delighted when Stephen invited me out to lunch as the new president settled into the Élysée Palace. We went to a marvellous restaurant near the BBC office, Les Amis du Beaujolais, not far from the Arc de Triomphe. As I was not expecting to work on my first day, I was keen to be as friendly as possible. We drank two bottles of Beaujolais before Stephen dropped a bombshell. 'Would you,' he asked, 'look after the *PM* programme?' I realized that I could not refuse.

The *PM* programme on Radio 4 starts at 5 p.m., but with France an hour ahead I had until six o'clock to sober up. It was a close-run thing. Fortunately other members of the office gave me all the help they could. The newspaper *Libération*, they pointed out, had been drenched in scent to smell like a socialist rose. Mr Mitterrand's menu had been issued, with a Château Talbot prominent among the fine wines. I was given the noise of the twenty-one-gun salute. My item was shaping up well.

I also had the advantage of having worked a lot for *PM*, even on occasions presenting it.

It seemed that Stephen did not entirely share my opinion that the piece had become a worthy item to lead the programme. After the broadcast, he stormed in. 'Get out of my studio,' he shouted. It was merely a symptom of the territorial imperative which often grips BBC offices abroad. They do not like someone coming onto their patch; and if these outsiders have to be tolerated, surely they should have the decency not to do the story too well?

A few days later Stephen went off on his holiday and I was left blissfully alone. Then the phone rang. It was the office in London asking me to go to Barcelona. I protested that I was settling down well in Paris, and that these were important days at the beginning of Mitterrand's presidency. But they would have none of it. More than a hundred people had been taken hostage in a Barcelona bank and I was the person who had to sort it out.

Fortunately the BBC man based in Madrid was my old friend from Saigon, Derek Wilson. We greeted each other in Barcelona like long-lost brothers. Our hotel was on Las Ramblas, the long street famous for its early evening perambulations, where people parade after the heat of the day. On this occasion, though, the army and police had blocked it off. A bank in the corner of the main square, at the end of the street, had been attacked by a group of political extremists, and the atmosphere was tense and full of fear. Derek and I decided to repair to his room.

We were very well placed. A telephone in the room allowed us to broadcast to London, and Derek's Spanish was good enough to enable him to monitor the radio for news of what was happening. It was time for dinner. Room service was duly ordered, and as the waiter pushed in a trolley groaning with food and drink, there was an enormous burst of small-arms fire just outside our window, aimed down Las Ramblas towards the bank. The army were getting involved. As old Vietnam hands, Derek and I were reasonably calm; it was clear that our hotel was not the target. We motioned for the waiter to bring the trolley further into the room. He did this very apprehensively as the gunfire continued. We settled down to enjoy our meal, accompanied at times by fresh bursts of firing. Somehow I guessed this might be my last story of this sort, and the way we tackled it seemed suitably surreal.

Every few hours we broadcast to London. The next morning I correctly predicted that the bank would be stormed; thankfully all the hostages were released unharmed. A young reporter from Independent Radio News staggered into the hotel foyer covered in dust. 'What a night,' he exclaimed. 'I was tied down by gunfire on the other side of the square, couldn't broadcast, but it was a great story. How did you get on?' The two Vietnam veterans did not have the heart to say how they had got on, but we did celebrate all afternoon over a long and very alcoholic lunch, before I flew back to complete my two-month tour of duty as the Paris correspondent. My days as a general reporter were over. I would soon be formally appointed a BBC political correspondent based at Westminster, but this would only be accomplished by strange, and some might say devious, means.

18

Finding a seat at Westminster

THE BBC HAS a tendency to grow. Like someone in middle age, unless some discipline is exerted it will put on weight; and in the BBC this means adding staff. Sometimes the reasons seem frivolous. I used to think that managers at the BBC found the ritual of the morning office meetings so compelling that, if there weren't enough people to make up a daily quorum in every department, more managers would be appointed.

There was also a tendency, very much encouraged under the leadership of John Birt, to create a parallel BBC. There was a strong body of people who made the programmes, and a distinct and quite separate line of managers who contrived to lead interesting lives without ever having to connect directly with the stressful business of broadcasting. They spent their time producing endless reviews on the future of the BBC, in writing needlessly complicated memos, and in working out reasons why various posts should be filled, or not filled, depending on the ebb and flow of management thinking at the time. There was a clear gap between programme makers and management, and during the Birt years that gap greatly increased.

The result of this divide was not always either efficiency or indeed fairness. One of those who held the post of director general while I was there, the underrated Alasdair Milne, said that at any hour of any day someone in the BBC with little talent was trying to stop someone with more talent from getting on with the job; his duty as director general was to find out where this was happening and make sure that those with more talent were allowed to proceed. To me this drag on the BBC's skills seemed rather like a branch of particle physics. There was talent and there was anti-talent. Encouraging the talent was relatively easy; keeping control of the anti-talent was far more difficult.

One of the central problems is working out what should be the proper disposition of staff in a corporation which as a result of the licence fee is to a large extent freed from the brutal realities of the market place. A guaranteed income of about £2 billion a year has a profound effect on the way the business is run. In private companies, how many people should be taken on and how they should be deployed can usually be determined on the basis of cost and potential profit. In the strange shifting politics of the BBC there is often nothing so simple as a bottom line.

It is sometimes hard to ascertain how many are employed in a particular area. The fear of overstaffing produces a clamp-down on the numbers officially on the books, but quite often there is a raft of extra people who have somehow managed to end up working there anyway. The skilful BBC manager learns how to do this without risk to his or her job. It can simply be a matter of bringing people in on contract. Some contracts are, amazingly, on a daily basis, others weekly, but usually they are renewable each year. Many of those involved are eventually given staff jobs. There are also people on attachment from other parts of the BBC, supposedly broadening their career experience. Then there are the very rare cases where the decision to give someone a post has never been formally taken by an interview board; it was into this category that I fell, in a rather ungainly fashion.

Everything depends on the willingness of managers to stretch the rules. I was fortunate that my old friend John Simpson had replaced David Holmes as political editor. For those who know John as the intrepid foreign correspondent it might seem strange to imagine him confined to Westminster and it has to be said that this was not the perfect posting for him. In private he pined to roam the world again, but from my point of view he was a vital ally in my time of need.

John phoned me in Paris, where I was completing my brief tour of duty, to ask me what I really wanted to do. 'To go to Westminster,' was my immediate reply.

'Isn't that odd,' he replied, 'I would like to be in Paris.' He then explained that there was a move afoot which would change my official position. When I was put in charge of European Parliament coverage I had, in the jargon of management, been 'seconded to a vacant Westminster post'. This was possible because although I had failed to become a political correspondent I had been deemed 'also suitable' by the interview board held the year before. Or at least that was the argument they used at the time.

'Well, can't you now just make me a political correspondent?' I asked.

'I will do what I can,' said John, and he arranged for me to be switched officially to the political staff. I had gained a vital toehold in the Westminster office, but I could not use it immediately as I had to finish my stint in Paris and, soon after, John Simpson left Westminster to become a television newsreader presenting the nine o'clock news with John Humphrys.

Sadly for John Simpson this would turn out to be a career move which did not work out, but it left a vacancy for a new political editor which was filled, to the surprise of many, by John Cole, whose strong Belfast accent and herringbone coat would help to make him a legendary figure. He could not take over immediately because he had to work out his notice with the *Observer* where he was deputy editor. There would be a gap of a month or so; and that gave me an opportunity.

I was back in London by this time and pacing up and down in my Broadcasting House office, with nothing much to do. I worked out a simple plan. If John Simpson had left the Westminster office and John Cole had not yet arrived, they must be short of staff. Surely I could help fill the gap in those weeks in which I was not covering the European Parliament? I went to see the director of news and current affairs, a Welshman with a laconic wit, Alan Prothero. He had a reputation for extreme tenacity, particularly when dealing with complaints from political parties. He was also credited with a marvellous comment, made when the BBC had lurched into some crisis or other. 'Well,' he declared, 'assistant heads must roll.'

He listened to my proposal with surprise and finally impatience. 'If you are a political correspondent,' he said, 'of course you should be allowed to go to Westminster.' He then picked up the most recent staff list, which had only just been updated. It looked like a small telephone directory, and was conveniently placed on his desk. 'Look,' he said. 'There's your name, and what does it say? Political correspondent. Tell them I've agreed.'

What Alan Prothero did not know was how badly this would go down with the Westminster staff. They were extremely reluctant to have their numbers increased. It was a small office, with a limited number of desks. There was no obvious answer to the old question: Where will I sit? There was also the suspicion that I would become a threat. Before long I would want to drop my role as European Parliament corre-spondent and begin to rise through the ranks at Westminster. Eventually, this is exactly what happened, but at the time I did not feel I was a threat to anyone.

I was assured that it was not personal, but I could not help but be upset when the correspondents sent a round robin letter to the management urging them not to move me to

Westminster. But I had the backing of Alan Prothero and also a good argument: they were short of staff, at least for the time being, and I was only offering to help.

There was an icy atmosphere when I turned up at the Westminster office. The six correspondents there felt tricked and outmanoeuvred; they were also annoyed that none of them had been made political editor. It was the worst possible start to an association with the BBC office in the Palace of Westminster, which would last for nearly twenty years. There were often times, at the beginning, when I dreaded going up the short flight of steps from the lift and opening the small door of the office. I had no desk. I would sit in an armchair with my briefcase. But I did have considerable advantages over my colleagues in terms of broadcasting experience, and an academic grounding in politics and economics, which I felt confident would allow me to win through in the end. And if they wanted to treat me like an unpopular boy at school they would soon learn that I had some playground skills as well.

My first task was to get on well with the head boy, John Cole. On his arrival he was told about the 'Sergeant problem', which he later admitted finding mystifying. After many years in newspaper management – he had been deputy editor of the *Guardian* before taking up the same post on the *Observer* – he longed to get back to his first love, reporting. Sorting out the impenetrable question of how someone who had been seconded to a vacant post should not necessarily be on his staff was not something he had bargained for as the new political editor of the BBC. He was more interested in whether I was any good and whether we could work together.

It was not obvious from the beginning that John Cole and I would become close colleagues and friends. I had some obvious drawbacks: my public school and Oxford background did not mesh with his more impressive rise as the son of an electrician who had learned his trade as a teenager on local papers in Northern Ireland. My time, though brief, with the television satirists of the 1960s was also rather questionable. John was serious, though full of humour, and to him those clever young men from Oxbridge were too fond of themselves to be funny. It did not help that in *Private Eye*, which carefully preserved the student humour of the sixties, John would be mercilessly pilloried for his Belfast accent. They insisted that he pronounced undoubtedly as 'hundootedly' and suggested that his pieces on television were unintelligible. In most editions there was a John Cole column, complete with photograph, linking up disjointed comments on the politics of the day. It was funny but it was also cruel, and I made a point of never discussing it with him.

I did, however, have some plus points. I had reported on the conflict which mattered more to John than any other political subject: the long-drawn-out agony of Northern Ireland. John, a Protestant Ulsterman, detested anything which smacked of appeasement to the forces of militant Republicanism. He felt so strongly that it was dangerous to make any comment, as it might be misconstrued. At least I had an advantage over many of my colleagues in that I knew the pitfalls. I had, to use the phrase he would invariably use, served in Northern Ireland.

I also had the advantage of being much younger than John; there was a difference of seventeen years. We competed a good deal as the years went by, as would any correspondents working the same patch for the same organization, but the age difference meant that we were not competing over his role in the BBC. We were not jealous of each other. When I made a speech at one of his many retirement parties, I described our relationship as like that in one of Hollywood's buddy-buddy movies, young cop and old cop. But it was my reference to a television series much closer to home which got the biggest laugh. I said that over the years I had learned to play Sergeant Lewis to his Inspector Morse. And that wasn't entirely a joke.

The most important bond between us was that we were both passionately interested in politics. He was a lifelong supporter of the Labour party but did not advertise the fact. He was open-minded and could never be accused of simply following the party line. During his eleven years as political editor, the Conservatives were continuously in power and some of John's best contacts and friends were Tories. He had an endless interest in political argument over matters of policy, and although the Tories suspected that he would not be voting for them, there were few complaints of personal bias. They knew that John was straight. If they told him something in confidence, he would keep it secret. If he gave an explanation of what was happening, he believed in what he was saying, and he was determined to get it right.

John's appointment as political editor marked a sea change in the way that British politics was reported on television. Up to this point the emphasis had been on balance, pure and simple. The easiest piece to write was to say that the Tories had said something, that Labour had disagreed, and that the Liberals had said they were both wrong. The BBC would loftily stay out of the argument and no one could accuse the corporation of taking sides. Variations on this approach still crop up today, but John introduced a more sophisticated approach, with a degree of sensible and proper comment that went further than any of his predecessors.

He would try to answer the more difficult questions: of why something was being said, and if tactics were revealed what their chances of success might be. He would put the argument into context and often refer to previous conflicts of a similar sort. John took delight in discussing the struggle for power behind the scenes. He would happily describe who was up and who was down in the cabinet, and who might take over in the unlikely event of Mrs Thatcher being run over by a bus. For many viewers he was providing all the missing bits, which in the past the newspapers alone had delivered.

The scope and range of the BBC's political reporting was dramatically increased; and the fact that this was projected by a bespectacled Ulsterman with a strong Belfast accent and an engaging manner no doubt helped it overcome much of the opposition which might otherwise have arisen. I would sometimes think that if I said some of the things John said, in a normal English accent, the roof of the establishment would fall in. The truth is that he was both highly experienced and thoughtful, and politicians would take it from him in a way they would not from anyone else.

But by no means everyone in the BBC saw John's performance in such a rosy light. The great political editor of the *Evening Standard*, Bob Carvel, who was also a brilliant broadcaster, gave John some sage advice when he arrived at Westminster to take up his new job. 'You have been appointed political editor,' he said. 'Now you have to be elected political editor.' John would have to convince senior members of the editorial staff that the managers had picked the right man. One of the BBC's great strengths is that those on the shop floor do not automatically obey instructions from on high. Editors have to be convinced that the correspondents assigned to them are up to standard and fellow members of staff have to be won over as well. The election of the new political editor would take some time.

The chief political correspondent, the hard-working Brian Curtois, had the most difficult job of all. There were times when the intense pressure would show and a white film of saliva would appear on his lips. He had to manage the team at Westminster, organize the rosters and holiday plans, and decide who should cover what story for which programme on

The BBC's chief political correspondent at work, not entirely sure
what he's going to say next.

How to become famous:

First, make it clear that the Prime Minister is not
coming out of the Embassy.

Second, have thirteen million viewers see that she's behind you,
while you have absolutely no idea what's going on.

Third, bring off the scoop of your life when she speaks
into your microphone.

Left: With John Cole, who taught me more about the ways of Westminster than anyone else.

Below: With Mrs Thatcher and Bernard Ingham in 1990, at the commemoration of the seventy-fifth anniversary of Gallipolli.

Enthroned in Cairo, during a trip with John Major in 1992.

En famille at Will's graduation from Edinburgh University in 1997. He's the one next to Mary. His brother, Mike, graduated from Cambridge the previous year.

Alastair Campbell revealing his skills as a press photographer on Tony Blair's first official trip to Washington, in February 1998.

A charity effort at 11 Downing Street, with Ffion Hague and a rather startled small boy.

With Jeremy Hardy on *If I Ruled the World*.

Appearing with Paul Merton on *Room 101*.

ROOM 101

Taking over from Michael Brunson as political editor of ITN.
In the end I didn't need his trademark mac.

television and radio. He also had to live with the uncomfortable fact that on two occasions, when John Simpson and John Cole had been appointed, he had been passed over as political editor. With me, he was always resolutely professional. 'Despite what has happened,' he told me when I arrived, 'I will put you on the rota.' It may seem like a strange welcome, but I was glad of it at the time.

Apart from John Cole, the strongest broadcasting personality was the parliamentary correspondent, Christopher Jones. They were much the same age but their approach to the job was entirely different, and it was only because of their innate good manners that they did not openly clash. Chris had spent many years at Westminster and was now at the height of his fame, the best-known reporter of the parliamentary scene. Chris was a fluent and sometimes witty broadcaster, able to sustain a long read in front of the camera; he stood out from his Westminster colleagues. When I first arrived, on attachment, he taught me a great deal, sometimes about relatively trivial matters. He was also a great story-teller and the tale I liked most was how he and another correspondent chose the final words spoken in the Commons by Sir Winston Churchill, who retired in 1964 at the age of eighty-nine. No one could work out exactly what he said, so Chris and the person working for *Hansard*, the official record, agreed on what the final words should be. They might have been tempted to try something along the lines of 'I have nothing to offer but blood, toil, tears and sweat,' but Chris assured me it was something far more mundane: Sir Winston thanked MPs for their good wishes on his birthday.

Chris was a master of the strange ways of parliament and a precise and quick judge of debates and personalities. After prime minister's questions, then held twice a week, he would rapidly decide who had won the exchanges. When I first went to Westminster, the battle was between the inexperienced leader of the opposition, Margaret Thatcher, and what Chris would often describe as the avuncular James Callaghan, then prime minister. Mrs Thatcher would invariably look as if she was being swatted aside like a fly, but her points were often good, and she had a sweet revenge when she won the election of 1979. I often found that leaving the press gallery with Chris Jones, hearing his quick asides on what had happened, was invaluable in deciding what to write in my early pieces from Westminster.

In those days we would broadcast from the bottom of the old New Scotland Yard building, renamed after its architect Norman Shaw and mainly turned over to offices for MPs. The BBC had a studio in the basement, which we could operate on our own. When we were broadcasting on television we would use a very crude form of autocue: our script was projected on to a screen just below the camera and could be scrolled up or down by using a foot pedal. Chris carefully pointed out the danger of the script moving in the wrong direction, describing how one correspondent had appeared to the viewers to be like a drowning man, desperately trying to read a script which was moving down instead of up.

Chris also gave me a useful tip for working under stress: try to reduce your choices. There were two ways to go between our offices in the Palace of Westminster and the studio in Norman Shaw. You could either turn right into the subway which took you to the Embankment, or turn left and come out at the entrance to Westminster tube. Either way you seemed to travel exactly the same distance. As you went over, clutching your script, with only minutes to go before a broadcast, it was important not to be troubled with a choice. Chris ordained, and I followed his advice rigidly, that on the way there you should turn right and on the way back you should use the entrance to the tube.

The main problem Chris had to contend with towards

the end of his career was that his kind of reporting from Westminster was gradually becoming obsolete. The great divide in those days was between parliamentary correspondents and lobby correspondents. Chris believed that the position of the political correspondents who had easy access to the politicians in the lobby of the House of Commons was open to serious abuse. Throughout his long career he had insisted on observing events from the gallery, without fear or favour. Hobnobbing with politicians, he believed, was the first step towards corruption. But the equally upright and strong-minded John Cole profoundly disagreed. For John the essence of good political reporting was to understand what was happening and not simply to report what was being said. To do that without talking to those closely involved in the arguments behind the scenes seemed to be unnecessarily puritanical and in practice plain wrong. Chris was only as prominent as he was for so long because parliament in those days was not televised. For most of his career it wasn't broadcast on radio either. Being a parliamentary correspondent was far more rewarding when people could only hear what had happened in the House of Commons through your descriptions. When that gap was filled, first by radio and then by television, the skills of the lobby correspondent dedicated to finding out what was going on behind the scenes came much more to the fore. You could broadcast excerpts from the exchanges on the floor of the House; listeners and viewers then wanted a quick explanation of the thinking behind the speeches and comments.

I have plenty to thank Chris Jones for: he taught me how to read a debate and how to measure prime minister's questions. He also taught me how far a BBC correspondent simply working in the press gallery could introduce comment. As with the example set by John Cole, it depended on how you did it, as much as what you were trying to get across. When I eventually learned those skills, it was surprising how much could be packed into a short parliamentary piece. My start as a fully fledged political correspondent of the BBC may have been uneasy, to say the least. But my time at Westminster was to become the most important part of my journalistic career.

19

Mrs Thatcher goes to war

As EVERY PARENT KNOWS, there is no perfect way to bring up children; and also, as every parent knows, you have to try to do your best. With my two sons I attempted to shield them from distress, and to keep my word. Sometimes that policy had strange effects. When I went to Northern Ireland I promised to bring them back *Star Wars* toys, which were then all the rage. I kept my word, but did not dwell upon other aspects of life and death in Northern Ireland. As a result, at the height of the terrorist violence, my two little boys would jump up and down and say, 'Daddy, Daddy, why don't you go to Belfast again?' Mary and I would look at each other and resist the temptation to reveal how grateful they should be that I was not going to Northern Ireland.

I also promised to take them swimming each week at the municipal baths in Harrow. At this stage our home borough of Ealing did not have such facilities. Each Sunday, whatever my other engagements, I was on parental duty. I would sit groggily beside the pool wondering just how this promise had been extracted. On one occasion I arrived back home on Sunday morning having flown overnight from the United States. Protesting about tiredness and jet lag cuts no ice with two determined small boys, and in any case I was too weak to complain.

Breathing in the clammy chlorinated air of the Harrow pool, I tried to give the impression of a responsible parent quite capable of looking after his sons. But my mind was still on the other side of the Atlantic. Two days before, I had been standing in the Oval Office of the president of the United States. It had been a memorable but pointless visit to Washington, carried out to placate a single-minded and impressive French politician, Simone Veil. A Jewish victim of a German concentration camp with her camp number still tattooed on her forearm, she was the most popular woman in French politics; she was also the first president of the directly elected European Parliament. The expenses for a group of French journalists to accompany her to see President Jimmy Carter were paid by the European Parliament; and to ensure that this would not be seen as an entirely French affair, a few journalists from other European countries were invited to join the party.

I got on well with Simone Veil. With her determination and strength of character, you did not need to know the story of her life to realize how extraordinary she was. We did not share a common language: she would try to understand my English, and I would try to understand her French. We were both interested in Margaret Thatcher. 'Will she be re-elected?' she asked. I had my doubts.

'These are not very good times to be in government,' I suggested. It was a theme Mme Veil warmed to, because she was hoping that when economic circumstances improved she would return to government in France, as she eventually did. I went on to conclude, 'To be re-elected, Mrs Thatcher will need the economy to pick up.'

It is often forgotten how difficult Margaret Thatcher found her first period in government. She nearly doubled VAT in her first budget; she put up taxes in 1981 when the country was in recession; and she was not fully in charge of her cabinet, which still contained a fair number of 'wets'. This was her term for those people who did not have stomach for the fight and for them it became a badge of honour. With the wets happily accepting that title, Mrs Thatcher's supporters became known as 'dries'.

What she needed to guarantee success in the next election was a good war. But when it came, in 1982, I was trapped by another promise to my two sons. All those outings to Harrow had paid off in one respect: they were both competent swimmers. And at some point in their long swimming training I had promised that were they to succeed I would buy them a boat.

At the Earl's Court Boat Show, which is held each year in January, we bought the *Mirror* dinghy on display. The sail number was 6600 and we called it *Lois Lane* in honour of Clark Kent's girlfriend. All members of the family, with the possible exception of Mary, were desperate to sail her as soon as possible. We joined the Datchet Water Sailing Club, which gives access to an enormous reservoir under the main flight path for planes taking off from Heathrow. The sailing season proper starts on the first day of April.

The timing could not have been more inconvenient. For weeks we had planned to make our first sail on Saturday, 2 April. But the day before, the Falkland Islands in the South Atlantic had been invaded by Argentina. For the first time in recent history it was decided that the House of Commons would meet on a Saturday to debate the crisis. When an appeal was made for volunteers to work on that day, I stayed mysteriously silent. There were more than enough correspondents willing to take part. But it did take some of the shine off the inaugural voyage of *Lois Lane*, and afterwards I was more than anxious to do my bit to cover the conflict, which began as a disaster for Mrs Thatcher and then became her greatest triumph.

The Falklands War is an interesting example of how a partisan press, anxious to please the government of the day, would not have produced the desired effect. To start with, everything seemed to go wrong. The Argentinian government were given the impression that Britain would not attempt to retake the islands, and the invasion itself came as a complete surprise. All three foreign office ministers, including the highly regarded Lord Carrington, resigned. It looked as if, far from clinching Mrs Thatcher's victory in the coming election, the conflict could have sealed her downfall.

At Ealing Broadway tube station when I set off for work there was a blackboard with a stark appeal for members of the Parachute Regiment to report for duty. The military sent a task force to the South Atlantic which would recapture the islands, and do so with a surprisingly small number of casualties. Like a wasp in winter, right at the end of the country's long colonial history, Britain was still able to produce a stinging response. It was the making of Mrs Thatcher. But her political victory was only possible because the media had not shrunk from telling the bad news first. It made the triumph all the more telling when it came.

For the BBC the war posed peculiar difficulties, which were not always successfully resolved. At the heart of these was the old problem of being fair to both sides. What were the two sides? There was a strong case for Britain not risking lives in an old-fashioned colonial war, and there were left-wing Labour MPs ready and willing to argue the point. The simple issue of going to war or not going to war was also a matter which could easily be understood, a great advantage for a mass medium such as broadcasting.

Although it is the duty of the opposition to oppose, for the Labour leader, Michael Foot, outright opposition to the Falklands War was both wrong and foolish. When British forces are engaged in difficult operations overseas the duty of the opposition is almost invariably to join in the support for 'our boys'. There was also the constant problem which politicians have to face, that before long the electorate will have their say.

So the political divide between the two main parties at Westminster was far from clear. Our problem as broadcasters was getting a fair balance, often having to choose between a clear argument for or against the war, and the much more complicated, sometimes deliberately obscure argument raised by the opposition. This often happens at Westminster; it is one of the reasons why many people find politics difficult, and frequently boring. It might have been much simpler for us if Labour had come out strongly against the war, but they had sound political reasons for not doing so. Instead, they spent a great deal of time stressing the importance of the United Nations in resolving the dispute by every means short of war. The government was also anxious to consider all the various peace iniatives, which had the advantage, for them, of distracting attention from the slow build up of British forces in the South Atlantic.

To me, much of the Westminster debate was annoyingly beside the point. Argentina gave no impression that they were prepared to give up what they called the Malvinas. If the Falklands could be retaken by force, without too many casualties, that surely was the only acceptable outcome. It was hard, otherwise, to see how Britain could overcome the clear loss of power and influence which would result if the Argentine invasion were accepted.

These were private thoughts. The BBC had to take an Olympian stance, above all these matters, however much they might touch the core of the nation's psyche. Or was that wrong? Margaret Thatcher certainly thought so; she could not understand why, in time of war, the BBC should not instinctively respond to her call to the colours. There was something wonderfully funny, but also poignant, when she stood with her defence secretary, John Nott, on a dark night in Downing Street, to announce the recapture of the island of South Georgia. The response from the small band of media folk, mostly cameramen and soundmen was hardly inspiring, and her disappointment showed. 'Rejoice, just rejoice,' she shouted before sweeping back into Number Ten.

The truth is that the BBC rightly feels very uncomfortable in the role of cheerleader. Like so much in British public life this stems in part from the seminal event of the twentieth century: the rise and eventual defeat of Nazi Germany. A deep revulsion to propaganda, particularly through the power of the mass media, became embedded in the BBC which, in different hands, could have become one of the great forces of misinformation; and the relentless cold war cynicism of the communist media merely reinforced this revulsion. For those in government, anxious for public approval, this view could easily be misunderstood. Their thoughts could be politely expressed in the exasperated question: 'Who do the BBC think they are?'

Even before the Falklands War Mrs Thatcher had plunged into this argument, but without appearing to have given the matter a great deal of thought. After the inner-city riots of 1981 she complained, 'If the television of the Western world uses its freedom continually to show all that is worst in our society while the centrally controlled television of the communist world shows only what is judged advantageous to them, how are the uncommitted to judge between us?' Fortunately the position of the BBC rested on broader principles than a simple calculation based on the idea that the end – beating the communist bloc – might justify the means – a controlled media. But this was an argument which was never resolved. The prime minister's beady eye was always upon us.

Some of the issues Mrs Thatcher raised were relatively trivial. She objected to Peter Snow on *Newsnight* on BBC2 referring to 'British' forces, rather than 'our' forces. The BBC was able to counter this by pointing out that the Argentinian forces could not be called 'the enemy'. In this we were helped by the fact that Britain had not formally declared war on Argentina. But a BBC executive made an unfortunate speech at a conference in Madrid. He suggested that when, as a result of this conflict, a soldier died, the BBC saw no difference between a widow in Buenos Aries and a widow in Portsmouth.

This may be true in terms of a moral debate; it is certainly not true in the way that a news programme is put together. BBC bulletins, of course, considered British casualties to be far more important than those on the other side. We were never as nationalistic as the *Sun*, which produced its famous headline 'Gotcha' when the Argentine cruiser the *Belgrano* was sunk. But the BBC naturally treated news of the missile attack on the British destroyer HMS *Sheffield* as a serious blow to our country's hopes, and it provided me with my one scoop of the war.

At Westminster, information is a kind of currency. It can be exchanged for other things such as power and favours, and it can sometimes be converted into real money, though this should be avoided. It is the stuff of journalism. As with any sort of currency, information can be used wisely, but often it is hoarded for no good reason. The value of information varies enormously, depending crucially on whether it is new. Old news finds no takers. For the journalist, the best supplier of information is someone who finds it exceptionally difficult to keep a secret.

I will not reveal who my source was that evening, though he might be pleased if I did; so long after, he might see it as a kind of battle honour. But often it is impossible to work out why you are being sworn to secrecy; and on this occasion I certainly was. The information could not be divulged on the phone. I had to descend to the lobby where, in those days, strict rules applied. As a lobby journalist you were forbidden to take notes on what your informant said; you were not meant to listen to other people's conversations; and overexcitement, as you hurried back upstairs, could be penalized because you were not allowed to run in the corridors. Duplicity and decorum seemed to go hand in hand.

The information was incomplete but was clearly important. One of our ships in the South Atlantic had been badly hit; the news would come out at 9 p.m. I immediately informed the newsroom at Television Centre; and when the nine o'clock news started they went straight over to a news conference at the Ministry of Defence. In his strange monotonous voice, the MoD's chief spokesman, Ian MacDonald, read out the grim details. The destroyer had been hit by an Argentinian Exocet missile, and subsequently sank. There were about forty casualties. At this early stage in the conflict, before the task force arrived, the vulnerability of the navy's vessels to missile attack was obvious to all.

When the war was over the change in Mrs Thatcher was marked: she had more confidence, she had proved herself as a war leader, and in politics there is no substitute for success. I was thankful that for once in my BBC career I did not have to feel guilty about not being close to the action. Other reporters, notably my old Oxford friend Robert Fox, and Brian Hanrahan, would make their names as a result of the conflict, but I could begin to settle down to a different kind of journalism at Westminster. It might be tempting to say that I missed the excitement of war reporting, but that would not be true. When I had gone on dangerous assignments in the past people in the newsroom had often said, 'Keep your head down.' It was a relief to know that my physical safety was no longer at risk.

But life is seldom simple. At the very moment when the course ahead seemed if anything too predictable, I was struck down by illness. It came on quite slowly, with a series of uncomfortable nights and unpleasant dreams, when we were on a family holiday in southern Brittany. On the way back I felt oddly tired when we were waiting to catch the ferry at St Malo. But it was only when I reached the Highcliffe Hotel on the cliffs at Bournemouth at the start of the Liberal Party conference that I realized it was something serious. I could not get out of bed without considerable difficulty; I seemed to be nearly paralysed.

For the best part of six weeks I spent the days lying on a sofa in our Ealing home. The family doctor had no idea what I was suffering from. I suggested it could be psychological in origin. 'Oh, no,' he said firmly, 'you're too vital for that.' It was a flattering thing to say, but given that I had almost no vitality at that moment, it did not seem very helpful. All kinds of blood test were carried out; each time I was told they were negative, I felt as if I had failed. The BBC, in the shape of one of my least favourite managers, Gerard Schlesinger, was beginning to get anxious.

'But Gerard wants to know what you've got,' I was told by the secretary in our office at Westminster; and I couldn't help thinking rather bitterly, 'I bet he does; so do I.'

It was only when Mary was struck down in a similar fashion six months later that we had any clue as to what had happened. She tested positive for toxoplasmosis, a parasitical infection which can be caught from cats. Our lovely Persian cat, Fluffy, had to be put down. It is not supposedly an illness which lasts for very long, but with us it lingered on, albeit in a less serious form, for many years.

By the time Mary fell ill, I was back at work but still finding it difficult to walk any distance, and standing for more than about ten minutes was simply not possible. The great Labour veteran, Barbara Castle, once told me that one of the most important things in life is to be lucky with your bad luck. Fortunately I was able to continue my work at Westminster; if

I had still been a general reporter, I would have had to be switched to other duties. Even at Westminster I felt my illness was something of a guilty secret. One day I confessed to one of my colleagues that I could not walk as far as Victoria station. 'Oh,' he replied dismissively, 'you're just a hypochondriac.' After that I decided to keep my health concerns to myself.

When Margaret Thatcher called the election for 9 June 1983, I was chosen to conduct the first interview following the announcement, which would be carried live on *PM* on Radio 4. I should have been thrilled at the chance to make a bit of history, but I was too worried about whether I would be able to walk the short distance from Westminster to Downing Street. The illness was a continuing worry, though fortunately it did not show; and as my role in the forthcoming campaign would be largely sedentary, I was able to play my part to reasonable effect.

Most of my work was for radio, compiling reports from news conferences and speeches. The morning bulletins on Radio 4 were obviously the most important, and one of my broadcasts inadvertently damaged a politician I rather liked, the foreign secretary, Francis Pym. He had made the mistake of suggesting on *Question Time*, with Robin Day, that he hoped the Conservatives would not win a landslide victory. He said, 'Landslides on the whole don't produce successful governments.'

To me this was a great news story. One of my colleagues vehemently disagreed. Surely, he argued, this was a statement of the obvious. 'Governments with big majorities become complacent, and don't take parliament seriously.' He could not be persuaded otherwise and I was drawn into a quarrel. It is often distressing to argue about news stories, because usually journalists rely on instinct rather than logic. The newsworthiness of this story, I thought, was fairly straightforward. At the start of an election campaign the foreign secretary was suggesting his party should not go all out for a thumping victory. It was hardly the way a leader should rally his troops.

The story was not touched upon in the newspapers but my version led the morning radio bulletins. Mrs Thatcher, who did not get on with Francis Pym, was privately furious. She wrote in her memoirs that he had struck the wrong note, upsetting those Conservative candidates standing in marginal seats. But she tried not to show her displeasure at the morning press conference, which was dominated by questions about Mr Pym's remarks. 'I think I could handle a landslide majority all right,' she insisted, and then referred to Mr Pym's natural caution, as a former chief whip. 'You know there's a club of chief whips,' she went on. 'They're very unusual people.' Her comments did not, however, stem the tide. It was the main election story of the day, and when Mrs Thatcher came to form her new government after the election, Mr Pym was dropped. From foreign secretary to backbencher was quite a fall, and it was clear that the election gaffe had played a part.

When people look back on the election of 1983 they invariably say, 'Oh, yes the Falklands.' But if they research Margaret Thatcher's speeches they will find only one substantial reference to the Falklands conflict, and that was in Perth just before the start of the election campaign proper. She and her advisers decided that she could not raise the subject without appearing to use the bravery of the armed forces to further her cause. Talk of the 'Falklands factor' started immediately after the election was over. The truth is that her position in the opinion polls had hardly dropped below 40 per cent since the end of the conflict, the economy had begun to pick up and Labour were still going through a fearsome internal battle. The shadow foreign secretary, Gerald Kaufman, produced the most famous description of the Labour manifesto of 1983. It was, he said, the longest suicide note in history. It advocated unilateral nuclear disarmament and withdrawal from the European Community. Ironically, that was the manifesto on which Tony Blair fought his first general election. A good deal of the fun of reporting politics is that nothing is ever quite as it seems.

20

'What is the next surprising thing?'

ON THE DAY OF her successful re-election in 1983, Mrs Thatcher celebrated with Cecil Parkinson. She had it in mind to make him foreign secretary; for her he would be a perfect replacement for the lacklustre Francis Pym. It was only then that her party chairman admitted to an affair with his former secretary, Sara Keays, which, the prime minister revealed later, 'gave her pause'. Mrs Thatcher was not censorious. There were others who might be shocked, but she was usually cool about such matters. As the story was relayed to me, her immediate response was, 'But if it's now over, that shouldn't matter.'

It was left to Cecil Parkinson to blurt out, 'But what about Victorian values?' This was the phrase usually associated with her moral outlook.

'But you are going to stay with your wife,' Mrs Thatcher replied. She needed, though, a night to think about it; the shape of the government would depend on the outcome.

Cecil Parkinson was invited to lunch at Number Ten the next day, but before he arrived there was a dramatic intervention from Sara Keays' father. He sent a personal letter to Mrs Thatcher revealing that his daughter was pregnant with Cecil Parkinson's child. The prime minister was surprised but not deterred. She decided it would not be sensible for him to take up such a sensitive and senior post as foreign secretary, but she was determined to have him in the cabinet, as the trade and industry secretary. Sir Geoffrey Howe became foreign secretary. The secret was kept for a few more months and then the affair was admitted in a joint press statement from Cecil Parkinson and Sara Keays, issued just before the Conservative party conference in October.

As the most junior political correspondent, I had been left in London on the assumption that the most important stories would happen at the Labour or Tory conferences, which are usually held in consecutive weeks. It was therefore up to me to stand outside the Department of Trade and Industry and pontificate on whether Cecil Parkinson would be forced to resign. There are many broadcasts which I would be happy to forget; this is one of them. I took the view he would survive and not be pushed out of office, and it is no consolation to read in Mrs Thatcher's memoirs that at the time she held the same view.

John Cole used to remind me that the more significant a story, the more important it is to leave in some 'weasel words'. These can be introduced so as not to interrupt the flow, and when you wake up worrying in the middle of the night you will be glad they were there. Phrases such as 'at this stage' or 'from what we can gather at the moment' or 'it looks as though' or even the all-purpose 'it seems to me'. Any of these phrases is better than an assessment made without qualification, in a situation where you cannot know all the facts, and which can soon be overturned by events. Over the years, I have also tried to include a further check to see that I am not getting overexcited, or simply misjudging the moment. It is the 'one week on' test. The idea is to imagine how your remarks will seem a week after they have been broadcast. It stops you saying 'This is the most incredible thing that has happened' when, a week later, the story has been largely forgotten. The 'one week on' test should not make you overcautious; one of the worst mistakes you can make as a political correspondent is to downplay an important story, often the mistake that junior correspondents make, believing that the cautious approach makes them sound more authoritative.

But these tricks of habit and custom are of only limited help. I have often been asked to make an impossible assessment when facts are limited and the situation is changing rapidly. Then you have to fall back on much older notions of 'discretion being the better part of valour' and the old newspaper adage 'If in doubt, leave it out.' There are occasions when a correspondent says they do not know what is happening, or why, and viewers heave a sigh of relief. At least they know what is not known and sometimes that is more revealing than a long waffling answer from someone 'on the spot'. With news now seen as a twenty-four-hour commodity, mistakes are more likely. In my earlier years as a correspondent it was much simpler because most of what we did was carefully scripted. Going back even further, when television news started after the war, BBC managers were fearful that newsreaders might betray their personal views in their facial expressions, presumably by raising an eyebrow or looking downcast, if there was anything in the script which disconcerted them. Happily, newsreaders turned out to be far less sensitive than that, but many years passed before correspondents would be asked questions on highly controversial matters and be expected to respond spontaneously.

As a natural communicator, John Cole brought to the BBC a set of fresh skills as an expert in what is usually called a 'two-way' or in ITN 'a live'. These are the occasions when the correspondent is asked questions by the newsreader. John had been answering questions like this for many years. The first time we met, nearly ten years before he joined the staff of the BBC, he was deputy editor of the *Guardian*, and I was asking him about the situation in Northern Ireland for the *Today* programme.

John liked the questions to be spontaneous as well as the answers; he disliked having to discuss with newsreaders what they were going to ask. This often caused difficulties because newsreaders tend to be a vain lot; they long to prove they are sentient human beings and not simply the purveyors of other people's scripts. Questions from newsreaders could often be tortured attempts to cover the ground the correspondent is about to cover, or they could be just plain daft. On one ghastly occasion, a newsreader on the six o'clock news said to me, 'What has happened this afternoon is very surprising, John, what is the next surprising thing that is going to happen?'

Despite the fact that one of the best jokes made about newsreaders is both unfair and in poor taste, I cannot resist repeating it. Chris Cramer, before he left to become overseas head of the American satellite news operation, CNN, was the news editor of BBC television news. When Martyn Lewis left ITN and joined the BBC as a newsreader, Julia Somerville left the BBC for the same job at ITN. Chris gave a snort and announced, 'Tit for tat.'

None of this deep knowledge about the relationship between correspondents and newsreaders, and how they relate to the public was any help to me as I stood outside the Department of Trade and Industry in October 1983 trying to work out whether Cecil Parkinson would be forced to resign. My assessment that he was unlikely to do so seemed a reasonable assumption, on the basis that there was no obvious pressure on him to go from his colleagues or his constituents. But in these situations, many of those who might be tempted to throw stones stay inside their glass houses. What we had not allowed for was the intervention of the one person who now more than anyone else wanted to encourage his downfall, Sara Keays.

There was a lot of talk at the time about the dangers of a wronged woman – 'Hell hath no fury like a woman scorned' –

but there were plenty of others who were pleased she had decided to take her revenge. On the eve of the Conservative Party conference, she gave a long interview to *The Times*. As with other resignations – which were to become a regular feature of the Conservative period in office – it was often when it looked as though someone might hold on that the rug was pulled smartly from under them. Cecil Parkinson was whisked away from the Blackpool conference after John Cole had managed to get an exclusive interview with him. He did not return to the cabinet for four years, until after the next election, and any hopes he might have of becoming prime minister or leading his party were finished for ever.

I have to say I never thought he was quite in the top drawer of politicians. Mrs Thatcher might have liked him on personal grounds, for his good looks and manners, but I found him too ingratiating to be impressive. He did not seem to be real; and when you knew that his father had had a lowly job with British Railways you longed for him to sound and behave more like what he really was, and not so 'proper'. He was, though, good with journalists, knowing just how indiscreet he could be without causing the roof to fall in. He knew the limitations of saying 'no comment' and when news of his affair came out, he tried to ease the plight of the journalists outside his house by sending out a bottle of Scotch to help them through the night.

In the early 1980s the Conservative government was lucky in the general state of the opposition. Since the 1979 election Labour had been crippled by an internal battle which at times resembled a civil war. When the group known as the Gang of Four – Roy Jenkins, David Owen, Shirley Williams and Bill Rodgers – left to form the Social Democratic Party, that was not the end of Labour's problems. Michael Foot had proved ineffective as leader, even though as a man of the Left respected by the Right he had straddled the internal divide. Labour did poorly in the election of 1983; in the popular vote they were only just ahead of the Alliance, which brought together the Liberals and the SDP under the leadership of Roy Jenkins and David Steel. When the election was over, Michael Foot announced he would stand down as party leader.

I was acquainted with the new Labour leader, Neil Kinnock, from the Welsh referendum campaign of 1979, when he had successfully fought off what he saw as the threat of devolution. How the wheel turns. Less than twenty years later, it was, of course, the Labour Party under Tony Blair's leadership which set up the Welsh Assembly. During that campaign Neil Kinnock and I spent a happy morning with his wife, Glenys, making a film for the *Westminster* programme; I was struck by his charm and his extraordinary skill in front of a television camera. He was able to appear completely natural. Television is often unfair to people. Conventional good looks do not always help; indeed they can be rather off-putting. In the Hollywood phrase, some performers do well because the camera likes them, and Neil Kinnock fell easily into that category. There were plenty of times later when we were far from chummy, particularly when I tried to interview him about the Militant Tendency as he strode through a crowd of reporters outside Labour headquarters in Walworth Road, but I did not subscribe to the view many people had, that he could never become prime minister.

A divided party, though, does not impress the public. The Militant Tendency, with its dedication to extreme left-wing politics, looked as if it could not be contained. It had success-fully infiltrated the Labour Party, and the argument that if you cannot run your own party, how can you hope to persuade voters you are ready to run the country is a telling one. There was also the problem of the left wing in parliament, and the difficulty of coping with the charismatic Tony Benn. His move from the centre to the left, from support for Europe to

Euro-scepticism, has been well chronicled, but it is the effect he had on mainstream Labour support which was so irritating to the party leadership.

Denis Healey had managed, only just, to beat him in the election for the post of deputy leader at the party conference in 1981, but this did not take the wind out of Mr Benn's sails. A few years later, at the time of the miners' dispute, Mr Benn was attempting to rally support for Arthur Scargill and the other miners' leaders. Like Tony Benn, Mrs Thatcher's views were also clear-cut, though completely the opposite. For her, the miners represented 'the enemy within', and Arthur Scargill was as implacable a foe as General Galtieri of Argentina. She clearly believed that defeating the miners could be as useful for her in her second term of office as the Falklands War had been in her first.

It was the Labour leader, Neil Kinnock, who faced an agonizing choice. He did not want to be associated in the public mind with union militancy. As the police battled with the miners' pickets in the worst scenes of industrial unrest since before the war, the Labour leadership were on a hiding to nothing. If they supported the miners in the way Neil Kinnock, with his strong roots in the South Wales mining community, might have wanted, they would have lost middle-class support essential for victory at a general election. But by seeming to be ambivalent, he attracted the scorn of the Conservatives and the wrath of Labour's powerful left wing.

During the miners' strike, I occasionally presented *The World this Weekend* on Radio 4. An interview with Tony Benn seemed a useful way to explore Mr Kinnock's dilemma, and perhaps make a bit of news as well. I had always, I thought, got on rather well with Mr Benn. My first contact with him had been in 1971 when the People's Republic of China was allowed into the United Nations and given a seat on the Security Council, replacing the Chinese Nationalists. Mr Benn had recently visited China and I thought he might be able to do a quick telephone interview to talk about the first Chinese ambassador to the UN. 'I haven't got my notes with me,' he replied, 'but how long do you want?'

'Well, to be honest,' I said, 'I am looking for about a minute.'

When the equipment had been set up at Broadcasting House, I asked him baldly, 'What do you think of the man the Chinese have appointed to represent them at the UN?' I did not risk trying out my limited pronunciation skills by mentioning his name. Mr Benn took this in his stride. Not only did he remember the man's name, he spoke it with great confidence and proceeded to give a fluent description. At the end, he came to a perfectly rounded conclusion.

There was a pause, and then he said, 'Well, there you are, sixty seconds, one minute. I don't have many party tricks, but that's one of them.' As a former BBC producer he could not resist underlining the point. It was quite impressive.

When I set off to do my interview with him for *The World this Weekend*, more than a dozen years later, I knew it could not be such a successful encounter. I walked up the short path to the red-painted door of his house in Holland Park with some trepidation. At that time Mr Benn was making a good deal of the idea that the BBC was a propaganda tool of the government. I deeply resented the charge. But that did not deter Mr Benn.

When he opened the door, I immediately noticed a small tape recorder, which he thrust forward, with its red light on, showing that it was recording. 'Hello,' he said; and I did not know whether to reply to him directly or speak into the tape recorder. I said hello to the machine. He then proceeded to give me a short lecture on the unfairness of the BBC's coverage of the miners' dispute. I took this in reasonably good heart, but knowing that all my remarks were being recorded I said nothing which might be used against me.

We began negotiations about the coming interview, discussing the questions I might ask and the ground we would cover. This is often a delicate business which can lead to misunderstanding, and in the past the BBC insisted on keeping any such negotiations private. Thankfully, they are now more open about the terms on which an interview may have been granted. They are now prepared to reveal when a politician has refused to take part in a programme, and sometimes it will be made clear that the interview is only designed to cover a particular field and not any subject the interviewer wants to talk about. But this was not true for much of the time I worked for the BBC. There was an unwritten rule that any agreement or the details of any negotiation beforehand would not be made public. It was just not done.

On this occasion, Mr Benn wanted to avoid making a personal attack on Neil Kinnock; there may have been particular reasons why this was important to him at the time, and it certainly fitted in with his frequently stated wish to concentrate on issues rather than personalities. But his rectitude would not help me explain what was going on within the Labour Party and I was anxious to point up the fact that he was attacking his own leader, however skilfully disguised that attack might be. I was convinced that if I did not make this clear in my questions the interview would be much harder to understand, but I reluctantly agreed that there would be only two questions mentioning Neil Kinnock. I thought that would be enough and honour could be satisfied.

But when I asked the two questions about Neil Kinnock's leadership the answers were far from satisfactory; they were deliberately vague. Instinctively, having momentarily forgotten our agreement, I asked a follow-up question, and Mr Benn exploded. I was, he suggested, an agent of government. My actions had proved it. He would not continue with the interview; indeed he insisted that what we had recorded so far should not be broadcast. This was moving from a skirmish into a serious incident, so I decided to ring my editor, Jenny Abramsky, an old friend who subsequently went on to become the head of all BBC radio programmes.

She decided that, in the circumstances, we should not continue with the interview. While she was telling me what she thought, I looked round and saw to my astonishment that Mr Benn was moving what looked like an electric iron over my tape recorder. In fact it was a demagnetizing device to wipe tapes. The interview was being obliterated. Fortunately, I kept my temper; it was, for me, a very rare case of being struck dumb. I could not believe that anyone would think I was so untrustworthy that they should take it into their own hands to remove the evidence of what had happened. I left as quickly as I could.

In a strange way, this incident had a direct effect on the course of Labour politics. Instead of Tony Benn, I turned to his close colleague, Eric Heffer, who had exactly the same views about the leadership's attitude to the miners' dispute. In the interview, which was broadcast at the start of *The World this Weekend*, he laid into Neil Kinnock with barely disguised venom. Mr Heffer had never been close to Mr Kinnock but after this interview was broadcast they were never able to mend their differences. When Mr Kinnock made his famous speech at the Labour Party conference in Bournemouth in 1985, in which he attacked the Liverpool council leader, Derek Hatton, and the Militant Tendency, he had barely started when Mr Heffer, a member of the Labour National Executive Committee, walked off the platform in disgust. I once suggested to Mr Heffer that everything might have been different if he had refused to do that interview with me on *The World*

This Weekend. 'Oh, no,' he said. 'It wasn't just that interview. I couldn't forgive Kinnock for what he did during the miners' dispute.' But when I told Mr Heffer that I only interviewed him because Mr Benn had practically thrown me out of his house, he was very surprised. 'I didn't know that,' he said. 'Tony never told me.'

I was personally affected by the incident in a rather different way: I was far more careful about making any agreement prior to an interview which I might later regret. It also strengthened my view that if possible it is better to have interviews broadcast live, or as close to live conditions as possible. Then the audience can decide whether your questioning has been unfair. I did not bear a grudge against Tony Benn and, later, he did apologize. As a political correspondent you cannot disapprove of politicians with strong convictions; it so often provides grist to your mill. But it was some time before he and I were back on an even keel.

A couple of years later I went back to his house to interview him again. Instead of coming across as an agent of government, I hoped to strike a friendlier note. I mentioned that my father had once sent him a ten-shilling postal order, to help with his campaign more than twenty years previously to renounce his peerage. Tony Benn's father had been given a hereditary peerage and my father, who had no connection with him, was upset at the idea that if Mr Benn inherited the title his political career in the House of Commons would be over. As a result of the campaign the law was changed, to allow people to refuse a peerage. As soon as I raised the subject of my father's contribution, Mr Benn left the room to check his records downstairs. Within ten minutes, he was back. 'There we are,' Mr Benn said. 'He was a clergyman, wasn't he? Look.' And there, typed out, was my father's name: The Rev. E. N. C. Sergeant, of Walton, Somerset.

When I told him later, in one of the last conversations we

had, that he had helped to reconcile Tony Benn and me, my father was typically self-effacing. 'If I can be of some small service,' he said, with a smile. He died of a heart attack soon afterwards, at the age of seventy-three.

21

Helicopters and Heseltine

WHEN SOMEONE FAINTED during an interview with me, I have to admit I was rather disconcerted. Working for years in television it is sometimes easy to miss the simple point that for most people appearing in front of millions of strangers is a far from natural event; it can be a great strain, particularly if you are being asked to lie. This poor woman, who turned a deathly white and slumped in her chair, was trying to be a loyal Tory after one of the most unpopular budgets of recent times. She was desperate to think of something positive to say; I had merely asked her what she thought of the budget.

We were in the North Yorkshire constituency of Leon Brittan in the spring of 1981. He was chief secretary to the Treasury, intimately connected with the budget, which had been brought in by the chancellor, Sir Geoffrey Howe. Unemployment had risen by nearly a million in the previous year. The country was in recession, and the tax-increasing budget appeared to make things worse. Because of higher petrol duties it hurt people more in rural areas, such as North Yorkshire. The budget would later be heralded as the basis for Mrs Thatcher's economic success, but at the time it was highly controversial, provoking a now-famous critical letter to *The Times* signed by 364 economists.

I was sent to Leon Brittan's Cleveland and Whitby constituency to gauge reaction among Conservative grass roots. It was my first contact with one of the prime minister's rising stars. He had recently married, and my short film for *Newsnight* could have helped his political profile. But the instructions I had been given would not have pleased him; I was to record the genuine anger which was felt even among Conservative supporters. Mr Brittan was, on the surface, extremely helpful. It was just that not one of his official supporters seemed to have a bad word for the budget. The producer I was working with was Tim Gardam, a young high-flier who became editor of *Newsnight* and later a senior manager with Channel 4. He was rather nervous and at one stage, in the general excitement, he drove us the wrong way up a dual carriageway. Fortunately there were no cars travelling in the right direction and we managed a rapid U-turn.

After the woman member of Leon Brittan's constituency association fainted during my interview, we decided that the only way we could get any critical comment was at the Conservative Club in Whitby, where I asked people at the bar what they thought. They were more than happy to heap scorn on the budget. We had the criticism that we needed, which could then be balanced by the strongly pro-budget comments of the chief secretary to the Treasury.

There seemed to be a less than subtle attempt by the government to get its own back after the film had been transmitted. The chancellor, Sir Geoffrey Howe, complained unofficially to the BBC about the size of the film crew we employed in North Yorkshire, but it did not grow into a major incident. For a time, though, it did rather colour my view of Leon Brittan. He seemed determined to win, even in circumstances when it would have been wrong for the BBC to allow him to do so. The same approach was used in a far more dramatic way when he was promoted to home secretary and attempted to stop the BBC broadcasting a programme featuring Martin McGuinness. McGuinness has since become Northern Ireland's education minister, but was then widely regarded as a leading member of the IRA as well as Sinn Fein. The film, *Real Lives: At the Edge of the Union*, attempted to show that he had a normal life, too. It was not really a programme to go on strike for, but most BBC staff stayed off for a day to demonstrate that the home secretary should not decide these matters. There was solid support in the Westminster office, even though John Cole was – perhaps unsurprisingly – not an advocate of the programme. We were secretly encouraged by management to take a stand and the programme was eventually shown, but the incident increased Mrs Thatcher's determination to 'do something about the BBC'. It was one of the factors that led eventually to the BBC management, under John Birt, keeping a far tighter editorial control.

At the time, however, it was Leon Brittan who suffered. Mrs Thatcher saw the way he had attempted to control the BBC's editorial policy as a mistake, and it was one of the reasons he was demoted in the next cabinet reshuffle, in September 1985. He was switched from the Home Office to the Department of Trade and Industry, a post he was soon forced to leave after one of the defining moments of Mrs Thatcher's time in office. From small beginnings, it turned into a vicious public fight, which led to the resignation of two cabinet ministers and threatened Mrs Thatcher herself. One could argue that it lit the long fuse which eventually destroyed her career. It was called the Westland Affair.

The whole sweep of recent Conservative Party history can easily be seen in terms of one proposition: they failed to get to grips with Europe. Another way of putting it is that Europe was the fault line which ran through the Conservative Party and made earthquakes inevitable. Whatever their leadership attempted, they were brought up against forces outside their control, pulling the party apart. On the issue of Europe, there was never a safe place for their leaders to stand. This was the position that Mrs Thatcher found herself in, and John Major later fared even worse. The Westland Affair was the first of the earthquakes.

It was also the first major political story in my career which could not be almost entirely conducted from the BBC office at Westminster; it soon spilled over into my life at home. Mary would come back from the telephone, looking rather surprised. 'It's Michael Heseltine.' On other occasions it might be the Department of Trade and Industry, or indeed Number Ten. For weeks, often to the mystification of millions of our viewers and listeners, the Westland Affair took centre stage.

Even in retrospect, it is hard to see how this relatively minor issue of defence procurement should have grown to threaten the government. The initial problem is easily stated: Westland was the only British helicopter firm; should it link up with American or European partners? It is only when the personalities are brought in that the real problem emerges. Mrs Thatcher was on the side of the American solution; her defence secretary and potential rival for the leadership, Michael Heseltine, favoured a European deal; caught in the middle was the new trade secretary, Leon Brittan, desperately keen to please Mrs Thatcher.

Other characters, too, became vital players in the drama; among them Bernard Ingham, Mrs Thatcher's press secretary throughout her time at Number Ten, and the solicitor general, Sir Patrick Mayhew, later to become Northern Ireland secretary. Sir Patrick was persuaded to write a letter suggesting there were 'material inaccuracies' in a statement from Mr Heseltine claiming that all relevant European governments would withdraw business from Westland if it didn't remain in European hands. An official at the Department of Trade and Industry, with the backing of Downing Street, leaked the most damning parts of the letter to the Press Association news agency. Mrs Thatcher, with help from Leon Brittan and

Bernard Ingham, was immediately suspected of authorizing this extraordinary breach of government security in order to get back at Mr Heseltine. She always denied being responsible, but there is no doubt that she wanted Sir Patrick's critical remarks made public as soon as possible, and an internal government inquiry concluded that the civil servants involved had acted in good faith.

When the cabinet met three days later the defence secretary took his fateful decision. The cabinet had just been told that all future ministerial statements on Westland would have to be cleared with the Cabinet Office. Mr Heseltine said quietly that he could not accept that decision and that he must therefore leave the cabinet. He walked out of the door of Number Ten, catching the BBC cameraman by surprise. There was no correspondent present, but Mr Heseltine did not want to be interviewed. He simply announced his resignation and then set off for what I later described as the longest walk of his life, out of office, down the road and across Whitehall to the Ministry of Defence. He never again worked with Mrs Thatcher, though he did eventually precipitate her downfall.

As often happens in the aftermath of a political disaster, someone had to take the blame. The hapless Leon Brittan, who proved to be the weakest link in presenting the government's position, was forced to resign after pressure from Conservative MPs, some of it in appallingly bad taste. One leading Tory called for a red-necked Englishman to take over the Department of Trade and Industry, an obvious reference to the fact that Mr Brittan is Jewish. His resignation did not end his life in politics – he went on later to become a distinguished member of the European Commission – but his career at Westminster was over.

The Westland Affair taught me how important journalists can be when politicians fall out. We can do more than simply alert the public to the battles taking place; we can suggest who is winning and who may have to take the blame. Politicians cannot wait for history to decide, they have to win with the tools at hand, and that often means capturing the media agenda. For the Labour leader, Neil Kinnock, the Tories' problems should have been an open goal. When he failed to score against Mrs Thatcher in the final debate it damaged him greatly. For the public, much of the detail of the Westland Affair may have been far too complicated, but when the smoke cleared one thing was obvious: Mrs Thatcher had not been defeated. It added to the image she fostered, of being the strongest man in the cabinet.

For the prime minister the key objectives were to escape blame and to protect those officials, like Bernard Ingham, who had been loyal to her. For Mr Heseltine and Mr Brittan contacts with journalists were not enough, although they might have been forced out earlier without them. At the centre of it all was Bernard Ingham, controlling information and even saying which cabinet minister should appear on which programme. After the Westland Affair, if anything his power seemed to increase. But it demonstrated yet again how much the power of officials stems directly from the minister who carries the can. Bernard Ingham, like other Downing Street press secretaries, depended totally on the patronage of the prime minister.

It was an American journalist who invented the term spin doctor to describe those, like Bernard Ingham, who put a favourable gloss on the facts to benefit their political masters. Mr Ingham resented the term, believing it implied that he lied and twisted the facts; and certainly the most cynical type of spin doctor could not survive in that job. Success as a Number Ten press secretary depends on being close to the prime minister. If press secretaries are caught lying or twisting the truth then the prime minister may suffer, and the official spokesmen will lose their authority. Their greatest strength lies in their ability to brief senior journalists, sometimes in private as well as during the regular meetings of the lobby correspondents, and their prime role is to handle information in such a way that the government will more often than not win the vital battle for the agenda.

Sometimes, as was obvious during the Westland Affair, it is not possible for Downing Street to keep control of the main political story of the day. Michael Heseltine and other key players were in direct contact with journalists, giving their accounts of what was happening. Those sources were carefully protected at the time, but Number Ten was well aware of what was happening. There were also limits to the extent to which Mr Ingham could control which ministers appeared on the various news programmes. For the political journalists these are the most testing moments, when the machine is breaking down, or in the jargon of the trade 'when bodies start falling out of the windows'. The adrenalin flows; the excitement is palpable.

It is wrong to think, as many people seem to, of the Westminster lobby journalists as a supine lot, anxious not to bite the hand that feeds them. If a story is running strongly, there is little the government can do except mount diversions by giving journalists other stories to work on, and try to put the best possible gloss on what ministers are doing. Ministers should do nothing to give the damaging story any extra momentum, and press secretaries should be careful about describing the mood of the prime minister. Some of the funniest moments in the lobby briefings at Number Ten were when Bernard Ingham complained that we were describing Mrs Thatcher as angry about something. Very angrily, he would say she was not angry.

Ministers at the time bitterly criticized Mr Ingham for the way he savaged their careers. There were two well-known examples. He once compared Francis Pym with Mona Lott, the character in a wartime radio comedy programme who was always moaning. This marked the beginning of Mr Pym's fall from grace. The other victim was John Biffen who, as leader of the House of Commons, angered Mrs Thatcher by his public comment that the government should concern itself more with consolidation, not radical change. Mr Ingham told a lobby briefing that Mr Biffen was 'semi-detached'. At the next cabinet reshuffle, Mr Biffen was out. On each of these occasions, of course, Mrs Thatcher's press secretary was faithfully transmitting her view; that was very much his skill. There were often times when he gave her view, even though he had not had a specific discussion with her about the matter in hand. He even had an uncanny way of sounding like her when he talked. But unlike Alastair Campbell, Tony Blair's press secretary whom in many ways he resembles, Mr Ingham clung to his status as a civil servant and head of the government's information service. He had not known Mrs Thatcher before she arrived at Number Ten. She had simply asked for the best press secretary in Whitehall and he was recommended. At one stage the gruff right-wing Yorkshireman had worked happily with Tony Benn when he was a Labour minister. He was in many ways a deeply committed civil servant, although he started his career as a journalist. It was during his eleven years with Mrs Thatcher that he became a political operator; and it was only after retiring, soon after she resigned, that his political views became widely known.

The lobby journalists usually have the best opportunity of getting to know the prime minister and the Downing Street press secretary on trips abroad, and no trip was more illuminating for me than Mrs Thatcher's visit to the Soviet Union just before she announced the general election of June 1987. It was a pivotal moment in relations between the Soviet Union and the West. Mikhail Gorbachev had driven through an astonishing programme of reform since becoming Soviet leader two years previously, and at a recent summit at Reykjavik with the American president, Ronald Reagan, he had even suggested the elimination of all strategic nuclear weapons within ten years. The key question facing all Western governments was whether Mr Gorbachev was really going to bring radical change or had he simply devised new ways of dressing up an old discredited system. If anyone had suggested that within a few years we would see the break-up of the Soviet Union and the introduction of democratic elections they would have been dismissed as absurd.

As we gathered at Heathrow on Saturday, 28 March 1987, for the flight on an RAF VC-10 to Moscow there was still very much a cold war atmosphere between the two countries. It was the first visit by a British prime minister to the Soviet Union for more than twelve years and the Russians even thought it might be cancelled at the last minute after what they regarded as a hard-line speech by Mrs Thatcher the week before. She was not at all anxious to lose the Iron Lady sobriquet, which the Russians had bestowed on her before Mr Gorbachev came to power, and relished the idea that one of her roles was to put 'backbone' into the American president, when it came to dealing with the Soviet Union. She was also totally committed to the retention of nuclear weapons. But she was also highly intrigued by the reformer Mikhail Gorbachev and made much of the fact that after their first meeting, some years before, she had announced that he was a man she could do business with. For weeks she had been preparing for this visit, being briefed by the most senior advisers on the Soviet Union.

The group of about twenty journalists were installed in the back of the plane. Conditions were fairly cramped, but we knew that RAF hospitality was of a high standard and soon after take-off we were assured by Bernard Ingham that we could look forward to our dinner undisturbed. Proper crockery plates, not the usual airline plastic, were laid out and the main course arrived. At this moment, right behind me, Mrs Thatcher appeared. I was taken by surprise and without thinking stood up. Plates, glasses and food shot on to the floor. 'Oh, that's all right,' she cooed in her most motherly manner. 'You stay where you are.' She then proceeded to clear up the mess, before stewards rushed to her aid. As I looked down on the prime minister I thought to myself, 'This really isn't my day.' But I think Mrs Thatcher rather enjoyed the incident. She liked to give the impression that we were all incompetent men and only she could sort us out. As she rose from the floor I managed to push a microphone under her chin and, somewhat to her surprise, launched into a long radio interview about the Soviet Union. My colleagues in the lobby were kind enough not to interrupt; and the interview only ended when she rather delicately put her hand over the microphone. But by then I had Mrs Thatcher at her best, fluent and interesting, unloading herself of all that detailed briefing, but doing so in a way that was easily understood. It was the best interview she ever gave me.

Later in the flight there was a bizarre incident when Mrs Thatcher once again came to the back of the plane. In tow was the foreign secretary, Sir Geoffrey Howe, literally so. She pulled him down the gangway between the seats, her hand gripping his casual sweater. 'Look at Geoffrey's new jumper,' she told us with almost schoolgirl delight. Sir Geoffrey gave no impression of being disconcerted, but in a few years' time he would get his own back for this and other humiliations. For many people it was his resignation speech in the House of Commons which led to her downfall.

Later in the four-day visit, I found myself on the receiving end of her sharp tongue. Looking glamorous in her fox fur Russian hat, she swept around a Moscow housing estate, shaking hands and behaving as if she was running for office. At the top of an apartment block I had the gall to suggest that she was electioneering – after all the election in Britain could not be far off. 'I am,' she snapped, 'simply doing my duty.' She implied that I certainly was not, and for a moment I thought she might push me down the steps of the tower block. Looking back on this incident some weeks later, when she announced that the election would be held in June, I had a burst of satisfaction. Her visit to Moscow naturally featured in the Conservative election broadcasts.

The most interesting aspect of the trip was the extent to which she and President Gorbachev clearly got on well. When we went to the Bolshoi Theatre for a performance of *Swan Lake* the interval appeared to go on for ages. After what seemed like half an hour the two leaders had still not returned to their box and the performance was further delayed. She later told me that among the subjects they were discussing was Mrs Thatcher's insistence that what the Soviet Union needed was to establish the rule of law; otherwise legally binding contracts and Western-style business were impossible. If only the Russian leadership had been able to take her advice.

The trip ended with a brief diversion. We flew from Moscow far south to the Soviet state of Georgia, which is now an independent country. Outside the capital, Tbilisi, around two million people had taken time off work to line the roads from the airport. It was an amazing demonstration of Mrs Thatcher's popularity. She was a star, not least because she was the world's most prominent woman; almost everyone knew who she was.

One of her most effective performances on the trip was in a television discussion with Russian journalists about nuclear weapons. She lectured and argued with them in a way they had never encountered before. When we had taken off from Tbilisi and were on the way home, I was hoping to have a chat, but she looked as if she might walk past me. 'Prime

Minister,' I said, 'can I just say how good you were in that television interview?' The incident in the apartment block might never have happened.

'Oh, do you think so,' she purred, and granted me ten minutes of her time. Even the Iron Lady couldn't resist a little flattery.

22

The highs and lows of Thatcherism

FOR ME, THE HIGHLIGHT of the 1987 election campaign was when Mrs Thatcher defended her decision not to use the National Health Service. At a news conference in Conservative central office, she told us with great conviction that she used private health care so that she could go into hospital 'on the day I want and with the doctor I want . . . I exercise my right as a free citizen to spend my own money in my own way.' The wise heads of the lobby concluded that she had made a serious mistake. It was, in Westminster parlance, a gaffe. Ironically, at that particular moment, her statement was also misleading. She was suffering badly from an abscess under a tooth, and she could not have it treated properly by her private dentist, on the day she wanted, because she was in the middle of an election campaign. It was not made public, but she had to rely on aspirin to dull the pain.

The commentators generally agreed that those who had to rely on the National Health Service would not be impressed by her determination to use private medical care. The controversy rattled her advisers, who were already worried by an opinion poll showing the Tory lead cut sharply to only 4 per cent ahead of Labour. The day became known as Wobbly Thursday. Later, even Mrs Thatcher admitted that there had been an atmosphere behind the scenes of near panic, with frenzied discussions about the Conservative advertising campaign and indeed about their whole election strategy. But there was no crisis. Public opinion reacted calmly to Mrs Thatcher's commitment to private medicine; most people were not surprised by her comments. The next opinion poll put the Tories well ahead, as they had been throughout the campaign, and in the end they won with a majority of 102 seats over all the other parties. Mrs Thatcher became the first leader since Lord Liverpool in the 1820s to win three elections in a row; looking back, her victory was the high point of Thatcherism.

The 1987 election was the first in which I was concerned solely with television coverage. I was responsible for all the election coverage on the lunchtime television news. This involved, at one stage, working with four different producers and we had to work hard to sort out all the material from the morning news conferences. At the end, though, I could not help but reflect that, despite all the drama, the result of the election was pretty much as we had expected at the beginning of the campaign. Not for the first time, I concluded that the power of the media to influence the outcome is often exaggerated.

The non-crisis over private medical care gave me cause to reflect on how we, as a family, tackled these problems. During my time at the BBC we did not subscribe to a private medical scheme; but, after much wrestling with doubts in the early days, we did send our children to private schools. I sympathize with all parents who find this a difficult decision. For many there is no choice because private schooling is simply too expensive, but we decided that if we reduced unnecessary expenditure and spent our holidays in Britain, we could afford to pay the bills. Our two sons started in a state school, North Ealing Primary, but then went to a prep school, Durston House, in the road in which we lived, and then on to Westminster School, conveniently close to my work.

One of our main concerns was that they would both go to the same school. William was accepted at Westminster and we were inordinately proud of his achievement. The pressure was on Michael to do the same. We need not have worried. Preparing for the interview, when he was ten years old, I warned him that they might refer to my job. When he came out, I was waiting in the courtyard and we made our way back to the tube. 'Well, did they ask you about politics?' I asked. 'Yes,' he replied, 'they wanted to know if I was interested in politics and I said, no, but I have read *Animal Farm*.' George Orwell's satire on communism was one of the books he had been told to read at school. He had skilfully managed to switch the conversation on to a subject he had prepared. His father, who had grave doubts about whether children of his age should be subjected to tests of this kind, heaved a great sigh of relief. Michael went on to become joint head boy of the school.

Mrs Thatcher's triumph in the 1987 election left the other parties desperately searching for rejuvenation and reform. Neil Kinnock had done well enough in the campaign, with considerable help from Peter Mandelson, to justify his continuation as Labour leader, but there would have to be more changes in policy and organization before they could give themselves a serious chance of winning. The Liberals and the Social Democrat Party, who had fought as the Alliance under David Steel and David Owen, would have to make a final attempt to solve their differences. Britain's electoral system does not favour multi-party politics, but David Owen found it impossible to accept the merger idea, a problem many people put down to the size of his ego. The real reason, I believe, was personal in a different way: he could not see himself as the successful leader of a merged party. His latent Tory sympathies led him eventually to back John Major for prime minister and if he had become the third party leader he would have found himself permanently at odds with most of his party members.

In January 1988 David Steel was about to make the biggest mistake of his career. He was negotiating with Robert

Maclennan, the less than charismatic leader of the Social Democrats who had taken over from David Owen when the party agreed to merge with the Liberals. It was five in the morning and I had been waiting all night with a television crew at the bottom of the main staircase at the headquarters of the SDP at Westminster. We were the only journalists present and, in our own way, we contributed to the debacle. At that time in the morning, the negotiators should have been able to slip away without being noticed, but they had to get past us, and they decided to come down the stairs and announce an agreement. Instead of this simply being a mixture of the policies the two parties could agree on, they had mistakenly decided the merged party should have a fresh programme. There were a number of ideas, such as abolishing mortgage interest tax relief, which neither of the two parties had agreed beforehand. When I broadcast the details on BBC radio and television news programmes that morning, opposition on both sides grew rapidly and the planned news conference to launch the merger, due to be held a few hours later, had to be cancelled. The only way out was for the document to be disowned by David Steel and the others involved. He likened it to the dead parrot in the *Monty Python* sketch and from then on it was known as 'the dead parrot document'. But it killed David Steel's career as well. When the parties did agree on terms for the merger later that year, Mr Steel decided not to try for the leadership, and Paddy Ashdown became the first leader of what eventually became known as the Liberal Democrats.

During the 1980s, the activities of the Gang of Four, then the SDP and finally the Alliance were given an enormous amount of coverage. Much of it demonstrated sharp differences in personalities and policies. It is a mistake to think that smaller parties are cosier and more homogeneous. Their politics often seem quite the opposite, vicious and small-minded. I was frequently puzzled by the way leading members would be prepared to make statements which could only have a damaging effect on their party's unity. To our delight and the parties' discomfort, they could not resist basking in the limelight. The fact that it put them further and further away from real power seemed a secondary consideration. After the 1987 election, the Liberals had only seventeen MPs; the SDP had five.

In the spring of 1988 my career at Westminster began to take off. In the BBC there can be long periods when there are almost no changes among the senior personnel then, with the suddenness of an avalanche in the Alps, the scene suddenly changes. It was the arrival of John Birt as deputy director general, just before the election, which triggered the changes, but they took some time to have an effect. He appointed Ian Hargreaves head of news. Like John Birt he had a cold analytical approach, which could be very unnerving. All the political correspondents were interviewed by him for half an hour and at the end of the process, apart from John Cole, I was the only member of the old guard who would stay on; all those who had signed the original round robin against me were told they would be moved on or moved out. It was the biggest bloodbath of correspondents in the whole of my time at the BBC. The new management had decided that my colleagues were simply not up to the job. It was as if a thunderbolt had struck, and somehow, to my great relief, I had been spared.

But my problems were not over. Among those who were brought in to cover politics at Westminster was John Harrison, who had worked there some years earlier. He had done particularly well when the IRA almost succeeded in blowing up Mrs Thatcher and half the cabinet during the Conservative Party conference in Brighton in 1984. I had not covered myself in glory that night, having gone to bed early with a streaming cold, hardly able to speak. I was staying in the Old Ship Hotel, not far from the Grand, where the bomb went off. But I slept on undisturbed. John Harrison was one of the correspondents who had shared an award for the BBC coverage. That was the start of our long rivalry.

We were very different as personalities: he had built up his career as a political correspondent on the *Daily Mail*; I was less keen to rush about and liked to think I was more thoughtful. The BBC management could not decide whose style they really liked and the interview boards for the two posts – chief political correspondents for television and radio – were dead-locked. After ten days of dithering, Ian Hargreaves telephoned me at home at eight o'clock in the morning. They had decided to appoint both of us to the post of chief political correspon-dent, taking it in turn to do television and radio; we would change over every six months. It was a recipe for war between us, which only one of us could win, but both John and I tried hard to keep the temperature down. It is never good politics in the BBC to engage in open combat with colleagues.

In January 1989 it was my turn to take over the television coverage and I was immediately involved in a strange visit to Moscow, which resulted in the Labour Party ditching its policy of unilateral nuclear disarmament. Of course, the tortuous process by which this unpopular policy was dropped took far longer than the three days we were in Moscow, but the visit enabled the Labour leadership to put the idea firmly in the public domain, and after that there was no going back.

Two of the key figures in the Labour delegation were the shadow foreign secretary, Gerald Kaufman, and Peter Mandelson, whose reputation as the power behind Neil Kin-nock's throne was already well established. Mr Mandelson had worked hard to build up the impression that Labour's defence policy was changing, despite conflicting comments made by his leader since the election. Senior Labour sources, otherwise known as Mr Mandelson, had featured in my preview of the Moscow visit, stressing that Labour's fresh approach would be tried out on the Russians.

It was an extraordinary trick to try to pull off. The Russians were not very interested in talking about the party's defence policy while Labour was still in opposition but, when pressed, one of the experts I interviewed on the Russian side made clear that a British unilateral move would confuse rather than assist disarmament negotiations. This helped to provide the vital cover sought by Mr Kaufman and Mr Mandelson. Speaking to a group of journalists in Red Square, the shadow foreign secretary suggested that the Russians would prefer a Labour government to adopt a multilateral approach to nuclear disarmament. The implication was obvious: if the Russians were not impressed by unilateral nuclear disarmament, why should the party continue to back the idea? At the Labour conference later that year the historic shift on nuclear policy was confirmed. One more part of the drive to make a Labour victory possible was in place.

Our visit to Moscow had been highly useful to the Labour leadership and I suppose it raises the question: were we used by them to help change their policy? The answer is certainly yes, but I think that was unavoidable. Modern political reporting cannot confine itself to a description of simple facts. Increasingly it has to deal with the shifting sands of policy formulation. It would be a dull kind of political journalist who tried to stay aloof from the arguments behind the scenes just at the point when they were having a crucial effect. Journalists inevitably play an important role in deciding what and how certain issues are raised. It is up to politicians to guess what questions we are likely to ask, and whether giving an answer would be in their best interest. Sometimes they have little choice.

When George Bush Senior, recently elected American president, paid his first visit to Mrs Thatcher in June 1989, I was phoned at home and told to go to Downing Street to ask them a question after their talks had finished. I was not briefed on what the question might be, but fell back on my usual practice of trying to think up the most difficult question to ask in the politest way possible. When I arrived at Downing Street I was irritated to be told to stand in a group, penned in by crowd barriers, with correspondents from ITN and Sky News. We were like prisoners in a dock, stuck in the middle of the street with the two leaders standing some distance away. To make matters worse, several hundred members of the two countries' official delegations were squashed into the end of Downing Street to watch the event. The whole scene was transmitted live to the television newsrooms. The arrangements were probably not designed to intimidate but they certainly had a disturbing effect, and I was all the more determined that the two leaders should not be given an easy time.

As the senior correspondent it was agreed that I should have the first question. 'I would like to ask the president a question,' I started.

'Don't you want to ask me?' Mrs Thatcher interrupted, sensing correctly that a question to her visitor might be more dangerous.

'You can both answer, if you like,' I replied, pleased to have the initiative. 'This is the question: is Britain still America's most important ally in Europe?'

Everyone in Downing Street knew that in the political climate of the time the truthful answer was no; Germany was America's most important European ally. Communism would soon collapse and the Germans were at the centre of a complicated argument with the Russians over disarmament. Mrs Thatcher moved towards me as if she was physically trying to shield President Bush from the question. She obviously feared he might say no. In an ungainly way he tried to move towards me as well. After what seemed like an age, he managed to say that Britain and the United States were 'partners in leadership'. Unfortunately, this was exactly what he had said the week before on a visit to West Germany, describing that country's relationship with the United States; and it was not what Mrs Thatcher wanted to hear.

In her memoirs, she admits that she was highly concerned at the time that the close cooperation she had established with President Reagan was now being put on ice by Mr Bush; that he was much more concerned about relations with Germany. Reading that added to the satisfaction I felt at the time. To go by tube to Westminster, to disconcert the prime minister and the American president, and then return quietly to Ealing must rate as one of my happiest experiences in journalism. For Mrs Thatcher it was just one more example of how, in her last period in office, she was endlessly dogged by the problems of European politics. In the same year it would lead her into sharp disagreement with the most senior members of her cabinet: the foreign secretary, Sir Geoffrey Howe, who was demoted to leader of the House of Commons, and the chancellor, Nigel Lawson, who was forced to resign. For her it was the beginning of the end.

Apparently, the final blow for Mr Lawson was that she insisted on bringing back one of her trusted advisers who had been working in America, Sir Alan Walters. But in reality it was nothing to do with that; the chancellor had fallen out with the prime minister over Europe, as had Sir Geoffrey Howe. The issue, which it was said later should be engraved on her heart, was formally called the exchange rate mechanism of the European Monetary System, but for ever afterwards was known as the ERM. The government had said that Britain would formally link the pound with the other European currencies in the system 'when the time was right'. Sir Geoffrey Howe and Nigel Lawson were both convinced that the time had come. For a period of about a year, Mr Lawson tried to achieve entry by stealth, tying the value of the pound to the German currency; that was until Mrs Thatcher insisted that there was no question of the pound shadowing the Deutsch-mark. It was an extraordinary dispute, right at the heart of government, and one that was bound to end in tears.

On the day that Mr Lawson resigned in October 1989, I had lunch with the new foreign secretary, John Major. He had only been in the job for a few months and had just arrived back from a bruising encounter with journalists at the Commonwealth conference in Kuala Lumpur. He was clearly taken aback to learn the extent to which he was now regarded as fair game by the media circus. All his politeness and affability, which had taken him so far in the Conservative Party, was of limited use in preventing unflattering stories suggesting he was out of his depth. At the end of the meal, he asked me what my advice would be. It was not a question I expected from a foreign secretary. 'Be brave,' I muttered rather unconvincingly. When we said goodbye, neither of us had an inkling of the dramatic events which were about to unfold.

At six o'clock that evening I was sitting in the BBC television studio at Westminster with a telephone clamped to my ear. The editor of the news programme was watching me intently on a monitor at Television Centre. 'When he puts the phone down,' he said to one of his assistants, 'we'll go straight to John.' Luckily, when the call was over, I had Nigel Lawson's resignation statement and was able to explain the background to his departure. I was also able to confirm that the new chancellor would be John Major. From then on, over the following months, there took place a series of events which later seemed like stepping stones, leading inevitably to my dramatic encounter with Mrs Thatcher outside the Paris embassy. Much of this ground has been well covered by others, but here are a few steps on the way.

I was keen to do a radio interview with Michael Heseltine as he was desperately concerned to appear loyal to Mrs Thatcher, while at the same time devoting all his energies to undermining her. He had agreed to do the interview on the basis that it would be an attack on the Labour Party. 'If you attack the prime minister,' I said sternly, 'I am afraid I will have to switch off the tape recorder.' He roared with laughter and it completely broke the ice between us. From then on he was one of my most useful contacts.

When the result of the leadership election that autumn was announced, Sir Anthony Meyer only received thirty-three votes from Tory MPs and there were about the same number of abstentions. But both John Cole and I considered that this was 'a shot across the prime minister's bows'. The only trouble was that we said this in reports which followed each other on the nine o'clock news. The next day the editor of the programme said rather sardonically, 'Well, at least you both took the same line.'

There were two more resignations from the cabinet before Mrs Thatcher's demise. The next to go was the trade secretary, Nicholas Ridley, in the summer of 1990; he had been one of her most faithful supporters in the government. I once interviewed him on the advantages of her most unpopular policy, the poll tax, and the lights in the studio went off. In the darkness I encouraged him to continue because, as I reminded him, this was a radio interview. Amazingly he did so. But even his loyalty was insufficient protection when the *Spectator* published his private view that the Germans were intent on taking over Europe, which he phrased without any attempt at diplomacy. I was brought in early by the *Today* programme to deliver a damning verdict on his remarks to the *Spectator*, which had been leaked to us the night before. Two days later he resigned.

The last resignation was surprisingly the most spectacular. For years Sir Geoffrey Howe had been the picture of discretion, difficult at times to listen to because he did not raise his voice; but in his resignation speech he burst into life. The impact was greatly increased because television cameras had, at last, been allowed into the Commons. In my report on the six o'clock news I spent nearly seven minutes describing his carefully crafted indictment. He denounced Mrs Thatcher, particularly, for isolating Britain at the European summit in Rome and he ended by suggesting that this was a time 'for others to consider their own response to the tragic conflict of loyalties with which I have myself wrestled for perhaps too long'. Michael Heseltine needed no more encouragement.

23

After the fall

FOR A POLITICAL JOURNALIST, feeling sorry for a prime minister is a strange emotion, not something to be encouraged if your job depends on keeping an objective eye on the political scene. John Major would be annoyed to discover that quite often I did indeed feel sorry for him. Being prime minister puts you at the top of the Westminster tree and the rest, even sceptical journalists, should look up to you with a certain amount of awe. His problem was that he was not Margaret Thatcher; but anyone following such a dominant figure would have been an anticlimax. On many occasions he seemed out of place, even out of his depth, particularly at the beginning of his time at Number Ten, and it is hard to resist the idea that for Mrs Thatcher this made him the perfect successor. It was certainly her intervention which proved decisive in the leadership election following her downfall.

There was little that Michael Heseltine could do to over-come one of the inexorable laws of politics, that he who wields the dagger cannot inherit the crown. The hatred the true Thatcherites felt for the person they accused of regicide is difficult to exaggerate, and Douglas Hurd, the third contender, had a disastrous campaign, summed up in the excruciating scene when he tried to appear relaxed by wearing a cardigan. Cynics fell back on an old Westminster joke: 'If Douglas Hurd is the answer, what was the question?'

'Nice' was how most Tory MPs described John Major. He had impeccable manners, an ability to listen, and in the jungle of egos which normally surrounds the cabinet table, he was able to appear modest and sincere. It was only later that some of his less desirable qualities became known, including moodiness, a sharp temper and a thin skin under criticism. He was, to my mind, far too concerned about what journalists thought of him, and he was too conscious of the fact that, as he put it later, he had not been properly educated, having left school at sixteen.

One of his earliest moves was to bring Mr Heseltine back as environment secretary, with the task of replacing the hated poll tax. The longest walk in politics had eventually led him back to cabinet meetings in Downing Street, but it had taken nearly five years; and it took him even longer to regain his old sense of belonging. At the Conservative Party conference in 1991 he told me after his successful comeback speech that a handful of protestors could have destroyed the occasion. 'All they had to do,' he said, 'was to unfurl a banner from the balcony, saying "Traitor", and I would not have been able to go on.'

My relationship with Michael Heseltine was helped by a running joke, which he pursued up until the time that he left office as deputy prime minister. When things were particularly bad, and that was quite often during this period of Conservative rule, he would sometimes say to me, without a hint of irony, that it had been 'another triumph'. It was impossible for anyone to accuse him of disloyalty, and there was something marvellously inappropriate about this phrase. I remember him coming out of Number Ten, after a cabinet meeting and mouthing to me, 'another triumph', to the complete puzzlement of the other journalists. To me, it meant things really were as bad as they seemed.

I was concerned, to start with, that relations with John Major would be difficult; he was slow to grasp how we needed him to add interest and depth to our news programmes. His

first trip abroad was to Italy to try to repair some of the damage
Mrs Thatcher had inflicted on Britain's relations with Europe
at the first Rome summit. She proudly summed up her own
position with the ringing declaration 'No, no, no' but her
isolation at that summit on the single currency and other
matters was for many of her opponents the last straw. At
the second Rome summit, little more than a month later, all
John Major had to do, in the atmosphere of relief which
greeted his appointment, was to say the equivalent of 'Maybe,
maybe, maybe'.

After his first meeting with the other European leaders
I was anxious to 'doorstep him'. This is the usual term for a
brief interview, sometimes with only one question. I was
gratified to see that he had received my request and was pacing
up and down preparing what he was going to say. So it was
all the more disappointing when he came out and all he could
manage was, 'It's been a very interesting morning.' It was
some time before John Major grasped the importance of a
pithy sound bite; and some of his early speeches were equally
uninspiring.

But it was not only the other European leaders who were
relieved to see the departure of Mrs Thatcher. Mr Major's
appointment was popular with the public, and of deep concern
to Labour. When he reported to the House of Commons after
the summit, I used a split screen technique to demonstrate his
different approach to Europe. On one side of the screen Mrs
Thatcher was seen rejecting proposals out of hand, which she
saw as moves towards a federal Europe; this faded to reveal Mr
Major on the other side of the screen giving a much more
polite response to the same proposals.

I thought it was an effective way of making the point on
television, but Labour were furious. At their Christmas party
for the media, the head of Neil Kinnock's office, Charles
Clarke, who became a minister under Tony Blair, angrily

insisted that I should have compared Mr Major with Mr Kinnock. I explained that the public wanted to know how the government had changed. But it was obvious why Mr Kinnock's aides were so annoyed: if Mr Major represented change, would the electorate be so keen to vote for the change represented by Mr Kinnock? At the next election we would find out how right Labour were to be worried.

Mr Major needed to gain authority, and it was fortunate for him that within weeks of taking office, this unwarlike man was taking the country to war, with the total support of the leaders of the other main parties. The die had been cast the summer before, when Saddam Hussein of Iraq had invaded Kuwait. In the intervening months a powerful force with a strong British contingent had been assembled by a Western coalition led by the United States, and it was now ready to drive the Iraqi forces out of Kuwait. When the Gulf War ended with a ceasefire, I was one of the journalists who expressed concern to Mr Major about the continuance in office of Saddam Hussein. In an interview with me, the prime minister suggested that internal forces would finish off Saddam, but this turned out to be a serious miscalculation. Long after Margaret Thatcher, the American president George Bush Senior, and John Major had left office, Saddam Hussein was still the undisputed dictator of Iraq.

Not much more than a year after the end of the Gulf War, the prime minister had to call an election, even though the opinion polls were not favourable. The government was running out of time; by the summer of 1992 parliament's five-year term would be up. For broadcasters too, there are important decisions connected with an election which can have a devastating effect on individual careers. Towards the end of 1991 the BBC decided we should go on election alert and this brought to a head the uneasy relationship between John Harrison and me. Although we were both called chief political correspondent, only one of us could expect to be involved in television coverage during the election; the other would be assigned to radio. With the backing of David Aaronovitch, then my line manager at Westminster, it was decided that I had won the battle; John Harrison would be going to radio. He was devastated. He could not accept the decision, and decided to apply for the post of South Africa correspondent, which had fallen vacant. Eighteen months later, while serving in South Africa, he was killed in a car crash. It was a terrible tragedy, made all the more poignant for me because we had been locked in such close rivalry for several years. For the rest of my time in the BBC, I was the sole chief political correspondent, working on both radio and television.

John Major surprised many of us, including myself, by winning the election, if only with a tiny majority. It was a success made all the sweeter for him because most people at Westminster believed Mrs Thatcher would have failed. Neil Kinnock took the blame; it seemed the electorate did not believe he was up to the job. In retrospect, harsher judgements could have been made of Labour's treasury spokesman, John Smith, whose shadow budget published a few weeks before the election promised to increase income tax, enabling the Tories to scare voters with Labour's tax bombshell. But politics does not always work in straight lines; Mr Smith succeeded Mr Kinnock and, before his early death, became one of the most popular Labour leaders in recent years.

Soon after the election, my own career faltered. John Cole retired as political editor and there was a struggle for succession. Elinor Goodman, the political editor of ITN's *Channel 4 News*, and I were shortlisted, but Robin Oakley, the political editor of *The Times*, was appointed. I had a bitterly disappointing interview in which the BBC's director general, John Birt, and two other senior managers gave the impression that my long service with the BBC was not necessarily an advantage. Looking back, there was only one moment of grim comedy when I suggested, in answer to a question about a possible new privacy law, that both Prince Charles and Princess Diana might be using their contacts with the media to further the arguments between them. John Birt gave me a withering look and said, 'And what evidence have you got for that?' As the months went by, and the suggestion I had made became a known fact, I could not help but remember John Birt's response that day. We never really got on.

Mr Birt's skill was in giving the impression to politicians of all the main parties that he was certainly not against them, and might even be counted on their side. Given that the BBC's continuing survival ultimately depends on the goodwill of politicians, his career as director general must be judged a success, but like many people in the BBC, I was disappointed by his lack of warmth and leadership skills. The great joy of spending so much of my career in the BBC was the high quality of the people and their enormous commitment to making programmes. In all sorts of ways, not least in his insistence that senior managers should be paid so much more than the rest of us, he became a kind of alien force, far removed from what I thought of as the true spirit of the BBC. He often gave the impression that it was the managers, and not the creative staff, who really mattered; but then senior managers would grumble that he did not think much of them either.

Robin Oakley and I settled down as best we could. It was never an easy relationship, although he was a thoughtful kind professional, with long experience at Westminster. My colleagues realized, of course, that potentially our relationship was explosive and there was general delight when the story went round of how I responded to Robin's first major broadcasting disaster. He dried up on air. 'We've all nearly done that,' I was widely reported to have told him. Unfortunately, this became the defining story of our relationship. Mostly,

though, the obvious tension between an experienced broadcaster who had failed to get the job and someone who had
spent their life as a print journalist was kept reasonably in
check. After all the fun and debate provided by John Cole, it
felt a little like the transition from Mrs Thatcher to Mr Major:
life in a lower key.

A fairly strict division of duties eased the problem. He
tended to appear on the *Nine O'Clock News*, while I usually
handled all the main political stories on the *Six O'Clock News*.
At lunchtime, I was happy to concentrate on *The World At
One* on radio, while he looked after television news. The most
difficult problem was in the morning on radio. Robin got very
cross if I appeared on *Today*, and as a result the editorial team
decided that, on most days, neither of us should be on. After
more than twenty years working on the programme, I was
extremely annoyed, but it was essential to maintain peace in
the office. It was not as though either of us was short of
outlets, and the political story was as strong as ever. The idea
that the Major years would be boring was soon shattered, and
as the prime minister's difficulties mounted the beneficial effect
on our business was obvious. In politics it really is an ill wind
that blows nobody any good.

If Mrs Thatcher should have the initials ERM engraved
on her heart, it would not be a bad idea to do the same for
Mr Major. When he was chancellor, Mr Major's greatest
achievement was persuading Mrs Thatcher that Britain should
join the European exchange rate mechanism after ten years of
prevarication. I remember him telling me some weeks before
it happened, in October 1990, that 'the Rubicon has been
crossed'. I reported this on the *Today* programme as the words
of 'a senior minister'; I could not say that it was the chancellor
of the exchequer without breaking a confidence. Two years
later, Mr Major was prime minister and the pound was ejected
from the ERM; it was one of the biggest setbacks suffered by

a British government in peacetime. According to the opinion polls, it was a blow from which Mr Major never recovered, and it paved the way for a massive Labour victory at the next election.

No one has devised a sensible way for a government to handle devaluation, except by taking the decision out of its hands and allowing the pound to find its own value by floating against other currencies. When exchange rates are fixed the government is forced, at times, to defend a weak currency, and when that fails the government's credibility is devalued along with the currency. Six days before what became known as Black Wednesday, Mr Major could not have been more determined to support the pound. I reported his confident assertion to the Scottish CBI: 'The soft option, the devaluers' option, the inflationary option, would be a betrayal of our future.' When that policy stood in ruins the most dangerous development for Mr Major came from within his own party. The Eurosceptics, who had always bitterly opposed ERM entry, were now emboldened to take on the prime minister across the whole range of European policies; the Tory fault line was exposed.

When opponents scent a prime minister on the run, it is difficult for him to recover. In a weakened state, Mr Major made a half-hearted attempt to defend the culture secretary, David Mellor, after the tabloid press had revelled in his antics with an actress, Antonia de Sancha. There was a sharp dis-agreement in the office about whether this was a story the BBC should cover. I successfully argued that the story made him look ridiculous as culture secretary and, if his continuance in government was in doubt, then it certainly was a story. After revelations involving a holiday paid for through friends with Palestinian connections, Mr Mellor reluctantly resigned. The next time we discussed culture was some years later when I joined him to choose classical records on his radio programme on Classic FM. I was once asked, in a BBC promotional film, why I liked reporting at Westminster and I said that one of the joys was that however much careers might come crashing down, no one was killed. David Mellor's fall and rise is a perfect example.

The prime minister was more successful in hanging on to Norman Lamont, who many believe should have resigned as chancellor when Britain was forced out of the ERM. Unlike Mr Mellor, he fulfilled a useful role in helping to take the blame for the debacle. He was the lightning conductor. Had he gone immediately after Black Wednesday, Mr Major would have been more exposed. But the chancellor's reputation had been badly damaged, and his position was not helped when he continued in vain to see 'the green shoots of economic recovery'. Finally, eight months after the crisis, Mr Lamont was sacked. After the announcement, I went to Paris to cover an Anglo-French summit and was surprised how frank Mr Major was prepared to be in a private chat. He said the trouble with Norman Lamont was that nobody now believed him. 'If he says it's Wednesday, people think it's Thursday.' I relayed this comment on the *Nine O'Clock News*, as being from 'a senior government source', and was slightly embarrassed when Mr Lamont complained that he did not know why he had been sacked. I knew only too well. But he got his own back in a blistering attack when he made his 'resignation' speech in the House of Commons. He accused the government of giving the impression of being 'in office, not in power'. It was a fitting epitaph on the Major years.

The appointment of the strongly pro-European Kenneth Clarke as chancellor was another dagger in the heart of the Eurosceptics. Whichever way Mr Major turned, the subject always seemed to come back to Europe. His own views were increasingly difficult to ascertain. He began with a clear declaration, made in Bonn, soon after he became prime minister, that he wanted Britain to be 'at the very heart of Europe'. Later that same year, with considerable skill, he negotiated the Maastricht Treaty without any serious cabinet dissent, after managing to ensure that Britain could opt out of the single currency. He then had the problem, after winning the election, of getting the relevant legislation through the House of Commons. With his tiny majority, this only proved possible with the support of the Liberal Democrats.

In the autumn of 1992, on his chartered plane flying back from Egypt, after celebrating the fiftieth anniversary of the Battle of El Alamein, he gave me a passionate defence of the Maastricht Treaty. After about ten minutes, I said, 'Well, why does anyone think of you as anything but a strong pro-European?'

He looked at me as if I had said something quite shocking. 'But, John,' he said, 'I am the biggest Eurosceptic in the cabinet.' For most of his time in office he was forced to sit on the fence over Europe; and he never found it comfortable.

In the Commons, the dramas over the European bills, the tight votes and the endless complexities were meat and drink for us, but most of the public were bored and bemused. Every now and then a clear picture would emerge, but often only by mistake. The best of these moments came when John Major was celebrating the parliamentary ratification of the Maastricht Treaty in July 1993. In a private chat with the political editor of ITN, Michael Brunson, which became public because their microphones had been inadvertently left on, Mr Major said, 'What I don't understand, Michael, is why a complete wimp like me keeps winning everything.' It was in the course of this conversation that Mr Major notoriously described three of his Eurosceptic opponents within the cabinet as bastards. Like Mrs Thatcher's wets, some Tory MPs adopted the term as a badge of honour, and despite Mr Major's Maastricht victory continued to harass him to the end.

In the autumn of the same year there was speculation that Mr Major's leadership was under threat, and Norman Lamont was forced to deny that he was involved in a plot. Labour were eighteen points ahead, according to an opinion poll. I was one of a group of journalists accompanying Mr Major on a trip to Japan. To my annoyance his remarks on the plane, responding to the Eurosceptics and the possibility of a leadership challenge, were deliberately made off camera. Knowing that this would dominate the coverage of my newspaper colleagues, I insisted on asking Mr Major about this in a doorstep interview at the British embassy in Tokyo. Mr Major was furious, believing that the BBC intended to sabotage news coverage of the trip, and sent his press secretary, Gus O'Donnell, outside to confront me. 'You jerk,' he said, in front of a group of other journalists. I would not normally have made a fuss, but I thought this overstepped the mark and immediately demanded an apology. Being a charming and sensitive man, O'Donnell withdrew the remark, but news of the row quickly reached London. To the delight of some of my colleagues I was asked on *Today* whether it was really true that the prime minister's press secretary had been forced to apologize.

For Mr Major the trip went from bad to worse when more of his private and intemperate remarks about the Eurosceptics leaked out. A tape recorder left on by a journalist recorded him saying that he could hear 'the flapping of white coats' when his 'barmy' Tory critics complained about his leadership. Mr Major's struggle with the Eurosceptics quickly became one of the most telling themes of his period in office. In the summer of 1995 Mr Major decided to bring the matter to a head. He stunned us all by announcing that he would resign and put himself up for re-election as party leader. It was the traditional challenge from a leader to his critics: put up or shut up. He hoped to flush out the 'Barmy Army' and force them to admit that they were not prepared for an open contest.

The prime minister left for a European summit in Cannes. It turned out to be one of my most enjoyable stories. In perfect summer weather, with the beach at Cannes providing one of the most glamorous backdrops in Europe, I could enjoy a great political story without having to worry too much about who or what we would film. The foreign secretary, Douglas Hurd, helped us by walking barefoot across the road after swimming in the Mediterranean; the chancellor, Kenneth Clarke, was appearing with me live on *Today* when I was told over my headphones from London that John Redwood had decided to stand in the leadership contest; and we had plenty of access to the prime minister, who had such a small part in the summit that at one stage a television camera panning along the line of European leaders stopped before reaching him. There was a pause and then the camera moved on to reveal our prime minister. It was both funny and poignant. Even his victory in the leadership contest seemed to have little effect. The impression of a weak leader of a divided party remained.

After Mr Major left office he worried that history would not be kind to him, that he would be seen as an interim leader who held office between Mrs Thatcher and Tony Blair. It is certainly true that with his tiny majority, which eventually disappeared altogether, he could not hope to equal their parliamentary dominance. He was almost always fighting for survival and in his second term had more than his fair share of bad luck. His government had to grapple with the quite unprecedented problems caused by mad cow disease, or BSE. He made a brave start in trying to produce a settlement in Northern Ireland, but it was far from complete when he left office. Above all, he had to cope with the European issue, which even Mrs Thatcher had found impossible. Mr Major was also unfortunate in finding himself up against a formidable opponent. Tony Blair was able to capitalize on all Mr Major's mistakes. After eighteen frustrating years in opposition, Labour were going to seize their chance.

24

The Third Way

WHEN JOHN SMITH DIED in May 1994, the shock was felt throughout Westminster. John Major announced the news to his cabinet colleagues, and one of those present told me that it sent a shiver through the room. The Labour leader was only fifty-five, younger than many members of the cabinet, and in political terms well within his prime. Much to his credit, Mr Major put aside political advantage and led the nation in mourning. Parliament was suspended after tributes had been paid, and some Labour MPs wept openly in public.

But politics never stands still. The death of any senior politician, however tragic, is always the signal for plots and intrigue. Finding someone to take their place can be described as a pair of shoes which cannot be filled, or even as the way ahead the deceased would have prescribed, if only he were here to guide us, but the simple question which faces those working behind the scenes is how quickly plans can be laid without appearing too hasty.

The news of John Smith's death came officially at 10.30 a.m. and very quickly the corridors buzzed with private comment about who might become the new Labour leader. Peter Mandelson had ceased to be the party's director of communications, or chief spin doctor, but he was far more powerful than his formal title of Labour MP for Hartlepool might suggest. He was the unofficial cheerleader for two of the most promising candidates, Tony Blair and Gordon Brown. Mr Mandelson's only problem was that he was not certain which way to jump. The three men had been extraordinarily close political allies, the core of what became known as the modernizing tendency within the party. The relationship had been based on the assumption that eventually, if a vacancy occurred, it would be Mr Brown and not Mr Blair who would go for the top job.

'So, who should it be?' Mr Mandelson asked me, as he waited to be interviewed on the lunchtime programmes. For me, this was not the burning question of the hour; it would not feature as a topic in the first broadcasts announcing the tragic death of John Smith. I was struck by the difference between those in the political world, and those who report it. But if your life and work depends on the next step up the political ladder, you cannot be blamed for having it high on your list of priorities. I did my best to reply.

'Tony Blair and Gordon Brown would both be good,' I replied. And then after a pause I said, 'I suppose it'll be Tony Blair.' He did not comment, but significantly he did not argue. It was the beginning of an anguished period for Mr Mandelson, and his decision had an important effect on Labour Party politics. He did back Tony Blair, but in doing so he produced a rift between himself and Gordon Brown, which even after years in government remained as deep as ever. The contest for the leadership also changed for ever the relationship between Mr Brown, who stood aside, and Mr Blair, who won without difficulty. They were never again each other's greatest friend in politics and there were always serious tensions between them. It is this sort of experience which led the Conservative politician Enoch Powell to conclude that in politics 'you don't have friends, you only have allies'.

I did not know Mr Blair well. Not long before Mr Smith died Mr Blair and I had lunch together at Quaglino's, Sir Terence Conran's new restaurant in St James's; I thought this supposedly fashionable locale would be suitable for the politician who was hell-bent on making the Labour Party electable. We swept down the stairs into the dining room, producing a suitable stir among the clientele, but it was not a very enlightening occasion. Perhaps wrongly, I concentrated on the issue of the European single currency, and he was almost mathematically exact in arguing the case both for and against. He was, though, extremely personable, as the electorate would eventually discover; and he seemed happily married, worrying about whether he had a wedding anniversary gift for his wife, Cherie. I would have been happier if he had made it clearer where he wanted the country to go, but he was so convinced of the iniquities of the Tories that details of what Labour might do seemed rather beside the point.

I had a closer relationship with Gordon Brown, perhaps helped by the fact that we are both the sons of clergymen. In Scotland, being the son of the manse may be different from being an English vicar's son, but it has some of the same effects: a life which starts in the public eye, providing status if not wealth. It is a background which can give you the confidence to look other people firmly in the eye, and it does not necessarily make you pious. My elder son, William, was then a student at Edinburgh University, and once, when Mary and I took him out to a restaurant, we came across Gordon Brown and his friend, the broadcaster Sheena Macdonald. Having just come back from a visit to Russia with John Major, I regaled them with an account of the prime minister's visit to the town of Nizhny Novgorod. Mary was convinced I had broken in on a romantic evening.

On this occasion in Edinburgh and at other times, I came to know Gordon Brown well enough to look forward to a visit he made to the United States just before the general election of 1997, which would propel him into government as chancellor of the exchequer. I was the only journalist travelling in his party, though of course the BBC paid my bills. It was obvious that Labour had a very good chance of winning, but victory was not assumed. So Mr Brown and his advisers booked on to the British Airways flight as ordinary passengers in tourist class, hoping that the flight personnel would look kindly upon them and upgrade their tickets. This was accomplished, partly through the charm of Geoffrey Robinson, then a little-known Labour MP, who accurately gave the impression of being a highly successful businessman.

It was not clear what role Mr Robinson had, but I assumed that he might become a Treasury minister, which he did; and he worked his way into my favour by ensuring that I too was upgraded and got to travel a few yards behind Mr Brown and his party. If Mr Robinson displayed any fault at this stage, perhaps he was a little too keen on the free drinks provided. On landing at New York, the impression of general bonhomie was enhanced when he decided I should travel with him in a white stretch limousine, rather than a taxi, and the driver provided a flask of Bourbon whiskey to help us on our way.

When we arrived at the Carlyle Hotel, where Princess Diana used to stay when she was in New York, there was a VIP welcome. The elegant manageress was waiting outside, and she greeted Mr Robinson as he slowly alighted from the limo. 'Hello, Dr Brown,' she said, to our amusement. We explained that we were only the advance party. Gordon Brown soon arrived and was filmed walking in. The son of the manse had made it. Although the visit was great fun, and we had a marvellous dinner in a private room at the Waldorf Astoria with Harold Evans and his wife, Tina Brown, this was far from being a frivolous trip. The shadow chancellor met Alan Greenspan, the chairman of the Federal Reserve, to go through with him the arguments for the government ceasing to have control of interest rates and making the Bank of England independent. This was Labour's secret plan, which was put into effect within days of winning the election in May and is widely seen as one of their greatest achievements. This was also the moment when Gordon Brown announced what became famous as the five economic tests he would apply before Britain could join the European single currency.

Geoffrey Robinson later became famous for inadvertently forcing the resignation of Peter Mandelson as trade secretary, when it was revealed that he had given him a loan of nearly £400,000 to buy a house. Mr Robinson left the government at the same time, but a couple of years later was kind enough to help me out in a cancer charity event at the Savoy Hotel. It was called Turning the Tables and involved Michael Portillo interviewing John Humphrys and Mr Robinson grilling me. To the general amusement of the guests, I kept complaining about my living arrangements, until Mr Robinson said to roars of laughter, 'You're not asking for a loan, are you?'

Another member of Gordon Brown's team was Charlie Whelan, who sometimes gave the impression of being a rough-talking yob, but was an extremely effective press secretary. Finally forced out of office, some of his mistakes were fairly obvious: he should have taken his mother's advice and called himself Charles, not Charlie; and he should somehow have avoided being regarded with intense dislike by the prime minister. Mr Whelan's obsessive loyalty to the chancellor, while cementing his relationship with Mr Brown, produced the opposite effect on Mr Blair. There was also a great fuss being made at the time over the role of spin doctors. One of the high points of Mr Whelan's career was in the autumn of 1997 when he told journalists the government's position over the single currency from his mobile phone while enjoying a drink at the Red Lion pub in Whitehall. The news he announced was that the government would not be seeking a referendum on the Euro during their first term of office. Although this turned out to be completely correct, there was one serious flaw: the prime minister had not yet decided that such an announcement should be made. It was only because of the strong backing of the chancellor, and Mr Blair's unwillingness to provoke conflict that Mr Whelan managed to hold on to his job for another year.

Many of Labour's problems in government stemmed from inexperience. Gordon Brown had never even been to Downing Street before he became chancellor of the exchequer. The brilliant campaigners in opposition had a far from certain touch when they reached office although the wave of euphoria which had greeted the election result was not quickly dispersed. The government enjoyed one of the longest political honeymoons that anyone could remember. Leading Labour figures might be forgiven for enjoying the credit lavished on them for the Tories' worst ever defeat, and some of the small changes were quite fun: it was a good idea to equip their supporters with Union flags to wave in Downing Street when Mr Blair took over and the scenes of wild enthusiasm will not be quickly forgotten.

For me, one of the most memorable moments came just before the election campaign started. I thought it was important for me to have some understanding of Sir James Goldsmith's Referendum Party, the anti-Euro group putting up candidates in almost all the parliamentary seats. I was ushered into his plush office in Kensington and was startled to be told that his organization had been looking into my background. I stared into the blue eyes of the billionaire; he was not stroking a white cat but otherwise seemed like a character straight out of a James Bond film. I felt rather dizzy. 'We have concluded,' he said after a dramatic pause, 'that your politics are unknown.' It was quite a relief.

During the election campaign, Alastair Campbell, Tony Blair's press secretary, complained that I was not spending enough time seeing how well the Labour leader was going down with voters. No doubt he would have preferred me to be confined to the leader's election tour, as I had been during campaigns in the 1970s, but my role was different now. I was expected to take a view of the campaigns of all the party leaders, and to help me, pictures and interviews were sent back to London. On one occasion when I was talking to Mr Campbell, he handed the mobile phone to Mr Blair and I found myself discussing the coverage for that evening. The Labour leader was keen on the more emotional moment in his speech when he seemed to catch his breath. It was the first time I was able to see the extent to which he is a political actor, concerned as much by the impact of the performance as the soundness of his argument. As on so many occasions I was left with a dilemma: how to keep my distance in order to ensure the necessary objectivity, while at the same time being close enough to know what is going on. It is a dilemma which can never be fully resolved.

When prime ministers are cocooned in Downing Street it is much harder to find out what they are thinking, and that is why trips abroad are so important. Then you see the government in miniature – only essential aides take part – and for journalists it is a useful way of discovering who really matters in the leadership. In the late autumn of 1997, after the election, I was one of a small group who went with the prime minister on a day trip to Bosnia, including a brief stopover in Sarajevo. It was my first visit to the Balkans and a chance to see the havoc created by the civil war: the pockmarked buildings, the craters, and the people, familiar from countless hours of news coverage, at last allowed to move about. In this unlikely setting, I was also able to observe the closeness of the relationship between Alastair Campbell and Tony Blair; they behaved as if they were equals. The ostensible purpose of the visit was a gesture to the British troops who would be spending Christmas away from home, but it made me wonder whether senior members of the government were perhaps too keen to treat each other like friends, and whether that held its own dangers.

For journalists, after all the dramas of the Major years there was a distinct sense of anticlimax, as the Blair government settled in. With their enormous House of Commons majority, ministers did not have to worry about backbench revolts; indeed many of them seemed to worry less and less about parliament. Mr Blair cut in half the number of times he had to appear for prime minister's questions, although the session was doubled in length, and public interest in politics seemed to suffer a sharp decline. The home secretary, Jack Straw, was one of the few ministers who would openly admit that this early period was not a recipe for good democratic government.

But politics, like nature, abhors a vacuum, and in the absence of many of the traditional political stories – of governments under attack, of revolts being planned – Westminster journalists began to concentrate on personal feuds instead. Accounts of the rifts between Mr Mandelson and Mr Brown, Mr Brown and Mr Blair, Mr Cook and Mr Brown, Mr Prescott and Mr Mandelson, all did the rounds. If friendship seemed to matter so much at one level, then so too did a lack of friendship. It gave heart to the despondent Tories. One former Conservative chief whip told me with relish, 'At least our differences were ideological; you can deal with that. Personal differences are so much harder; they don't go away.'

Tony Blair was acutely conscious of the need to set a clear direction for the government. By agreeing to the spending limits proposed without much conviction by the previous administration, his room for manoeuvre was limited, particularly in the first two years. But where change was not dependent on government funds, he pursued it vigorously. Promises to devolve government in Scotland and Wales were soon kept and he quickly committed himself to the Northern Ireland peace process started, but far from completed, by John Major. On Europe, Mr Blair was constrained by the decision to rule out early membership of the Euro. What the prime minster anxiously sought was a new philosophy, a non-socialist alternative to the Tories which he called the Third Way, and his most important ally in this quest was President Bill Clinton.

In February 1998, there was still a freshness and confidence about Tony Blair which made him want to visit the White House with a certain amount of style. Accompanied by his wife Cherie, he took a group of journalists across the Atlantic, and for the first time on a prime ministerial trip, we travelled by Concorde. I had been on the plane before, as a reporter on *Today* roaring off to Bahrain on a trial flight more than twenty years earlier, but this was now a standard way to travel; and it was only much later after the Paris crash that fears were raised about Concorde's safety. In a few hours we were there.

Mr Blair was determined to enjoy the trip. He had plenty of reasons to believe that his relationship with Bill Clinton would have as much impact as Mrs Thatcher's with Ronald Reagan. In opposition, the Labour Party and the Democrats had worked closely together; Mr Blair and Gordon Brown had made a much-publicized visit to Washington to ensure this would be the case. New Labour had followed New Democrat in party labelling, and many of the ideas which had triumphed in the British campaign had their origins across the Atlantic. If only it had not been for Monica Lewinsky. I asked a simple question on the plane. 'Do you believe the president when he says he did not have an affair with her?'

'Yes,' Mr Blair said firmly, 'I do believe him.' He went on to say how much Mr Clinton was a man he would trust. I suppose it was the only answer he could give; anything else might ruin his reception in Washington. But it seemed highly unlikely to be true.

It was during the visit that Mr Clinton made the celebrated

outburst that, for a time, seemed to silence his critics. At a news conference with Mr Blair he declared: 'I did not have sexual relations with that woman.' Alastair Campbell expressed his annoyance that Mr Blair's views on this matter were even being sought. As I had raised the issue on more than one occasion, I was the target for his tirade. He questioned not only my judgement, but also the entire purpose of the BBC. This did not particularly bother me. I was used to Mr Campbell's attacks, usually cloaked in humour but sometimes designed to wound as well. Other reporters, including Peter Riddell of *The Times*, were more upset. He wrote a story about relations between the government and the BBC which was featured on the front page of his paper.

One of the main items on the president and prime minister's agenda was the need for more discussion about their plans to invent a political philosophy based on the idea of the Third Way. Seminars followed on both sides of the Atlantic, and I attended one of the more bizarre occasions which was held at a law college in New York in September that same year. On the very day that the president's testimony to the grand jury was shown on television, Mr Blair was in New York with Mr Clinton where they were attending the fiftieth anniversary of the United Nations. In my television reports, I managed to weave together Mr Clinton's remarks at the UN with how he had managed to cope with several hours of his cross examination, complete with sexual detail, being shown in public. The most striking moment was when he arrived at the podium to make his speech to the UN, to be greeted with a standing ovation. In the evening, with his wife, Hillary, President Clinton made another public appearance, at the Third Way seminar, along with Mr Blair and Romano Prodi, then the prime minister of Italy. Mrs Clinton gave no impression of being under strain; she seemed to appreciate her husband's jokes and appeared to be listening attentively. I did not learn a great deal about how the non-socialist alternative might form a coherent philosophy, but I did get a clear insight into the workings of the American presidency. By chance, in a corridor, I came across two of Mr Clinton's closest advisers, and I asked them how the day's events had gone. They looked me straight in the eye and one of them said, 'I think we are generally agreed: it has been a good day for us.' Their argument, believe it or not, was that the president had given the impression that he was helping the grand jury. It was only on his last day in office more than two years later that he admitted to having lied.

The last time Mr Blair met Mr Clinton, while he was in office, was during a meeting of the G7 countries on the Japanese island of Okinawa in the summer of 2000. I was staying in the same hotel as Mr Blair, and as he passed with his party I could not resist making a formal bow in the Japanese fashion. The prime minister smiled and from the back of the group an unmistakable voice shouted, 'Lower, Sergeant, lower.' It was Alastair Campbell swiftly seizing the opportunity I had given him. But I have allowed my story to get ahead of itself. By the time Mr Blair attended the summit in Japan, I had changed my job. After thirty years and a series of dramatic and surprising events, I had left the BBC and had already started my new life with ITN.

25

Full circle

'TELL THEM NO.' The instruction on the email could not have been more emphatic. The subject of the message, as so often in the BBC, was a set of initials, bewildering to anyone not deeply immersed in the small world of media activities: HIGNFY. This was the way the head of the BBC's Westminster office, Mark Damazer, ordered me to turn down a request to appear with Angus Deayton, Paul Merton and Ian Hislop in the television comedy show *Have I Got News for You* in July 1998. There are those who believe that, like Nelson at the Battle of Copenhagen, I deliberately put a blind eye to the telescope and failed to read the vital message. The truth is that I had no idea that my office computer could receive emails, let alone reply to them.

I eventually obtained a copy of the message; it was extracted belatedly from the computer files and collected by me as part of the small number of vital documents I might need when I left the BBC eighteen months later. After the emphatic no, there is a brief explanation of why I should not return to my roots in student humour and fool about on the most popular BBC2 programme of that period. 'As discussed before,' the email from Mr Damazer says, 'I see some points you make are valid, but I'm afraid risk-free ascetic instincts are valid, and, on balance, right. I will compensate you with a lunch.'

If I had received the email and responded as requested, it is no exaggeration to say that the course of my life would have been quite different. Fortunately, the unregulated muddle of normal life, way beyond the grip of computers, conspired to produce a rare success. It all happened over the course of just four days. On Monday, when the producers of *Have I Got News for You* were let down by a potential guest, I was considered a possible replacement, as one of the old student comedy stars who somehow had slipped through the net and become respectable. One of the show's main producers, Colin Swash, had worked with me briefly a couple of years earlier on an Ian Hislop Radio 4 comedy, with me playing myself or a character so similar it hardly mattered. Remembering that and my time with Alan Bennett, he decided I could be a last-minute stand-in. He might also have felt it was a chance for one of these know-alls from the newsroom to be given a bit of a drubbing.

I was keen that BBC news should respond quickly and firmly; if we were going to say yes, which I thought we should, we should not give any impression of prevarication. After all, we were meant to be the people in the BBC who could respond to a political crisis at a moment's notice. Why should we dither about a comedy programme? Mr Damazer was in a meeting and could not be contacted; his assistant assured us he would agree. I decided to go ahead, subject to confirmation later.

Three days later, on the morning of the programme, I was travelling to work on the tube when I received a message to ring Mark Damazer. On my mobile phone, I told him that to pull out at this late stage would look very bad. But what about the email which he had sent the day before? I explained I knew nothing about the email system. 'All right,' I heard him say above the rattle of the tube, 'but it's up to you.' The implication was clear: if things went wrong, it would be my fault and I would have to take the consequences.

Spontaneous comedy is all the better for a little bit of

preparation. I did not have a great deal of time, but I knew that the shambles of the initial British intervention in the civil war in Sierra Leone was bound to come up. I was keen to suggest how a film could be made of the incident. Hollywood had already produced *Out of Africa* so this could be called *In to Africa*. Ian Hislop had an idea who might play the foreign secretary, Robin Cook. But I had prepared a neat reply, 'One thinks of Kenneth Branagh (pause) but would he get the laughs?'

'Why do you think the British company supplying mercenaries was called Sandline?' Angus Deayton asked me. 'Because,' I replied, 'they were anxious to draw a line in the sand.' And what about accusations that BBC news was 'dumbing down'? I swiftly rejected the charge. 'We are,' I said, 'dumbing up.' They were kind enough to show a videotape of my encounter with Mrs Thatcher on the steps of the Paris embassy, which gave me the chance to suggest their version had not been fairly edited; they had left out the bit where she said, 'John, what shall I do now?' I was on Paul Merton's team and he was wonderfully ready to take my side as the misunderstood victim of the Paris incident. It was very good fun.

The response from BBC news seemed cool. There was no word from Mr Damazer on the following Monday morning. Indeed it was not until a week later that I saw him again, walking through the Westminster newsroom with the news editor. 'Has John been told?' Mark asked him. It was only then I heard that a formal meeting of the programme review board had decided that for me the show had been a personal triumph. The public response was extraordinary. For the previous ten years I had been a regular contributor to BBC television news and was therefore hardly unknown. But my appearance on a comedy show had somehow turned me into a person people wanted to know. One man ran after me as I was getting into a taxi and as we pulled away he shouted,

'Great, really great, thank you.' Endlessly, strangers told me how much they enjoyed it; publishers became interested in my autobiography; and there were many requests from other comedy programmes. For me, it was not entirely comfortable: the dilemma of my early life was again exposed. What did I really want, to make people laugh, or to absorb myself in journalism? And the answer, as it always has been, was to try and do both.

At times, the sense in which my life had turned full circle was almost overwhelming. At one of David Frost's summer parties I met again my old producer from the Alan Bennett programme, Patrick Garland. John Bird was also there. I had been one of his fans since his satire shows of the 1960s and was flattered to be told that recently someone had asked him for his autograph thinking he was John Sergeant. But the most important response came from senior politicians, who could well have thought I should not appear on comedy shows. In the week that followed the programme, no fewer than six members of the cabinet told me how much they had enjoyed it; the deputy prime minister, John Prescott, often the butt of jokes on *Have I Got News for You*, was one of the most enthusiastic.

Paul Merton showed his support by inviting me to appear on *Room 101* on BBC2, in which a guest is asked to choose subjects or objects which they hate. I produced some fairly routine ones, such as over-attentive waiters and impossibly tough plastic wrappings, but it was really an excuse to tell funny stories. Paul was again a delight to work with because he obeys the classic rules of comedy: don't interrupt other people's jokes and give them opportunities to come back at you. The on-stage relationship is crucial because a television studio, with all the cameras and equipment, can be rather clinical, like an operating theatre. Fortunately, studio audiences know their job is to be easily amused, and the sound of their laughter can always be turned up. To my surprise I discovered that producers from rival shows were also there. Even before my appearance on *Room 101* had been transmitted, I was booked to be on another comedy chat show, with Mark Lamarr, because his producer had been in the audience. For that show I returned to the same studio at Television Centre in which, thirty years before, I had made comedy with Alan Bennett. Had I improved over the years? I was certainly more relaxed. I was also much better at playing myself.

On radio comedy programmes, getting an audience can be quite difficult. Many of the Radio 4 shows are recorded in the wonderful art deco radio theatre in Broadcasting House, designed in the 1930s. It is a small place which should be easy to pack, but we had a pitifully small number for a show hosted by my old political news editor, David Aaronovitch, called *True Lies*. Gyles Brandreth was also on the panel, but despite all our efforts we could barely raise a laugh. At the end of the show more than half the audience, about sixty people, stood up in a group; it turned out they were two coach loads of German students. Had we known we could have tried a few cracks about Gerhard Schroeder.

The News Quiz on Radio 4, chaired by Simon Hoggart in the same theatre, never seems to have that problem. A healthy number of fans are even prepared to queue in the rain, which can be embarrassing if you have to walk past them on the way to the warm and welcoming hospitality room. The regulars – Alan Coren, Jeremy Hardy, Linda Smith and Andy Hamilton – are immensely talented, but I try not to appear in awe of them. The first time I took part was at the end of a particularly difficult week: the Welsh secretary, Ron Davies, had resigned in mysterious circumstances and I had been granted the only interview with him on the day he left office. It was 27 October 1998. I thought I was being asked to interview the prime minister about the state of the economy. Usually the BBC are careful about responding to such requests, because once an interview of this sort has been recorded it is almost certain to be broadcast.

As I walked the familiar steps up Downing Street, I was not in a good mood. If there is anything worse than not having a political story, it is the feeling that you are being used to provide someone else's political story. The employers' organization, the CBI, had produced their economic report that morning, but it hardly merited a comment from Tony Blair. The prime minister's deputy press secretary, Godric Smith, met me at the door. 'We are not doing the interview here,' he announced. 'We are doing it in the Welsh Office.' My mood blackened even more. Not only was I being asked to do a story I did not believe in, I was being physically pushed around Whitehall as well. The Welsh Office is just across the road from Downing Street, and we waited in the small reception room on the ground floor.

The door opened and in came Alastair Campbell. He did not waste any words. 'The Welsh secretary has resigned; here's the resignation letter. He'll be here in a couple of minutes.' I read the resignation letter, which told a strange tale of an encounter on Clapham Common the evening before, with a growing feeling of disbelief. 'Whilst walking, I was approached by a man I had never seen before who engaged me in conversation. After talking for some minutes he asked me to accompany him and two of his friends to his flat for a meal. We drove, in my car, to collect his friends, one male, one female. Shortly afterwards, the man produced a knife and together with his male companion robbed me and stole my car, leaving me standing at the roadside.' I tried to make sense of this weird account and told the cameraman that he should be ready for anything.

'But aren't we here for an interview?' he asked.

'I don't know,' I replied.

The door opened again, and the cameraman immediately started filming. Mr Campbell came in with the resigning Welsh secretary. 'So we have finally got you to come to the Welsh Office,' said Mr Davies, pointing up the fact that this was not part of my normal beat. An exclusive interview with Mr Davies was then offered. I was still annoyed; and reading the letter had convinced me there was no proper reason for his resignation. If he had been the victim of a crime, he did not have to resign. To the surprise of Alastair Campbell and Mr Davies, I therefore questioned him along these lines. The matter was never fully resolved. A man was held for questioning by the police and then later released. Mr Davies never adequately explained what had happened, but it was the end of his political career.

On *The News Quiz*, at the end of that week, I was able to make fun of this mystery. I suggested that Mr Davies had told the prime minister that as he fully accepted the punishment why did he have to discuss the crime. I also said that if Mr Davies *had* given the reasons to me, we would not have been able to broadcast them, because too many children watched *The Six O'Clock News*. The narrow line that sometimes exists between high politics and low comedy had been satisfactorily bridged.

In show business, as the old saying goes, nothing succeeds like success. If one programme likes you, others are bound to follow. I was rapidly in danger of overexposure. As well as my normal work on BBC news, I found time to go to America for the *Holiday Programme*, going back to the scenes of my early adventures in New Orleans and Washington. I was a judge on *Masterchef*, chatting with the expert Rose Gray from the River Café restaurant on the drawbacks of amateur cooking. On *Call my Bluff* I suggested ridiculous definitions of words. I made after-dinner speeches and spoke at the Chichester Festival. I was a judge for one of the Cartoon of the Year awards and for the Channel 4 political awards. I reviewed books for Radio 4. I pretended to be a politician in a comedy programme on BBC2 called *If I Ruled the World*. On BBC1, on Christmas Eve, I appeared to be having an enjoyable evening with Dale Winton, though of course it had been recorded a few days earlier. On two brief trips to the Balkans I tried to convince the Croatians and the Macedonians of the importance of an independent media. Marvellous and amusing though many of these events were, none of them helped answer the central question: should I continue as the BBC's chief political correspondent, or should I make my escape?

The only job I really wanted on the staff was that of political editor, but Robin Oakley showed no signs of being ready to retire, and there was no hint from the BBC management that before the election, expected in 2001, they would act against him. At times he suggested I was plotting to succeed him, but as I explained to his face, there was little I could do along those lines. If the BBC wanted to get rid of him that was one thing; the idea that I could have him removed, simply because I wanted his job, was quite untenable. It is ironic, I suppose, that five months after I did leave, Robin was replaced by Andrew Marr. But by then Robin's patron, the director general, John Birt, had finally left the corporation, and the new man at the helm, Greg Dyke, was trying to put his stamp on the BBC.

I do not want to give the impression that I was unhappy at this time; far from it, I was at the peak of my career. It was simply that opportunities had opened up before me, and I was anxious not to miss out. One suggestion from BBC management was that I should present the breakfast television news programme. With memories of my less than successful time on *Today*, struggling into work at 4 a.m., I quickly declined. They even sent a senior person down to Westminster to try to get me to agree, but I was adamant. A more intriguing suggestion was that I should combine my present job as chief political correspondent with a quite different role: presenting the immensely popular Sunday television programme, *The Antiques Road Show*. I found that idea more appealing. My colleagues were far from convinced. It was even suggested that by doing it, I would be admitting to being something of an antique myself. As one of them put it, 'It takes one to know one.'

It was at this point that I received a call from Nigel Dacre, the editor of ITN, who provide the news service for ITV. He asked me if I was interested in talking about their plans for the next few years. I knew immediately what was in his mind, though I was taken completely by surprise. Michael Brunson, the highly respected political editor of ITN, was due to retire, and I had assumed they would be looking for someone much younger with popular appeal. It had not crossed my mind that I would be in the frame. For almost the first time in my professional life I was being headhunted. We met on a Friday afternoon in the Landmark Hotel, suitably placed halfway between Television Centre and ITN's headquarters in Gray's Inn Road. 'This conversation,' Nigel announced, 'may only take two minutes.' But that was only if I said no. When I expressed interest, it might have been appropriate for us to discuss the details of my career as a political correspondent but instead, to my great pleasure, he said, 'I liked you on *Room 101*.' Clearly he found the other parts of my life important as well.

We met again, for breakfast, at the same hotel the next Monday, with the editor in chief, Richard Tait. They had the details of how much they were prepared to offer. I said it would show how seriously they took the job. They had decided to be generous, and I rather regretted my pompous remark. I only just resisted saying yes, straightaway. BBC management were suitably shocked; they had been convinced

I would stay with them until I retired. 'Oh, ****' was the reaction of the head of news, Tony Hall, and then in a calmer voice, 'Congratulations.' It set the tone for a very friendly disengagement, which left me proud of all the years I had worked in the BBC. My leaving party, involving about three hundred staff at the Reform Club in Pall Mall, was quite an occasion. Robin Oakley made a generous, warm and humorous speech. The leaving video, which has become one of the ordeals of these gatherings, was surprisingly kind. In a recorded interview, Alan Bennett praised me as he had thirty years before when I originally applied. The *Newsnight* presenter Jeremy Vine, an old colleague at Westminster, tried an imitation of my style which was so bad it was really funny. Some of my female colleagues even cried, and I would have liked to, but thought it might be considered unseemly.

I settled quickly at ITN and soon enjoyed competing against the BBC. The job was sufficiently different to be interesting, and sufficiently similar for me not to feel a wrench. There were times in the BBC when it seemed as if that large and complex organization was making it difficult for me to come up for air. At ITN the task was more straightforward, the line between me and senior management much shorter and I was quickly made to feel at home. I was rather like a sailor reaching dry land after a long and arduous journey. My career was far from over, but I now had a chance to take stock, to look back at where I had come from. I turned my experience into this book and after reading it you may have some idea of what I am like. If you give me ten seconds, I will attempt to sum up: from an early age, and throughout my long journalistic career, I have always tried to chart my own course – to be myself.

Index

Index

Index